PRAISE FOR

ZODIAC UNMASKED

"[Graysmith's] access is as good as it gets. A meticulous reconstruction of the way the case evolved. By far the best book on the subject of the Zodiac murders, *Zodiac Unmasked* clearly illustrates that the elusive quality of the Zodiac had little to do with his cunning and everything to do with law enforcement ineptitude. *Zodiac Unmasked* also deals with the fans and the wannabes in fine detail. The case has always been a magnet for weirdos. Graysmith has managed to make his way through the minefield of quirky personalities involved."

—*New York Press*

"Fascinating . . . like reading a brand-new mystery. [Graysmith has] done a wonderful job in putting closure on the Zodiac case. A terrific job."

—Inspector Dave Toschi, the San Francisco detective who worked on the Zodiac case

"An excellent study . . . Now readers can learn all that [Graysmith] has learned in investigating the case further. A scary and disturbing account of pure evil." —*Booklist*

"Graysmith's evidence against Allen plays solidly."

—*Publishers Weekly*

Zodiac, *Zodiac Unmasked*, and *Auto Focus* have been made into major motion pictures by Warner Brothers, Paramount, Phoenix Pictures, and Sony Pictures.

ZØDIAC

Robert Graysmith

BERKLEY
New York

BERKLEY
An imprint of Penguin Random House LLC
penguinrandomhouse.com

ISBN: 9780425212189

St. Martin's Press edition published 1986
Berkley mass-market edition / April 1987
Berkley mass-market movie tie-in edition / January 2007

Printed in the United States of America
27   29   31   33   34   32   30   28

In memory of my father.
And with all my love for my mother,
David, Aaron, Margot, Penny,
and especially Pamela.

Acknowledgments

I am especially indebted to Inspector Dave Toschi, Sherwood Morrill, Paul Avery, Herb Caen, Margot St. James, and the Owl and the Monkey, Inc. Thanks to Richard Marek, my editor, for sensitive and perceptive directions on what path to follow.

Killing someone is just like walking outdoors.
If I wanted a victim, I'd just go get one. I
didn't even consider a person a human being.

—HENRY LEE LUCAS,
serial killer, 1984

We have madmen waiting. . . .

—*Mideast terrorist leader,
1978*

Contents

Introduction

After Jack the Ripper and before Son of Sam there is only one name their equal in terror: the deadly, elusive, and mysterious Zodiac. Since 1968 the hooded mass murderer has terrified the city of San Francisco and the Bay Area with a string of brutal killings. Zodiac, in taunting letters sent to the newspapers, has hidden clues to his identity by using cunning ciphers that have defied the greatest codebreaking minds of the CIA, the FBI, and NSA.

I was the political cartoonist for the largest paper in northern California, the *San Francisco Chronicle*, so I was there from the beginning as each cryptic letter, each coded message, each swatch of victim's bloody clothing arrived at the editorial desk. At first I was merely fascinated by the purely visual qualities of Zodiac's symbols. Then, gradually, a resolve grew within me to unravel the killer's clues, to discover his true identity, and, failing that, at least to present every scrap of evidence available so that someday someone might recognize the Zodiac killer.

When I started writing this book I realized that two obstacles lay ahead of me. First, the various suspects and few surviving victims had scattered and many of the witnesses were in hiding. To discover the missing facts I had to find the missing witnesses.

One had changed her name six times. Another who had escaped Zodiac had been hiding for a decade, using many different names. Eventually I found her through a postmark on a Christmas card. Second, the murders had taken place in different counties, and, due to interdepartmental jealousy, each police agency had vital information the others were unaware of. From each county, from garages where files had been taken as souvenirs, from files saved just moments from destruction, I brought all the elements together for the first time and began to paint a complete picture of Zodiac.

In 1975, after several years of interest in the case, I became aware that there were unsuspected Zodiac murders and that one of Zodiac's early victims may have known his true name. This victim, in the act of turning Zodiac into the police, had been murdered.

There is no defense against the compulsive, random killer. The serial killer is unquenchable in his bloodlust, and California seems to have more than its share of serial murders (just second in the country after New York). Multiple murders, a recent phenomenon, are now claiming between 500 and 1500 American lives each year, according to the Justice Department.

The Zodiac murders were not simply killings. They were sex crimes in which the killer reduced the victims to objects that existed only to give him sexual pleasure achieved through violent acts. The hunt for the victims was the foreplay and the attack the substitute for the sex act. Zodiac (a sexual sadist) achieved his sexual pleasure by torturing and killing because violence and love are hopelessly intertwined and confused in his mind.

Sexual sadists have a tendency (like most serial murderers) to be quite intelligent and become amazingly proficient at concealing themselves after their first killing. The cat-and-mouse game they play with the police may become the principal motive for the crimes. Once the killer is captured, his detailed and grisly confession itself is a brutal attack. Though no one knows what creates a sexual sadist many doctors suspect a damaged sex chromosome or an event early in life. Cruel and rejecting parents and peers may create pressures that are expressed in childhood by bedwetting, shoplifting, and animal mutilation and torture. With the awakening of puberty, the anger manifests itself in ever increasing, cleverly concealed acts of sadism.

If there is one key word for the entire story of the Zodiac mystery, it is *obsession*. The lure of the case has destroyed marriages, derailed careers, ruined health; as over 2500 Zodiac suspects were scanned, people were swept away by a tide of mystery, tragedy, and loss.

I wanted this book to accomplish something, to effect a change, to stop the killer. Slowly each strange symbol and cipher broke away and I learned how the killer wrote the untraceable Zodiac letters, why he killed when he did, and even the inspiration for his crossed-circle symbol and his executioner's costume.

This is the true story of a pursuit that spans almost two decades and still goes on. I have included hundreds of facts never revealed in print before. It is as accurate an account as eight years of research can provide. Over the years, only fragments of the Zodiac letters were released by the police or reprinted and reproduced by the newspapers. In this book, for the first time, is every word Zodiac wrote the police.

In a very few cases it was necessary to delete the last names of some witnesses. They are known by the police. The names of several major Zodiac suspects have been changed; some facets of their past work records, educational degrees, and geographical locations have been altered. In the cases where it was necessary to change a name this is noted in the text. In the chapter on Andrew Todd Walker limited portions of dialogue were reconstructed for purposes of narrative flow.

Witchcraft, death threats, cryptograms, a hooded killer still sought, dedicated investigators, and a mysterious man in a white Chevy who is seen by all and known by no one are all parts of the Zodiac mystery, the most frightening story I know.

—ROBERT GRAYSMITH
San Francisco
May 1985

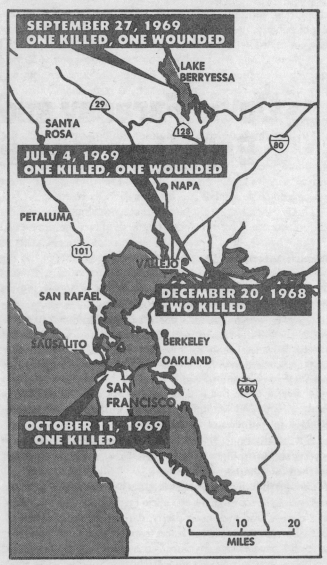

Map of Zodiac's Northern California victims.
Map by R. Graysmith.

David Faraday and Betty Lou Jensen

Friday, December 20, 1968

When he hiked in the rolling hills overlooking Vallejo, David Faraday could catch glimpses of the Golden Gate Bridge, the saltwater fishermen, sailboats and speedboats on San Pablo Bay, and the wide, tree-lined streets of the town. He could make out the black skeletal derricks, the piers, battleships, brick smokestacks, and three-tiered warehouses of Mare Island, the great gray mass lying across the straits.

In World War II thousands swarmed to the area to do navy work, and Vallejo was transformed into a boom town. Cheap housing units of plywood and plasterboard were thrown up, temporary constructions. By the 1960s they had become permanent black ghettos, fosterers of race hatred and gang violence that reached into the high schools.

David Arthur Faraday, seventeen, a scholar and varsity athlete, was one of the top students at Vallejo High School. As 1968 drew to a close, David had met a pretty, dark-haired sixteen-year-old, Betty Lou Jensen, who lived across town. He had been going over to see her almost every day since. Today, at 5:00 P.M., David and Betty Lou were talking with some friends on Annette Street about

1

their date for that night. It was to be their first date together.

David left at 6:00, and at 7:10 drove his sister, Debbie, to a meeting of the Rainbow Girls at the Pythian Castle on Sonoma Boulevard. David told Debbie that he and Betty Lou might be going out to Lake Herman Road at the end of their date because he'd heard "a bunch of the kids were going out there tonight."

David returned home, to his parents' green, brown-shingled, T-shaped house on Sereno Drive, surrounded by a manicured hedge and two massive round shrubs, all dwarfed by the soaring poplar tree on the right.

By 7:20 David was dressing for his date. He wore a light-blue long-sleeve shirt, brown corduroy Levi-type pants, black socks, and tan, rough-leather, low-cut boots. He put his Timex wristwatch with chrome case and band on his left wrist, and shoved a dollar and fifty-five cents, all in change, in his right front pants pocket. He pocketed a white handkerchief and a small bottle of Binaca breath drops. On the middle finger of his left hand he fitted his yellow metal class ring with its red stone. David combed his short brown hair diagonally across his forehead, above large, intelligent eyes and a generous mouth, then slipped on his beige sportcoat.

David said good-bye to his parents and left the house at 7:30. He took a deep breath of the very cool night air (it was only 22 degrees), and walked to the 1961 Rambler brown-and-beige four-door station wagon that was registered in his mother's name.

He backed the Rambler out of the driveway and took Fairgrounds Drive to Interstate Highway 80 for the one and one-quarter miles to the Georgia Street exit. From Georgia David made a right turn on Hazelwood and rode on Hazelwood until he came to 123 Ridgewood, a low, flat house bordered by ivy and lean, tall trees. David pulled to a stop in front. It was 8:00.

Betty Lou Jensen, like David, was hardworking, studious, serious, and had a spotless reputation. As far as her parents knew she and David were going to a Christmas carol concert at her school, Hogan High, only a few blocks away.

Betty Lou took one last look in the mirror and adjusted the colored ribbon in her hair; her long brown straight hair framed her face and came down over her shoulders. She was wearing a purple mini-dress with white cuffs and collar that made her dark, widely spaced eyes look mysterious. She had on black T-strap shoes.

Betty Lou looked nervously over her right shoulder toward the window to be sure the blinds were drawn. She often told her sister Melody that she thought a boy from school was spying on her, and on several occasions Mrs. Jensen had found the gate open leading to the side of the house. A classmate? Or was someone else spying on her?

While he waited for Betty Lou, David spoke with her father, Verne. Her parents were from the Midwest, but Betty Lou had been born in Colorado, like David's mother.

When Betty Lou came out, David helped her with her white fur coat. Purse in hand, she kissed her dad good-bye, told him that they were going to a party after the concert, and at 8:20 left, promising to be back by 11:00.

Instead of going to the concert, the two went to visit Sharon, another student, on Brentwood, close to the school. At 9:00 Sharon walked them out to their car. They didn't say where they were going next.

At about the same time, out on Lake Herman Road, a few miles east of the Vallejo city limits, two racoon hunters, who had just parked their red pickup inside of the Marshall Ranch, noticed a white four-door hardtop '60 Chevrolet Impala parked by the entrance to the Benicia Water Pumping Station. There was a truck coming out of the pumping station gate onto the isolated road at the time.

At 9:30 an unusual incident occurred on this spot. A boy and his date had parked the girl's sports car just off the winding road so he could adjust its motor. Both saw a car, possibly a blue Valiant, coming down the road from Benicia into Vallejo. As the car passed the couple, it slowed, went a few yards down the road, and stopped in the middle of the road. They saw its white backup lights come on. And then the car started backing up toward them with excruciating slowness. There was such menace, such an aura of malignancy about the actions that the youth put his date's car in gear and took off at high speed. The Valiant followed them. When the couple got to the Benicia turnoff, they turned. The other car continued straight ahead.

At 10:00 P.M., Bingo Wesher, a sheepherder at the Old Borges Ranch, was checking his sheep in the area east of the Benicia pumping station when he noticed a white Chevrolet Impala sedan parked by the entrance to the station in front of the gate. He also saw the racoon hunters' '59 Ford truck.

After Betty Lou and David had a Coke at Mr. Ed's, a local drive-in, they drove east on Georgia and turned left onto Columbus Parkway. At the city limits of Vallejo, David turned right onto narrow, winding Lake Herman Road.

They passed the great towers of the SVAR Rock and Asphalt Paving Materials Company, its machinery eating away at an orange-and-tan mountainside. There were silver mines here, and David had heard of two men who planned on operating a quicksilver mine in the farmland. Small ranches crowded the road the first mile. By day the hillsides were dotted with black-and-white cows grazing on the pale yellow hills against sharp blue skies. Now, the night slid thick and black behind the beams of the Rambler's headlights. David and Betty Lou headed east to a remote lover's lane. Police traveled it periodically, warning couples of the possible dangers of parking in such an isolated area.

Just before 10:15, David pulled off the road to the right and parked fifteen feet off it, facing south, in the graveled area outside gate #10, the chainlink-fenced entrance to the Lake Herman pumping station. He locked all four doors, put Betty Lou's white fur coat and purse and his own sportcoat on the seat behind the driver's seat, and turned on the car heater. He tilted the adjustable front seat back to a forty-five-degree angle.

There were no lamp poles, and the rocky clearing was surrounded by gently mounded hills and farmland. The spot was popular for lovers because the kids could see the lights from any police cruiser as it came around the curve in the road, which gave them time to get rid of beer or grass.

At 10:15 a woman and her boyfriend, a sailor, drove by. When

4

they reached the end of the road and came back past fifteen minutes later, the car was still there, but was now facing out toward the road in a southeast direction.

At 10:50 Mrs. Stella Borges arrived at her ranch on Lake Herman Road, exactly two and seven-tenths miles from where Betty Lou and David were parked. As Mrs. Borges came in the door the phone rang and she began a conversation with her mother. They agreed that Mrs. Borges would pick up her thirteen-year-old son at a show later that night.

At 11:00 Mrs. Peggie Your and her husband, Homer, drove out to Lake Herman Road in their gold '67 Grand Prix to check out the sewer and water pipes his company was installing near the pump house. When they passed the Rambler, Mrs. Your saw David sitting in the driver's seat and the girl leaning against his shoulder. When the lights from the Yours' car illuminated the gate area, she could see David put his hands on the steering wheel.

After looking over the construction site, the Yours went to the bottom of the hill and turned into the Marshall Ranch to turn to go back toward Benicia. They could see the racoon hunters' red pickup parked in the field twenty-five feet in. The two hunters, in stocking caps and hunting jackets, were in the truck. After turning around, the Yours came back past the Rambler. David and Betty Lou were still sitting in the same position.

The racoon hunters had returned to their pickup by walking up the road on the side of the creek. They had been about to leave when they saw the Yours' car pull into the driveway. It was 11:05 when they finally left, and both men noticed the Rambler parked alone by the gate, now facing in toward it.

When another car came around the bend in the road and caught them in its headlights, like glowing eyes peeking over a hill, Betty Lou and David may have been holding each other. Instead of passing the station wagon, this car pulled up next to them, to their right, about ten feet away.

The figure in the car was probably in silhouette, hunched and stocky like the surrounding dark hills, flat as a paper cutout. In the darkness there may have been a momentary glint of light, as if from glasses. The man was wearing a windbreaker.

There the two cars sat, side by side, just off a desolate country road.

At 11:10 a worker from Humble Oil in Benicia was on his way home when he passed the Rambler at the gate. He noticed it, but the make and color of the other car failed to register with him.

The oil worker's auto disappeared in the distance.

A dry breeze rattled the frozen grass along the road.

This is what may have happened next:

The new arrival finally rolled his window down and spoke to David and Betty Lou, asking them to get out of the car.

Astonished, the young couple refused. The stocky man opened his car door. And as he got out, he pulled a gun from under his dark jacket.

The stranger stood glaring down at Betty Lou, whose window was open. Instead of forcing himself in through the most obvious entry—on the passenger side—the stranger began stalking around the car. He paused, aimed at the rear right window just off center, above the chrome stripping in its lower part, and fired a bullet. It shattered the glass. He moved to the left side of the car and fired a bullet into the left rear wheel housing. His intention seemed to be to herd the youngsters out of the right side of the car.

He succeeded. As both of the teenagers scrambled out of the passenger side, the stranger raced around to the right side of the car.

Betty Lou had gotten out. As David slid across the seat and turned his head getting out, the man reached through the open left window with the gun and pressed the barrel behind the upper part of the boy's left ear and pulled the trigger. The bullet angled horizontally forward, leaving behind the powder burns of a contact wound. It exploded the boy's skull.

Betty Lou screamed and ran northward, parallel with the road and toward Vallejo. Racing after the girl, gun extended, less than ten feet behind her, the stocky man shot Betty Lou five times. He hit her in a tight pattern in the upper right portion of her back.

This was incredible marksmanship: a moving target, a moving gunman running over gravel, on an almost totally dark country road.

Betty Lou fell dead exactly twenty-eight feet and six inches from the Rambler's rear bumper. The fleeing girl had never even reached the pavement of the road.

She lay on her right side, face down, her feet to the west. David was on his back, feet pointing toward the right rear wheel. He was breathing in an almost imperceptible rasp. A large pool of blood was beginning to form about his head.

The stocky man backed his sedan up and drove away down the dark, twisting road.

Mrs. Borges, still in her coat, hung up the phone and got her mother-in-law and daughter for the drive to Benicia. She glanced at the kitchen clock. It was 11:10.

It took her four to five minutes, at thirty-five miles an hour, to reach the site where David had parked. As she turned the corner of the road at the edge of the chainlink fence, her headlights illuminated the dreadful sight.

At first Mrs. Borges thought the man had fallen out of the car. Then, near a yellow diamond traffic sign, she saw Betty Lou. The right front door of the Rambler was still open; the hum of its heater was audible in the stillness.

Mrs. Borges accelerated down the narrow thruway to Benicia looking for help, reaching speeds of sixty to seventy miles per hour. Just north of Interstate 680 she saw a Benicia patrol car and began to honk and blink her lights to get their attention. The two cars pulled to a stop in front of the Enco Station on East 2nd Street and she told them of the horror at the edge of the road. It was 11:19.

The police cruiser proceeded with flashing blue lights to the scene of the attack and arrived in three minutes. The officers, Captain Daniel Pitta and Officer William T. Warner, detected shallow breathing from the boy and called for an ambulance.

They checked over the two-tone Rambler. The motor was lukewarm, the ignition switched on, the right front door wide open, the other three doors and tailgate all locked.

They found an expended .22 casing on the right front floorboard of the car. Because the ground and gravel area was frozen, there were no visible tire tracks or signs of a struggle.

They covered Betty Lou with a wool blanket. The large pool of blood that had collected around her body had come mainly from her nose and mouth. The trail of blood led back to the car.

David was lying face up. Captain Pitta could see from the dark area around the wound at his left ear that the bullet had been fired at close range. There was a large lump on his right cheek, and blood on his hands and the sleeves of his shirt. Warner made a chalk outline of the still figure, its feet close to the car's right front door.

The blackness was sliced by the red lights of an A-1 Ambulance. It slid to a stop. David was picked up on a stretcher and placed in the back of the vehicle for a mile-a-minute, siren-screeching trip to Vallejo General Hospital. On the way, a doctor worked over him.

At 11:29, Pitta called County Coroner Dan Horan. Since the attack had occurred in an unincorporated section of Solano County, out of the jurisdiction of the Benicia police, he notified the Solano County Sheriff's Office by radio and requested a unit and an investigator.

Horan dressed quickly. By midnight, he was at the now bustling scene, with Dr. Byron Sanford of Benicia. Horan had a habit of taking on all the stress of such a tragedy, notifying the families of the victims in person. (This stress contributed to a heart condition that eventually forced him to resign.) Sanford pronounced Betty Lou dead on the scene—D.O.S.—and ordered the body removed for autopsy. First, pictures were taken from as many angles as possible.

A reporter from the *Fairfield Daily Republic*, Thomas D. Balmer, had arrived earlier but was kept back until the Sheriff's investigator arrived at 12:05 A.M.

Detective Sergeant Les Lundblad handled two, maybe three murders in an entire year. Now he stood thoughtfully in the blackness and coolness of Lake Herman Road, his small-brimmed hat pulled down over his battered, weatherlined country face. He

8

had rarely been without that hat since he'd become a detective sergeant for the Sheriff's Office in 1963.

Lundblad made a sketch of the scene, working by his flashlight and the floodlights set up for the photographers and fingerprint men. The stillness was punctuated by the static of the radios from the police cars that now rimmed the road.

Lundblad ordered his men, Officers Butterbach and Waterman, to the hospital to get a statement from David. At 12:23 they arrived at the intensive care unit, sought out nurse Barbara Lowe, and were told that the boy had arrived at the hospital D.O.A. He had been pronounced dead at 12:05.

The officers called the Sheriff's Office and had Deputy J.R. Wilson come to the facility, where he took photos of the close-range powder burns on the boy's left ear, the lump on his right cheek, and the blood-matted hair.

Out on Lake Herman Road, the Rambler was dusted for latent prints. Then the policemen fanned out and began searching for the gun and other possible clues. The Benicia officers took measurements. Lundblad recorded them.

The photos and evidence gathered by the Benicia police would be turned over to the Solano County Sheriff's Office. Pitta and Warner had preserved a fairly good crime scene, the body had been isolated from its surroundings and nothing had been moved until it had been photographed, identified, and painstakingly measured so that the evidence could be brought to court untainted. Even so there were scant tangible clues. Checks were done for semen.

Beyond the chalk outline of the boy's head were even more empty shell casings; altogether, nine more expended casings were recovered. The murder weapon proved likely to be a .22-caliber J.C. Higgins model 80 or Hi Standard model 101. The bullets were Super X copper-coated long rifle ammo made by Winchester since October 1967, which made it pretty new.

A ricochet mark was found on the roof of the station wagon, and very slight shoeprints were found in front of the parked car, leading to the passenger side. Also, a deep heel print was found behind the pump house beyond the locked fence.

One of the ambulance attendants noted that he had never seen so much blood by the side of a road in his entire life. "It was an exceptionally gruesome case of double murder," concurred Lundblad.

At 1:04 A.M. Lundblad left for Vallejo General and then went on to the Colonial Chapels Funeral home, where he met with Butterbach and Waterman to confer with Horan on the position of the bullets in Betty Lou Jensen's body.

Lundblad stood in the shadows. Under the glare of the fluorescent lamps the mortician removed the clothing from the girl's body. Abruptly, an object fell from her white-and-pink panties and rolled across the floor to Lundblad's boots. The detective slowly bent down and picked it up. It was a 22-caliber pellet that had been trapped after passing through Betty Lou's body. Grimly, Lundblad placed the slug in a pill bottle, gathered up the bloody clothing, and returned to his office. Butterbach and Waterman worked until 4:30 A.M. and then called it a night.

An autopsy was performed on Betty Lou at noon, and on David an hour and a half later. It was at 1:38 that Dr. S. Shirai, the pathologist, found the bullet that had killed David, badly battered, flattened against the right side of the victim's skull. This was sent to Lundblad in cotton.

From the victims and the vehicle, seven slugs were reclaimed. Four of these slugs were in good condition, the remaining three in damaged condition. (Two were never recovered, lost somewhere in the field by Lake Herman Road.) Each recovered bullet had a right hand (clockwise) twist with six lands and six grooves —a "six and six."

When a gun is made, a rod studded with metal burrs, a "broach," is drawn through the barrel, leaving behind a spiral set of imperfections, the "rifling." This cuts into the fired bullet's sides, making it rotate and giving it better flight steadiness as it leaves the barrel. The process also leaves identifying markings on the bullet. These are called "grooves" (the spiral notches) and "lands" (the spaces in between the grooves). Like fingerprints, the imprints make the slug unique to the gun it was fired from. Under a comparison microscope, "ejector" and "extractor" marks can also link a spent shell to a specific gun.

As Lundblad put it, "The investigation would be handled like the limbs on a tree." He would methodically follow each lead as it branched from the facts. He began by making mileage and time studies, driving the distances from suspects' and witnesses' homes at various speeds. The victims' last day was exactingly reconstructed minute by minute; thirty-four detailed statements were taken. Lundblad investigated the private lives of the two victims, working almost around the clock. The family and friends of Betty Lou and David were questioned, as well as the routine local suspects. Among other possibilities, there were 290 registrants from Napa State Hospital for the Insane living in the area.

From Betty Lou's family Horan learned that there was a love-sick boy who had been "bugging" her at school and who had threatened David ("I'm thinking about using brass knucks on you"). They also suspected this boy might have been the one prowling about the yard at night. Horan passed this information on to Lundblad, who discovered the suspect had an airtight alibi: After his sister's birthday party the boy watched *Global Affair* on TV until 11:00—in the company of a Mare Island policeman.

Leads from the public were followed up ("Look for a dark car without any chrome . . ."). But there seemed to be no motive to the brutal slayings—outside of killing for the sheer joy of it. Lundblad could find no attempt at robbery or sexual molestation of the victims. Perhaps the killing itself had served as a sexual release for the murderer.

The news from Criminal Identification and Investigation (CI&I) in Sacramento was no better:

In addition to subjecting to further tests any J.C. Higgins, Model 80 automatic pistol recovered, further tests should be made on any weapons having the following characteristics:
  a. Cartridge cases: Semicircular firing pin impressions at 12 o'clock position, small extractor markings at 3 o'clock position. Very faint ejector marking at 8 o'clock position (latter may not always be detectable).
  b. Weapon barrel or test bullets: Six right-hand grooves, land and groove ratio 1:1+. Bullet groove width approximately .056 inch. Bullet land width approximately .060 inch.

Due to lack of sufficient unique structure it appears that considerable difficulty will be encountered in positively identifying the responsible weapon if it should be recovered. . . . From our examination it appears that a conclusive identification of the responsible weapon will be extremely difficult, if not impossible, even though it should be recovered.

Examination of the dress (Item 9) revealed one hole in the front near the center and five holes in the upper right side of the back.

No smoke or gunpowder residue was found in the vicinity of any of these holes except the topmost hole on the back. Near the latter one single grain of gunpowder was found. From these examinations, it therefore appears that the weapon was held at least several feet from the victim at the time of the shooting. The minimum distance it could have been held cannot be established without testing of the responsible weapon when it is recovered.

There were no witnesses, no motives, and no suspects.

2

Darlene Ferrin

Saturday, December 21, 1968

"This is scary. I knew the two kids who were killed on Lake Herman Road," confided Darlene Ferrin to her co-worker Bobbie Ramos.

"You did?" asked Bobbie.

"Yeah, I'm not going up there again," Darlene said to her with a shiver.

"I was standing at the counter talking to her," Bobbie told me later, "I can remember part just plain. She was saying, ' You know it gives me an eerie feeling.' She knew them either from Hogan High School . . . I don't know how close she knew them, but she knew who they were, more so the girl."

Hogan High School was just over a block from Betty Lou Jensen's home. Darlene had been a student there.

Every Friday, Saturday, and Sunday night Bobbie Ramos worked with Darlene until three in the morning at Terry's Restaurant on Magazine Street in Vallejo.

"One thing about Darlene," Bobbie recalled later, "she talked to everyone. I used to tell her, 'Don't talk to everybody, everybody's not your friend. You just think they are.' She was so

13

friendly people waited in line to get in her section. Darlene had braces on. Twenty-two and she wears braces. She looked more like seventeen. And acted seventeen. She had a Kewpie doll look, braces on, short blond hair, the type you want to take home."

Darlene weighed 130 pounds and was five feet five inches tall, with light brown hair and a penetrating blue gaze. Photos of her taken five years earlier, when she was sixteen, showed a remarkable resemblance to Betty Lou Jensen.

"When she didn't put her eyeglasses on she wore false eyelashes. She used to buy them by the dozen for us," said Bobbie. "Darlene was happy, laughing, joking, outgoing, not shy. Talkative. . . . She didn't mind meeting new people, new friends."

Darlene, her second husband, Dean, and their baby girl, Dena, lived at 560 Wallace in a building owned by Bill and Carmela Leigh, Dean's bosses at Caesar's Palace Italian Restaurant, where he worked as an assistant cook.

Wednesday, February 26, 1969

Karen, Darlene's seventeen-year-old babysitter, went to the front window and looked out onto Wallace Street. The car had been there since 10:00 P.M., and she was sure the man inside was watching the Ferrins' ground-level apartment.

The car was an American-made sedan, white colored with a large windshield, but it was so dark out that she couldn't read the license number even though the car was parked only about eight feet away.

The glow of a match flickered inside the car. The man in it lit a cigarette, and Karen got a partial look at him. He was heavyset, with a round face and curly, wavy dark brown hair. She thought he was middle-aged.

Karen was so distressed that she went into baby Dena's room and stayed close to her crib until Dean got home from work. Karen went to the window, debating whether to tell Dean about the stranger, but decided against it when she saw the white car was gone.

Thursday, February 27, 1969

Darlene was in the bathroom putting on her makeup to go out when Karen told her about the stranger.

"What did the car look like?" Darlene asked.

Karen told her.

"I guess he's checking up on me again. I heard he was back from out of state." Darlene paused. "He doesn't want anyone to know what I saw him do," she said. "I saw him murder someone."

Darlene mentioned a man's name—a short, common name. But Karen didn't hear her. She was too intent on the fact that Darlene was obviously frightened of this stranger.

When Darlene dropped by Terry's Restaurant that night, she was told a stocky man had been asking questions about her.

Saturday, March 15, 1969

Pam Suennen, Darlene's younger sister, had previously found two packages on the doorstep of the Ferrins' home, but she had never seen who'd left them. However, today she opened the front door in time to see a man in horn-rimmed glasses delivering a third package. She had seen him before, parked in front of the house in a white car.

"And he told me," Pam remembered, "that under no circumstances was I to look in that package. He stayed outside the door. He stayed outside in his car for the longest time after he delivered the package.

"When Darlene came home she asked if anything had come for her. I gave her the package and she took it into the back room and when I asked her what it was, she didn't say anything. From that point on she seemed different. She was real nervous and she took the phone in her bedroom and made a phone call and then she rushed me out and she took me home real fast."

Pam was finally able to learn that the first package contained a silver belt and purse from Mexico and the second package white and blue flower-print fabric. Darlene planned to use this fabric to make a jumpsuit.

Bobbie Ramos thought that Darlene's ex-husband, Jim, was in Mexico and had sent the first two packages through a man he met there. Jim had married Darlene in January 1966 under an assumed name, Phillips, five months after his discharge from the San Francisco Army Presidio. "Honest to God! Darlene was petrified of him," Bobbie told me later.

A co-worker of Darlene's at the phone company in San Francisco, Bobbie Oxnam, recalled, "Darlene was leery of Jim. She wouldn't be in the same room with him by herself. . . . One of the reasons we kicked them out of our apartment was because Jim had a gun (a .22) and we didn't want that."

Friday, May 9, 1969

Darlene and Dean purchased a small house at 1300 Virginia Street, next to the Vallejo Sheriff's Office, for $9,500.

Saturday, May 24, 1969

It was the painting party that finally induced Karen to stop babysitting for Darlene. Darlene had most of her new friends over to the Virginia Street house to help her clean it up, and Karen stayed with Dena. Three young men arrived who were so strange that they made Karen uncomfortable and so she left the house. Too, she had grown tired of covering up for Darlene's running around with other men, a guilt that had preyed on her mind for the last five months.

Darlene's younger, rebellious brother, Leo Suennen, was at the party, as well as the Mageau twins, Mike and David, close friends of Darlene who outdid themselves trying to do her favors. The other guests were Jay Eisen, Ron Allen, Rick Crabtree, Paul the bartender (not his real name), Richard Hoffman, Steve Baldino, and Howard "Buzz" Gordon; the latter three Vallejo cops. The only other woman there was Darlene's friend Sydne.

Darlene called her sister, Linda Del Buono, at about noon and asked her to come over. It was Linda who had first pointed out Darlene's increasing nervousness and physical degeneration. Darlene would not admit to any problems. Dean saw no change in his wife.

While Linda was on her way over, another guest, a stocky man, arrived at Darlene's new house.

"At the painting party," Linda told me later, "she was so scared she begged me, 'Just go, Linda, just go.' This guy at the party had no business being at her house, and she told me to stay away from him. He was the only one dressed neat. Everyone else had old jeans on and was painting.

"I can see his face with my eyes open, I can see him with my eyes closed. I remember him from later at Terry's, and I remember him at the painting party and Darlene was scared to death. She didn't expect him to show up. I can see him sitting there in the chair. The dark-rim glasses, the hair curly, wavy, an older-type man, he did have the dark-rim glasses like Superman wears.

"Overweight . . . he was five feet eight inches tall or so. Of course he was sitting down most of the time. I remember going in a little bedroom with Darlene and I asked, 'Darlene, what's wrong with you?' She was so nervous, she was so nervous. This guy was scaring the heck out of her. I mean she couldn't eat. She wasn't smiling. She wasn't being the Darlene that I knew. Something was bothering her. When I showed up he was already there. And Darlene begged me, 'Linda, don't go near him. Just don't talk to him.'

" 'Well, who is he?'

" 'Don't talk to him,' insisted Darlene.

"She didn't want me to have anything to do with him. She asked me to leave 'cause she didn't want him to know any part of the family. It was really strange. I thought about that, but then I went to Texas on my birthday in June."

Pam, Darlene's younger sister, arrived at the painting party shortly after Linda left. "I remember seeing this man leave a package on the doorstep at Wallace Street," she recalled for me, "and I remember seeing him at the painting party. . . . He liked to talk to me because I'm always a pretty honest person. Darlene got upset with me because she thought I was telling him too much. Well, he would ask me something. Darlene said, 'Pam, I'm going to stop asking you to my parties if you don't stop talking to him!' I said, 'I thought you were dating this guy the way he talks.'

"He was a very well-dressed guy with glasses. He had dark hair. He had a wart on his thumb. For some reason, I think Darlene met this man in the Virgin Islands. She mentioned a little bit about drugs. Groups of people constantly went into the bedroom all the time. I was never allowed back there.

"Someone mentioned something to the effect that somebody had been following Darlene and Darlene changed the subject and said, 'Don't worry about it, nobody's going to hurt me.' She was one of the most trusting people I've ever seen. I would have been scared to death if I had known someone was . . .

"I said, 'Darlene, aren't you scared?' She said, 'Nobody's going to do anything.' "

When Pam left the party, there were still fourteen people left and more coming. Some of these guests overheard the well-dressed man badgering Darlene about her sources of income. The stranger had a short, common nickname. Pam thought it was "Bob." (This name has been changed.)

Sunday, June 22, 1969

Linda had just gotten back from Texas and wanted to tell Darlene how her relatives were, so early in the morning she and her dad, Leo, went to Terry's Restaurant.

"When I walked into Terry's this one particular day with my dad, the man from the party was sitting there, and he was watching Darlene all the time," Linda told me with a shudder. "He was constantly watching her, and as I walked in he held the paper up over his face 'cause he noticed me."

The stranger gave Linda a "cold stare" and then went over to

Darlene, saying something to her and then leaving. Linda told her father about the man. "My dad said, 'Ain't no big thing.' He didn't think anything of it."

Pam saw the man too. "He was sitting at Terry's. I sat next to him. I remember he was eating strawberry shortcake. And I remember Darlene was very nervous because I was sitting next to him. He was talking to me and she was very nervous about the whole thing. She kept whispering to me to get away from him.

"He wore a leather jacket. He always smelled of leather, even the time he came to the house to deliver that package. He was the guy who was asking about her at work, prying into her finances. He was asking me about Darlene's little girl and what was her relationship with Dean: 'What did she do with her tips?' and 'She's really got her head together' and 'I understand Dean never wants to watch the baby.'

"I was there for two and one half hours sitting at that counter and he sat there the whole time eating strawberry shortcake. Darlene kept telling me to get away but I didn't want to go home because Harvey, my husband, wasn't home.

"The man didn't wear his glasses all the time. He put them on when he looked at the check. They were rim glasses, dark rims, black, so black," Pam concluded, "and he drove this car with old California plates. This man's car was solid white."

"She was scared of somebody," Darlene's friend Bobbie Oxnam told me later, "she had been scared for some time. It started right after the baby was born."

"Did she ever mention the name of this stranger?" I asked.

"No. I wish I could say that she did. She would make a statement every once in a while that she was having trouble or she was terrified of this guy. She would never go into it in any sort of depth."

Bobbie Ramos recalled for me that "About the beginning of June, Darlene told me of a man watching her. She told us about him again when we took her and her daughter to the Solano County Fair." She turned to her husband. "Do you remember that guy in the white car that used to bother Darlene all the time,

19

used to sit out in front of her house all the time, who drove her over here one day?" Her husband didn't. "He was thirty to twenty-eight and not heavy. He wore glasses."

"It was real nice when Darlene and Dean first got married," Carmela Leigh, the wife of Dean's boss, told me later. "She was funny and we used to laugh all the time, and then all of a sudden, she went to work at Terry's after the baby was born and then nobody saw her anymore. She was still funny and joking and laughing and giddy, but she didn't have time for anybody. She'd fly into the restaurant and be real excited 'cause she was going somewhere, just letting her husband know she wouldn't be home when he got home. That rubbed me wrong because I didn't like her being superexcited about her going out with a bunch of friends when she was married and had a baby." Carmella used to go over and keep Darlene company while she was pregnant and after the little girl, Dena, was born she would stop in and have a cup of coffee when she collected the rent on the apartment. "I only knew her for probably two years," Carmella recalled wistfully, "she was chubby and wore braces, and after she had the baby she was even chubbier, a very sloppy dresser. Then all of a sudden she started dressing real nice and lost a lot of weight and started fixing her hair, which I thought was great. But then when that started, her relationship with her husband ended. She was just never home. She had a whole group of new friends and I never hardly saw her. I never knew any of her friends or where she went. Our friendship kind of dwindled because she was never around, never home. Dean never knew where she was and I never saw her because she was always gone."

Everyone seemed to notice the change in Darlene, who was excitable and even more high-strung than before. She lost so much weight that people attributed her nervousness to diet pills. Darlene would talk so fast that she would 1..ix up her words and run them together.

"Dean and her were kind of switchy at times," said Bobbie Oxnam. "They had their problems same as any newly married couple with a child. . . . She was very much outgoing. She just liked being around people and Dean didn't. I think that put a strain on their marriage at times. She was not a tramp; she was no angel but she was not a tramp either."

Carmela had often seen Darlene in good clothes and one day commented on a beautiful halter top with a blouse over it.

"Oh, I bought this at James Sears," said Darlene.

"Shoot," Carmela thought, "here I own my own business and I can't even shop at James Sears."

"And that's how I knew where she got her clothes," Carmela said to me later. "Now where did she get the money? Dean never knew where she got the money to buy clothes from. He was only a cook and she was only a waitress. She would say that she got them on sale, but I know she used to buy them at James Sears and that isn't a cheap store.

"So her husband didn't want to think of anything. It never crossed his mind that she was dealing in narcotics or something. He wouldn't think about it. He would say, 'It's just something she's got to get out of her system. She just turned twenty-one.' "

Among Darlene's friends it was no secret that she had been dating other men, including policemen from the Sheriff's Office.

"She used to go to San Francisco a lot," Bobbie Ramos recalled. "That's one thing we knew, too, 'cause she used to tell her husband. . . . You don't come home all excited and tell your husband, 'Oh, I had so much fun. I met these guys in the city and we went to the beach and did this and did that.' "

"A lot of times she'd just go by herself," Bobbie Oxnam said later. "She loved the surf area to think, she'd sit in the surf and watch the sun come up."

"I heard she didn't drive. What did she do, take the bus?" I asked.

"She drove. She drove without a license. She drove all the time. She was very capable. A lot of times she'd have a friend's car, Dean's boss' car," she said.

Distant from everyone, Darlene would come home almost at dawn when Dean was already asleep, creep under the covers, and with one leg out of bed rock herself quietly to sleep. By the time she awoke, Dean would have left for work.

Tuesday, June 24, 1969

Darlene told her younger sister, Christina, "There's going to be some big things happening in the next few days." Darlene said this in a very mysterious way. "And it's really something. Really something big is gonna happen."

"What?" asked Christina.

"I can't tell you yet but you'll read about it in the paper."

Christina had no idea what Darlene was talking about. "That was real confusing," she told Carmela Leigh. "I don't know if it's narcotics or a murder or a party."

"Then," said Carmela, "we thought Darlene knew something about a narcotics bust or something she had heard from one of her policemen friends."

"Darlene never verbalized precisely what made her afraid of this man in the white car," Bobbie Oxnam later told me. "He had something on her but what he had I don't know. I have a feeling it's connected with the Virgin Islands but that's just a hunch. Jim and her got involved with the wrong people while they were there on their honeymoon. That's why they left so fast. Now what kind of trouble I can't say."

The couple had hitched to St. Thomas and the Virgin Islands, panhandling, diving for shells, sleeping on the beach.

Pam suspected that this was where Darlene had seen a murder.

Friday, July 4, 1969

At 3:45 P.M., Dean Ferrin reported for work at the Leighs' Italian restaurant. Fifteen minutes later, Darlene called her friend Mike Mageau and made a date to go to the movies in San Francisco at 7:30 that evening.

Mike and his twin brother, David, had first met Darlene at Terry's. "Now this fellow Mike was a very peculiar fellow," Sergeant John Lynch said later. "When he and his brother came to Vallejo they went into the coffee shop and got to talking to Darlene. Apparently she was a really outgoing, gregarious-type person and they told her a lie, that they were wanted in Chicago for a shooting or something like that and I guess that's what intrigued her with the guy in the first place." Bobbie Ramos also recalled that "the twins gave Darlene a story about running away. One told her he was 'Warren Beatty' and the other that he was 'David Jansen.' They gave her some kind of line and she believed everything. She just fell right in with the deception. You know, she thought if you had a problem, she had a problem."

In reality they were the sons of the owner of a local pest control agency. An intense rivalry developed between the twins over the affections of Darlene and they often fought over driving her to work.

Linda remembered, "Both of these guys were jealous of Darlene. 'I want to do her washing.' 'No, I do.' Back and forth they fought over her. It was pathetic."

The twins were green eyed, black haired, six feet two inches tall, and extremely thin. They would be twenty in October. Their father said that Darlene called the Mageau house often, as much as twice a day.

At 4:30 P.M., Bill Leigh opened the doors of his restaurant at 80 14th Street. At 6:00, Carmela, who was pregnant and hadn't been working, dropped by Caesar's to spend an hour or two.

Thirty minutes later, she looked up to see Darlene and her fifteen-year-old sister, Christina, come into the restaurant. Darlene was wearing a jump suit that zipped up the front and had red, white, and blue stars all over it. They had come to see Dean on their way out to Mare Island for the Fourth of July celebration and boat parade on the channel. Christina was runner-up in the "Miss Firecracker" competition and they were to ride in the boat parade that night.

"Darlene went out to Mare Island to ride on one of the boats that was all lit up," Carmela told me later. "All I know is that she came into the restaurant and said she knew some people that had a boat . . . and she was going to go down there too."

"What time will you be home?" asked Dean. "I'm inviting some people from the restaurant over to our house for a little party."

"Oh, I'll be home about ten," said Darlene.

"Well, stop and get some fireworks," said Dean, "and we'll be there about midnight."

"O.K."

"She was going to take off and go down to the boat parade and then get the fireworks," Carmella recalled. "She was all excited. She had friends and didn't say who they were only that she was going to ride on their boat. Dean was kind of worried that if she went off with her friends she might not come home and he had already invited us all over."

At 6:45, Darlene went into Terry's to tell Bobbie about the party that was going to be held at her house.

"She just rattled on and on and on," Bobbie Ramos told me. "She stood right at the cash register, gave some rollers to Jane Rhodes to hold for her, and was talking about her sister winning 'Miss Firecracker' and she was going to have a party and she wanted me to come. Finally I said, 'O.K., O.K.,' but Darlene knew I wouldn't be there and then Harley, the manager, walked up. 'Get out of here and quit bothering my girls,' he said. He wasn't mad. She used to do it all the time. When Darlene left at 7:00 she said, 'I'm going to come back to see you.' "

An hour later, Mike received a call from Darlene saying that she had to spend some more time with Christina and would call or be by later. When Christina and Darlene returned from Mare Island they went by Caesar's again, and at 10:15 Darlene called the sitter to see how things were. The sitter told her that one of her friends at Terry's had been trying to reach her.

Darlene drove into Terry's parking lot at 10:30 and talked for about ten minutes with her friend. As she and Christina were leaving, Darlene stopped and talked with an older man in a white car in the lot. Christina noticed the conversation between the two was strained and she "sensed tension in the air." Christina observed that the stranger's car was bigger and older than Darlene's '63 Corvair. Darlene said nothing about the man on the way to the Suennen family home, where she let Christina off.

Darlene arrived at her new home on Virginia and the sitter, Janet Lynne, met her at the door. She told Darlene an older-sounding man had been calling all evening but wouldn't leave his name or any messages. "He said he'd call back," said Janet.

Darlene changed out of her star-spangled jumpsuit into a white and blue flower-print jumpsuit, which had been made from the fabric that had been left in a package on her doorstep by the man in the white car. Darlene woke up Dena and began playing with her and explained to Janet and her friend, Pamela, that "I'm having some friends over here tonight for a little party."

Darlene planned on taking the sitters home and then coming back to clean the house up. However, just as Darlene, carrying Dena, had the girls bundled up in the Corvair, the phone inside began to ring and she rushed to answer it. When she returned, she asked if the two girls would mind staying until around 12:15 and they agreed. Darlene explained, "I have to go back out and get fireworks for the party."

Darlene left immediately, taking Georgia Street east directly to Beechwood Avenue, where she made a left to Mike's house at 864 Beechwood, four-and-one-half blocks from the Jensen home. Mike lived just to the west of Hogan High (Betty Lou Jensen had lived just to the south).

Darlene stopped in front of the house, turned off the engine, and waited. In a moment Mike rushed out in such a hurry that he left all the lights blazing, the door standing open, and the television playing.

In the driver's seat, Darlene started the ignition and gestured impatiently for Mike to get in. As the bronze Corvair pulled off, they were trailed immediately by a light-colored car that had been parked in the shadows of the tree-lined street.

"We're being followed," Mike said.

Darlene sped off to Oakwood, took a right on Springs Road, and started out toward Columbus Parkway, the same direction as Lake Herman Road.

It was 11:55 P.M. now.

The car raced behind them at high speed. Darlene kept turning to lose the stranger. She began going down side streets, but the car behind followed closer and faster.

Mike kept telling her, "Oh, no, no, no, no, go straight . . . go straight!" Finally Mike said, "Just go this way." With the other car in hot pursuit, they were being chased inexorably toward the outskirts of the city.

Still within the city limits and only four miles from downtown Vallejo was Blue Rock Springs Golf Course, another well-known lovers' lane, and this was where Darlene and Mike were being herded. Darlene nervously turned right into the parking lot. Seventy-two feet from the entrance she hit a log and stalled the engine.

The parking lot was about two miles from the site of the Jensen-Faraday murders almost seven months before, but was not nearly as secluded. The lot overlooked the golf course; to Darlene's extreme right was a grove of trees. Hers was the only car in the lot.

The couple sat in the darkness only a moment when the other auto, similar in design to the Corvair, caught up with them in the lot, turned out its lights, and then parked eight feet to their left. The front of the car was nearly even with the back bumper of Darlene's car; Mike thought the car might be a '58 or '59 Falcon, with old California plates. He could tell the driver was a man.

"Do you know who it is?" whispered Mike.

"Oh, never mind," said Darlene finally. "Don't worry about it."

Mike didn't know if this meant she knew who it was or not.

Almost immediately, the other car roared off at a high rate of speed, heading toward Vallejo. Mike breathed a sigh of relief.

In five minutes, though, the car returned. Now it parked to their left and to the rear of the Corvair with its lights on. Mike noticed the other car had pulled up behind them at sort of an offline from their car, a cut-off technique used by highway patrolmen. Mike has been parked in the same lot once before and a police officer had come up in this same manner.

Suddenly, a bright and powerful light, like a policeman's spotlight, was beamed at them from within the other car. The lone occupant of the car threw open his door and, carrying a large flashlight extended in front of him, advanced toward the couple, all the while shining the glaring light from one face to the other.

The light went out. It was a "floating lantern" with a handle of the type Mike had seen on boats.

Thinking it was the police, Mike suggested to Darlene, "Here come the cops, you better get your identification out," and reached for his right rear pocket to get his wallet. Darlene took hers out of her purse and replaced the purse in the rear behind Mike's seat. The man strode to the passenger side of the car; the window was down.

Without warning, the blinding light exploded on again directly into Mike's eyes. The stranger was invisible. Mike heard the clink of metal against the window frame, saw a muzzle flash and smoke erupt. The roar of the shot filled his ears. The bullet hit with tremendous heat and Mike felt his blood flowing. Even though the shots seemed loud, Mike got the impression the gun had some sort of silencer on it. The man pumped more shots at the couple.

Darlene slumped forward over the steering wheel, hit by bullets that had passed through Mike's body and by bullets aimed at her. She was wounded by nine rounds. Two bullets caught her in the right arm and two in the left arm. Five bullets hit her in the right side of her back, piercing her lung and the left ventricle of her heart.

Mike reached for the door handle, his fingers scrambling frantically, and to his horror realized that it had been removed. He was helpless—unable to get away from the fiendish killer shooting at him. The boy had been wounded in the right arm and was in terrible pain while the attacker, without a word, turned and began walking away, his head down.

Mike let out a loud cry of agony.

The gunman, in the process of opening his car door and doing something Mike could not make out, stopped in the still, silent summer night, turned slowly, and looked over the shoulder of his Navy-type windbreaker in Mike's direction. With his hand on the door handle, the stocky man's profile was illuminated by the interior light of his car, and for the first time Mike saw the face of his attacker.

The man appeared to have a large face and was not wearing glasses. He seemed to be between twenty-six and thirty years old and had short, curly, light-brown hair worn in a military style crewcut. The man's build was "beefy, heavyset without being blubbery fat," perhaps 195 to 200 pounds. Mike estimated that he was one head higher than Darlene's Corvair, about five feet eight inches tall. His pants had pleats but Mike could see that he had a slight potbelly.

The intruder had stopped, looked back at Mike, and now was returning to finish the job. The stocky man leaned into the Corvair through the open window and fired two more shots at Mike. Mike kicked out with his legs in a pathetic attempt at self-defense. With nowhere else to go he leaped backward into the rear of the auto, legs thrashing spasmodically.

The man fired two more shots at Darlene, turned away, got into his car, and drove off just fast enough to make the gravel fly.

Mike, badly wounded in the left leg, right arm, and neck, finally was able to regain the front seat. He opened the passenger door from the outside and toppled from the Corvair onto the parking lot. Blood rushed from the wound to his cheek and neck; the bullet had entered from the right and exited from his left cheek, ripping a hole through his jawbone and tongue. It felt like a "sledgehammer had hit" him, and when he tried to speak he could only gurgle. He could not even call out for help.

In the front seat he could hear Darlene moan.

At about midnight, in his home eight hundred feet from the Blue Rock Springs parking lot, George Bryant, the twenty-two-year-old son of the course caretaker, was having trouble sleeping on such a hot night. George was in his bedroom on the second story of the house and lying on his stomach peering out the window overlooking the park.

He had gone to bed a half hour earlier and lay listening to people laughing in the distance and a few exploding fireworks. Suddenly George heard a gunshot. A short interval of silence and then another gunshot. A short pause again and then rapid fire. Soon he heard a car take off at "super speed and burn rubber." The attacker's luck was holding. George could see most of the lot, but the spot where Darlene's car was stopped was hidden by trees.

Three teenagers, Debra, Roger, and Jerry, were looking for a friend of Roger's. They had come to Blue Rock Springs after a day of celebrating the Fourth in the downtown area of Vallejo. As they passed the main parking lot they noticed Darlene's Corvair and they thought to check to see if this was the missing friend.

They decided it wasn't and were about to leave when they heard a muffled scream. Debra backed the car up and turned it to shine the high beams on the Corvair. They saw a man rolling in agony on the ground.

Debra pulled up as close as she dared and stopped. All three teenagers ran up to the injured man.

"Are you all right?"

"I'm shot," Mike was finally able to get out, "and the girl's shot. Get a doc."

"All right," said Jerry. "We'll get you one."

"Hurry."

Roger wanted to stay behind with Mike but Debra and Jerry urged him to come with them to Jerry's house to call the police. As the brown Rambler turned out of the lot and onto Columbus Parkway, the three teenagers thought they could see the red points of taillights disappearing down Lake Herman Road.

Debra called the police from Jerry's and told them what she had seen. As time went by the three became anxious and went to Jerry's uncle, who was a policeman. The uncle checked and found a car had already been dispatched to the scene. The four then went to police headquarters.

The Vallejo P.D. switchboard operator, Nancy Slover, had received a report from a female caller that "two persons were shot at the east side of the main parking lot at Blue Rock Springs at 12:10 A.M." Detective Sergeant John Lynch and his partner, Sergeant Ed Rust, were in their car in plain clothes when the report came through.

"I tell you the way this thing come down," Lynch told me later. "We worked Sonoma Boulevard and Tennessee Street, and we got a report there was gunshots out at Blue Rock Springs. I was

29

driving the car and made a U-turn and started down Tennessee Street. I talked to Rust and he says, 'Aw, it's the Fourth of July and there's kids out there shooting firecrackers,' ... so we kinda moped around and didn't roll on it. I guess about ten minutes later we got the call there was a shooting out there.

"It's the one thing I felt really bad about, that we didn't roll right away on that call. If we had went right out Tennessee Street that car would have had to pass us. 'Cause he came down Tennessee and then he turned on Tuolumne. ... I don't think he made any turn on Lake Herman Road. I got to the scene fifteen minutes after it happened."

Rust and Lynch could see Darlene's Chevrolet on the east side of the lot, pointed toward the park area. The car's head and taillights were on, the turn signal was flashing, and the passenger door was open.

Officer Richard Hoffman and Sergeant Conway were on the scene already, attempting to question Mike, who was bleeding badly from severe wounds in the neck, the chest and shoulder area, and the left leg. He was lying at the rear of the Corvair, at right angles to it. Lynch called for an ambulance from Kaiser Hospital.

"Mageau was really in great pain," Lynch said later. "To tell you the truth, when we got there I didn't think she was hit too hard. ... I thought Mike was the one who ... he seemed to be in great pain from the hit in the knee."

Lynch and Rust bent over Mike and noticed something weird. The boy was wearing three pairs of pants, three sweaters, a long-sleeved button shirt, and a T-shirt. On a hot July Fourth night!

They could see Darlene was wearing a white-and-blue flowered outfit and blue shoes. Behind the wheel she opened her eyes slightly; she still had her false eyelashes on. Lynch and Rust both knew who she was. "Lots of cops knew her and used to stop in at the coffee shop out there where she worked. I knew who Darlene was," said Lynch, "but I never talked to her. In fact, her family lives just down the street from my house. She liked to run in the ocean. She'd take her shoes and stockings off and just run through the surf.

"She dated a lot of officers. Apparently she was the type of person who liked policemen. When people work nights, usually those are the kind of people who like policemen."

Lynch noticed that Mike's position on the ground had been carefully outlined with white chalk by Conway. Mike's eyes were wide and he struggled to open his mouth to speak. When he finally did, blood gushed out. In halting words and between spasms of pain he told Lynch, "A white man . . . drove up . . . in a car . . . got out . . . walked up to the car, shined flashlight inside . . . started shooting.

"I got . . . out of car . . . I tried to get the people to come over . . . but they drive off. After . . . finally ten minutes . . . the policemen came."

"Do you know who shot you?" asked Conway.

"No."

"Can you give me a description?"

"Can't."

"Try."

"Young . . . heavyset . . . in a light tan car."

"Did he say anything?"

"No. He just started shooting . . . and kept shooting."

Again Lynch went to the driver's side of the Corvair, where Darlene was still behind the wheel. He could see she was wounded in the upper body and left arm and was still alive. She was making a soft moaning sound like the wind.

"Where is that ambulance?" muttered Lynch.

"I remember," he told me, "she was trying to say something and I put my ear over her like this to try to understand, but I just couldn't. The words she said were either 'I' or 'My . . .' " Her pulse was weak and her breathing shallow. Lynch got Darlene out and laid her on the ground.

Rust noted that both windows on the left and right were rolled down and the ignition key was turned to on. The radio was on and the car was in low gear. Even the handbrake had not been set. He wondered about this.

Seven shell casings were found a few feet away from the victims on the right side. Rust peered in from the right side and could see three bullet holes in Darlene, two in her upper right arm and one in her right side.

When the ambulance arrived, Lynch helped the steward lift Darlene into the vehicle. Hoffman accompanied the victims to the hospital in case Darlene should be able to say something.

Lynch had called out three fire trucks to illuminate the area with floodlights while Rust checked out the area where Mageau had been lying. Approximately where the center of Mike's back had been, he found a copper-jacketed slug, badly misshapen but recognizable as a 9-mm. or .38 caliber. There was no blood or skin on the slug. Rust bagged it and marked it.

Now Rust checked the place where Darlene had been slumped behind the wheel and found another slug, similar to the one under Mike but in better condition. He continued to inspect the inside of the car and found on the right rear floorboard two spent shell casings, brass, marked with a "W-W"; they appeared to Rust to be 9-mm ammunition. Lynch himself was not overly familiar with guns.

The inside of the Corvair was very bloody. Rust knelt down by the driver's side and, looking closely, found that a hole about one-half inch to one inch long had been made in the door handle area. He made a note for I.D. technician John Sparks to dig inside the door when the car was towed to the impound room at the Vallejo P.D.

Rust noticed a man's black leather wallet on the right rear fender, where Hoffman had placed it. Rust looked through it and then in the glove compartment, where he found registration papers for the auto in the name of Arthur Ferrin, Dean's father.

On the left rear floorboard he discovered a woman's quilt pattern purse, tied with a leather drawstring and covered with blood. There was only thirteen cents inside.

Rust could hear the static of their car phone. Lynch went for it. It was Hoffman calling.

Darlene was D.O.A. at 12:38 A.M.

At exactly 12:40, a man placed a call through an operator from a pay phone to the Vallejo P.D. Switchboard operator Nancy Slover answered.

"I want," said the man, "to report a double murder." There was no trace of accent in the voice and it seemed to Nancy that the man was reading what he was saying. Or had rehearsed it.

"If you will go one mile east on Columbus Parkway to the public park, you will find kids in a brown car."

The stranger's voice was even and consistent, soft but forceful. Nancy tried to interrupt him to get more information but he just talked louder, covering her voice. To her the caller sounded mature. He did not stop talking until he had completed his statement to her.

"They were shot with a 9-millimeter Luger. I also killed those kids last year.

"Good-bye."

When he said "good-bye," the man's voice deepened and became taunting. Nancy heard the sound of a receiver being replaced. She was left listening to the empty hum of the line.

After he hung up, the killer must have stood for a minute in a lighted phone booth. Suddenly the phone began to ring; a middle-aged black man in shabby clothes who was passing by looked over and saw the stocky man in the booth. Turning his head away, the killer opened the door of the phone booth, plunging it into darkness. To stop the phone from ringing he unhooked it and let it hang. After a moment, he walked briskly off into the night.

At 12:47, Pacific Telephone had traced the call to Joe's Union Station at Tuolumne and Springs Road, located right in front of the Vallejo Sheriff's Office and within sight of Darlene and Dean's little green house on Virginia. The stocky man may have looked in the house as he passed it after making his call. Dean was still working at this time, so the only occupants were Dena and the babysitter and her friend.

The police placed a call to Dean's father because the Corvair was registered in his name. Thus his father learned of Darlene's death first.

The police then tried to contact anyone at the Mageau residence by phone, and when this failed, they dispatched Officer Shrum and his partner to the Beechwood address. They got out of their squad car and approached the house carefully since the door was standing open and all the lights were blazing. Except for the blaring television, the two officers could hear no other sound in the building. They found the house empty.

After locking up Caesar's, the owners and help, including Dean, started west toward the Ferrins' house on Virginia for the party. Bill Leigh and Dean, in separate cars, stopped at Pete's Liquor Store and bought some liquor.

"After we closed the restaurant," Carmela remembered later, "the waitresses and all of us got in our cars and we all went over to his house. When we arrived there was a babysitter, two young girls Dean didn't know, never had seen before. They were daughters of a friend of Darlene's. Which made it embarrassing for Dean. He felt a little funny. They were supposed to be taken home, but Darlene never came back.

"That's why we were wondering, 'Well, where is she? What is she doing?' The sitters said that Darlene had said she was going to get some fireworks."

Dean left to find her. The phone rang at 1:30 and Bill Leigh picked it up. All he could hear on the line was heavy breathing. "Probably one of Darlene's goofy friends," he said to Carmela over his shoulder.

Bill was gruff. "Why doesn't she stay home with her husband once in a while," he said into the mouthpiece and hung up.

A few minutes later, Dean's parents received a similar call and could hear only deep breathing or "the wind on the end of the line." All they could tell was that someone was there.

Dean's brother got a crank call next.

Thus there were three anonymous calls to relatives of Darlene less than an hour and a half after she was shot, long before any mention of the crime in the paper or on the radio. Darlene's own parents, the Suennens, got no such calls; they had an unlisted number.

Was the killer searching for a specific person to speak to? Was it Dean he wanted to taunt, and did he know the sound of his voice? Although Dean and Darlene kept the same phone number when they had moved to Virginia Street, they were listed in the book as still living on Wallace. If the killer had been a stranger, he would have assumed that he was calling a house many blocks away; yet he used a pay phone within sight of the couple's new home.

"Finally, somewhere around 2:00 A.M., Darlene's husband came home," Janet, the sitter, told me later. "He said, 'I'll just take you home.' He seemed worried or upset, like something was bothering him, something was on his mind. He said something like, 'Darlene's not coming home yet,' and then he just took us right home."

"Dean took the kids home right away, whatever time it was then," Carmela recalled. "He was probably gone ten minutes. We heard about the murder when the police came to the door. We were still there hanging around. Yeah, we were all there wondering where Darlene was and where the fireworks were and we were just kinda sitting around the room talking for about an hour when there was a knock at the door. And then the police came to the door so my husband and Dean went to the police station, and as soon as they walked out of the door one of the policemen came in the house and asked us some questions about where Dean had been earlier that night. I guess immediately the husband is suspect in a case like that.

"So we told him we all worked together and we all came over for a party and we were waiting for Darlene and then we said, 'What happened?'

"He told us she had been shot and was with another man. 'Is she all right?' I asked him. He said, 'No. She's dead.' And boom! That shook it. It just upset everybody. He told us all, but Dean didn't know until he got to headquarters."

The police questioned Dean and Leigh for an hour, keeping as much information from them as possible.

"We heard she had a boyfriend," the detectives said to Dean.

"Well, Dean never wanted to know that," Carmela said later. "In fact, he didn't want to believe that. When she was going out all of the time people would tell him, 'Boy, you better find out who she's going out with.' He used to say, 'She's not doing anything wrong. She doesn't have a boyfriend. She's just young and has to get it out of her system.' So he really did love her and he used to protect her when people would tell him things about her. And after it was over, when he would hear bad things about her he would clam up. He didn't know any more than any of us. The last year he didn't even know her."

Bill Leigh told the police, "I don't know any reason anyone would want to kill Darlene."

The official police report of Bill's questioning in room 28 at Vallejo P.D. reads as follows:

William did state that he knew that she was running around a lot and thought she was seeing other men, could not give names or dates, places, of any of this. Stated she would go out and stay out until late nite or early A.M. Stated some of William's friends had said they had seen Darlene in different places with other men. William stated Dean allowed her to go out usually as she pleased and would not believe she was doing anything wrong.

William then stated he remembered a person known only as "Paul" [this name has been changed], who Dean had sold a '51 Ford pickup to. Stated he heard this Paul had tried several times to get Darlene to go out with him and she would not and this Paul became sarcastic, mean, and bitter about the fact she would not have anything to do with him. . . . William stated he had never met this Paul as far as he knows and does not know where he lives or works. Has heard that he is a bartender. . . . He heard that this Paul used to hang out around the bar (Jack's Hangout) that was next to Darlene's old place on Wallace, would come over when Darlene was home and pester her, trying to pick her up.

Bobbie Ramos found out about the shooting at a quarter after midnight from Officer Howard "Buzz" Gordon, a mutual friend of Darlene and Bobbie. "He called me up at work and told me. He might have been at headquarters when the call came in," she told me later. At 2:30 A.M., Sergeant Rust arrived at Terry's to talk with Darlene's co-workers.

Bobbie Ramos was first. She had spent some evenings with Darlene at the Coronado Inn, where she liked to dance. The only male friend of Darlene's that Bobbie knew was Mike.

(After Darlene's death Bobbie moved from the more isolated working area of Terry's to the Banquet Room, where she would see two hundred people at a time.)

Rust then talked with Evelyn Olson, who claimed that she had been told by Darlene that her marriage was about at an end. "Darlene thought her husband didn't love her anymore. She told me this around Christmas, and after she told me this she began dating other men. Darlene had many boyfriends but nothing serious," said Evelyn.

Just past 3:00 A.M., Rust spoke with Lois McKee, the cook, who told him that although Darlene had many male friends, she seemed to stick mainly with Mike, and in fact she knew of a trip to San Francisco the two had made within the last month.

Harley Scalley, the manager, confirmed that Darlene "ran around with several men." "Darlene dated a lot of guys?" I asked Lynch later, and he replied, "Oh, all kinds of guys. She was a goer."

But Bobbie, Evelyn, and Lois all recalled one particular individual, a short stocky man with black hair who kept trying to date Darlene. The man had a pink pickup and a brown car, possibly a Corvair, and "would get uptight when Darlene wouldn't date him. He would become very bitter about this." The women did not know the man's last name but they did know he was a bartender. And that his first name was Paul.

At 3:30 A.M., Darlene's body was taken to Twin Chapels and photos were made.

"I was pregnant at the time," Darlene's sister, Linda, remembered, "and I went into the mortuary and she was laying on this slab and they said, 'She's not finished yet,' and I said, 'I want to see her now.'

"And I broke through. . . . I had so much adrenaline in me. . . . I broke through those doors and touched her and I'll never forget that because it was like touching marble or a doll. And her hair was orange and her mouth still had blood on it. They had sewed up her mouth but it was still bloody. I kinda wish in a way I hadn't but that's what I wanted to do so I did it."

Lynch was still out at Blue Rock Springs at seven in the morning. "We were searching for whatever we could find. Ed Cruz made an elaborate sketch of the whole area. They dug a perfect bullet out of the car, one that wasn't smashed. It probably went through the fleshy part of her body and then just had enough momentum to penetrate the upholstry and they just dug that out."

As the barrage of shots fired by the killer in the parking lot was recovered, the detectives found nine 9-mm casings and seven copper-jacketed 9-mm slugs in various conditions.

Since the killer had fired at least nine shots and possibly as many as thirteen without reloading, they believed the weapon would almost certainly be a Browning. (Smith and Wesson did produce the M59 Pistol, a 9-mm Parabellum that operated on a Modified Browning system and had a magazine capacity of fourteen rounds. It has been marketed as a police sidearm.) All other semi-automatics considered—Star, Smith and Wesson, Astra, Llama, Neuhausen, Zbrojovka', Husqvarna, Esperanza and Parabellum (Luger)—had only a magazine capacity of eight or seven bullets. The Browning 1935 High Power (FN GP35), manufactured in Canada by the John Inglis Company since World War II and used by the Canadian army, holds thirteen cartridges in a double-rowed, staggered box magazine.

Rust arrived at Blue Rock Springs with a still badly shaken Linda and her husband. Linda told Lynch that Darlene's three closest friends were Sue, Dean's cousin, and Bobbie, "the blond at Terry's," and a man known only as "Bob," who used to bring Darlene presents from Tijuana. Linda also mentioned Paul. "Paul tried to date Darlene but she didn't like him particularly. He was a neat dresser, short, stocky, with dark hair," she said. "He visited Darlene frequently; he was very emotional."

Lynch spoke with Mike's father, who had stayed the night of the killing at Kentwig's Motel, and he said that "Darlene had called several times on Friday." As for Mike's twin, he had supposedly been living in L.A. for four to five weeks before Darlene's death, but there were conflicting claims to this.

At 8:25 A.M., Mike was operated on. During the emergency

surgery his fractured jaw was wired and his left leg repaired with the use of three metal pins and protected with a full leg cast. One slug was removed from his thigh by the doctor; this was put in a glass bottle and delivered to Lynch. Most of the delicate surgical work was done on his arm because of some splintering. Mike's acute tongue injury still prevented him from being able to speak without great pain.

At 9:30 A.M., John Sparks, the I.D. man, gave the Corvair a through going-over in the police garage.

At 11:15, Lynch and Rust went to the Suennen family home. Darlene's father, Leo, said that Darlene had no known enemies but "at times she appeared to be afraid of Mageau."

Even though he was heavily sedated, Mike was finally interviewed from his hospital bed by Lynch. Carefully Mike emphasized it was "dark out and hard to see." In weak, halting words he related to Lynch the events of the tragic Fourth. Only one part of the story was altered: "Darlene picked me up at 11:40, and since we were both hungry we headed down Springs Road west toward Vallejo, but at Mr. Ed's we turned around at my suggestion and drove to Blue Rock Springs so we could talk."

From a confidential report I learned of another change in Mike's story. Sue Ayers, a legal secretary, claimed that she had talked to Mike in the hospital after the shooting and he told her that Darlene and another man had an argument while he was present in Darlene's car at Terry's the night of the shooting, and that when they drove away the stranger followed them to Blue Rock Springs, where the argument continued. And that they were shot by that man. Mike also told her that they were followed "at least from the time she picked me up at my house."

In subsequent interviews Mike said the attacker wore a blue shirt or sweater, weighted about 160 pounds, and combed his hair "up in kind of a pompadour and then back." The car was changed to a light, tan Chevy.

Darlene's sister, Pam, stated that Mike told her at the hospital that "the guy came up and shot. . . . He knew Darlene because he called her by name. She was known to her close friends as 'Dee' and he called her 'Dee.' "

"Why do you think Mike doesn't want to tell certain things to the police?" I asked Pam later.

"Well, he was in love with Darlene," she suggested. "Mike wrote her letters. When Darlene died they found three letters from Mike, all signed by a different name. Mike liked to pretend to be different people."

The police contacted the sitters and asked them to come down.

"They were very pushy. So definite. We'd say something and the policeman'd say, 'No, that couldn't be,' until you just figured, 'No, it couldn't be.' You don't argue when you're that young with a police officer. You know you're really young when you're fourteen," Janet told me some years later. "It's really strange. They take you to a police station and you have nightmares for weeks afterward, but you try to remember everything."

"I have here," said Lynch, "that Darlene came home at 11:00 and cleaned the house."

"No," said Janet. "It was actually around 11:35."

"There was a big discrepancy," said Janet, "between the police report and the time she really came home. They kept telling us that she had to be home at 11:00 and we kept telling them it was later. They didn't even bother to write it down. What time did you say she was murdered? Midnight. She didn't even leave until almost midnight 'cause we were watching a program that doesn't come on until almost midnight and she was murdered like five minutes later. How could she get out there in five minutes? And she picked up somebody else, too. We thought it was important. You can't get all the way out there that quick."

A hot pursuit would explain the speed.

As in the Lake Herman murders, there was no sexual molestation or robbery. In both cases the killer had fired a fusillade of shots and had left behind no identifiable tire tracks or footprints. The slayer did possess a thorough knowledge of the geography of Vallejo. Was he a resident of Vallejo, perhaps a neighbor of Jensen or Faraday, or even a common friend of all the victims?

Lynch contacted Lundblad, who compared both crimes and decided the phone call to the police was not a ruse. Lundblad spoke to the press and told of the similarities in the murders, but did not mention the call or elaborate on the evidence.

A Vallejo policeman who had dated Darlene fell under suspicion, was cleared by Lynch, but eventually left the department.

Sunday, July 6, 1969

At 12:02 A.M., Carmen, Mike's mother, arrived in Vallejo from Los Angeles. She and Mike's brother talked to Lynch. "Darlene had no known enemies," said Mike's twin.

A man and his son next phoned Lynch and told him that they had witnessed an argument between a man and a woman at Terry's parking lot around 10:30 P.M. on July Fourth. The man was thirty, about six feet tall, and weighed about 180 to 185. He had hair the color of champagne, combed straight back.

At 6:45 P.M., Lynch talked with the three teenagers who had come upon the murder. At 7:00 P.M., Darlene's father picked up Christina and the two sitters and took them to Darlene's house on Virginia, where they met Lynch and Rust.

Out of five detectives, Lynch was assigned as chief investigator on the murder. He assessed every possible motive from jealousy to revenge, but none of these panned out. The nature of the sick phone call led the detective to concentrate his search for a maniac.

"She was a beautiful girl. I was at the autopsy. I had no days off at all. For a town like Vallejo this was a real big deal, especially after those two other kids," Lynch said mournfully.

Monday, July 7, 1969

The Corvair was returned and Linda and her father had to move the car down the hill away from the house to clean it. "It was all full of blood," said Linda, "and there was Dena crying for her mother. It was heartbreaking."

Dean brought all of Darlene's diaries, phonebooks, and papers to Lynch. He discovered a yellow photo envelope with strange words written on it. Dean was unable to explain what the writing might mean. The words "hacked," "stuck," "testified," and "seen" were on the edge of the envelope in Darlene's handwriting. Lynch could make out a series of partial words as well. They made no sense to him. They were "acrqu," "acci," "calc," and "icio." In addition she had circled the printed words "on," "by," and "at" and scratched out the word "highly." A phone number on the back proved to be that of Mr. Ed's Restaurant and Drive-In.

There were other disturbing things for Lynch to think about. Darlene had left to get fireworks on the night of the Fourth and yet her sister said she had already bought them. When Darlene was found, she had neither fireworks nor the money to buy any; only thirteen cents was found in her purse. "Seems to me," Lynch recalled, "she drove over to Mike's house and told him they were going to have a fireworks display at her house and she asked him to go with her so they could buy the fireworks. . . . There were booths all over town."

Tips to the police hinted that Darlene's murder involved narcotics, witchcraft from the Virgin Islands, and even a Satanic church, a devil cult in Vallejo.

I asked Linda about the witchcraft connection.

"Darlene was really into it even when she was seventeen. She believed in reincarnation and voodoo and stuff like that. The Virgin Islands, that's when she really got into it."

Carmela later told me, "She was probably in an occult. She probably was mixed up with some goofy people only 'cause she loved excitement. . . . Her being married previously to the kind of guy she was, it could have been a life-style for her."

"Darlene mentioned the witchcraft angle to a certain degree," Pam related, "knowing this guy that was sitting at the counter up at Terry's, just the way he talked, the way he was into that skull with the dripping candle. Darlene said that he was the one who kept it lit and talked about these weird things and witchcraft.

"But there was no ritual. Darlene's friends would just come over and tease, but the one who would start it all would be this guy, the man who delivered the package. The man at the painting party."

I spoke with Bobbie Oxnam about the newspaper stories about Darlene and drugs.

"The stories printed made a lot of us angry. . . . She might have taken marijuana once in a while but drugs were strictly taboo to her."

"I guess," Bobbie Ramos explained to me, "the police didn't ask me the right questions. All this talk of drugs turned me off. . . . Darlene got into something I don't think she could have got out of and she was afraid. So I think she did want to get out of it and the killer said, 'Well, I'll just do away with her 'cause she'll probably just go to the police.' "

However, Linda had her own theories. "The money put on the new house," she said forcefully, "none of it come from Dean. It came from whatever she was doing with this man in the white car. . . . I was constantly, twice a week, taking her to the bank, Crocker Citizen's on Georgia."

And why was Mike wearing three pairs of pants and three shirts on a hot summer night? And what about the missing door handle? Dean stated that the inside passenger-side door handle was always attached and Christina said that it was attached when she left the car at the family home.

But the most chilling and inexplicable thing was that, after the couple had been found at Blue Rock Springs, after they were taken to the hospital, and after police had sealed off the area, the missing door handle on the front passenger-side of the Corvair was mysteriously replaced.

Friday, July 11, 1969

Right now Lynch was concentrating on the search for the bartender, Paul. He owned a '56 Chevy, blue over white, a red Pontiac, and the pickup he had purchased from Dean Ferrin. Paul would often have breakfast at Terry's at 2:00 A.M., after the bars closed. A source told Lynch that Paul was constantly bothering Darlene and had followed her many times. Darlene was "deathly afraid of him and was friendly only in an effort to keep him at a distance." Lynch told me, "Paul wasn't real aggressive, but he was the type of guy who was tough to put off and he had been coming in there at the coffee shop bothering Darlene. It took us a week to find him." Finally Lynch received a tip that the Paul they wanted to talk to was employed in a bar in Benicia. They got in touch with Benicia Detective Sergeant Bidou, who found a 1966 address for Paul. First Lynch and Rust checked out several bars in Benicia unsuccessfully, then they went to the old address on "D" Street and talked with the landlady, who stated she had seen Paul a month earlier. She described the bartender as "kind of plump with dark straight hair."

At 8:00 P.M., she called Rust at the Vallejo P.D. and said she had made some calls and found out that Paul was in Yountville, between Napa and Lake Berryessa. The detectives drove there immediately and spoke with Paul, who was now a boilermaker, at his home.

"I don't know any friends of Darlene's," he snapped.

"We just want to know where you were on July Fourth."

"I was in a soft ball game with a team sponsored by the Napa Police Department. I like cops," he said curtly. "The game started at 10:30 A.M. and when it was over I came straight home. After supper I attended a veteran's fireworks display and was home by seven and stayed there."

Paul's new wife confirmed this.

Lynch was very disappointed. One of his fellow detectives told me, "The whole investigation originally seemed to focus on this guy. I mean, everybody was kinda after this Paul, Paul, Paul. The guy had even worked out at the Elk's Club at Blue Rock Springs. But we checked it; that alibi was airtight."

Lynch and Rust dejectedly went back to headquarters.

Mike moved to a tiny second-floor apartment, his "hideout," dyed his hair red, and was driven back and forth to the hospital by his father for treatment on his leg and disabled arm. Later he would go to live with his mother and brother in Southern California.

"We felt," Carmela told me later with a chill to her voice, "that Mike must have known who the killer was, because if I got shot, I don't know if I'd move out of town. Then we thought maybe she knew. Maybe she did."

Lynch finally had to ask Mike why he was wearing so many sets of clothes. Lynch told me, "He said that he was embarrassed by being so thin and wore extra sets of clothes to make himself look huskier."

"Not very comfortable on the Fourth of July," I said.

What of the missing door handle that was mysteriously replaced after the Corvair was in police custody? The implication was that the killer had to be a cop or someone close to the police in order to reattach the handle. Then I remembered that Rust's note to the police I.D. technicians read: "Dig inside the door handle area for bullets." The technicians may have done this and when finished automatically replaced the door handle, perhaps finding it under the front seat where the killer could have thrown it.

Jack Mulanax, the tough, broad-shouldered cop who would inherit the Ferrin case in the months ahead when it would become more than anyone had ever dreamed it would be, even tracked down Darlene's first husband in Santa Cruz and questioned him. "The guy's a little guy. I was thoroughly convinced that he was not the killer," he told me.

Rust and Lynch met with Linda to prepare a composite sketch of the man at the party. "I sat there with the police and the artist did the drawing from my directions. I spent hours with the police," she told me. "Afterward they gave me a long list of names and I was to circle any names of people I saw at the party. They could account for everybody but the guy in the suit. After Terry's, I never saw him again."

The envelope that arrived at the *San Francisco Chronicle* was postmarked in San Francisco and had two six-cent Roosevelt stamps on it, placed vertically, one above the other. The letter inside, written in a small, cramped style that trailed off toward the right as it came to the bottom of the page, was cold and menacing. With the letter was one-third of a neatly printed cryptogram composed of strange symbols.

It was a letter to the editor. In it, the writer took credit for the murders of David, Betty Lou, and Darlene.

Zodiac

Friday, August 1, 1969

In the offices of the *San Francisco Chronicle* at Fifth and Mission Streets, I joined the two editorial writers, Temp Peck and Al Hyman, in the editorial conference at 10:00 with the newspaper's publisher, Charles deYoung Theiriot. We met each morning to discuss the news and to decide on the topics for the next day's editorial page. I would scan the papers, draw six cartoon roughs, and the editors would select one. After I redrew it in ink on illustration board, it would be the editorial cartoon for the next edition.

It was to this office that the first letter from the Vallejo killer arrived, signed only with a crossed-circle symbol. In addition, the killer had enclosed a cipher message composed of arcane symbols.

A long tradition exists of writers and artists attempting to solve true crimes in their works of fiction. From Poe ("The Mystery of Marie Roget") and Mary Roberts Rhinehart ("First Mate Bram Murder Case"), to Arthur Conan Doyle, and Agatha Christie, who was instrumental in solving an actual aconite poisoning case. Oscar Wilde and the nineteenth-century British painter Walter Sickert both claimed to know who Jack the Ripper really was.

Wilde planted clues in his *Picture of Dorian Gray* and Sickert hid references to the killer in his portraits of knife murders. In recent years, for a brief time, Sickert was actually a Ripper suspect himself.

This was in the back of my mind as I looked at the small printing on the letter. I was seized by several emotions, but primarily I felt a rage at the coldness, arrogance, and insanity of the murderer. As an editorial cartoonist you develop a strong sense of justice, a need to change things, and as a painter and cartoonist I worked with symbols every day. The tools of my career were being misused, appropriated by a murderer.

At this time, no killer since Jack the Ripper had written the press and taunted the police with clues to his identity. The letter's strangeness ensnared me. Irretrievably hooked, immediately obsessed, I wanted to solve what I felt was to become one of the great mysteries.

The letter, in blue felt-tip pen, read:

> Dear Editor
> This is the murderer of the
> 2 teenagers last Christmass
> at Lake Herman & the girl
> on the 4th of July near
> the golf course in Vallejo
> To prove I killed them I
> shall state some facts which
> only I & the police know.
> Christmass
>   1. Brand name of ammo
> Super X
>   2 10 shots were fired
>   3 the boy was on his back
>   with his feet to the car
>   4 the girl was on her right
>   side feet to the west
> 4th July
>   1 girl was wearing paterned
>   slacks

2 The boy was also shot in
   the knee.
3 Brand name of ammo was
   western
   (Over)

Here is part of a cipher the
other 2 parts of this cipher are
being mailed to the editors of
the Vallejo times & SF Exam
iner.

I want you to print this cipher
on the front page of your
paper. In this cipher is my
identity.
If you do not print this cipher
by the afternoon of Fry. 1st of
Aug 69, I will go on a kill ram-
Page Fry. night. I will cruse
around all weekend killing lone
people in the night then move
on to kill again, untill I end
up with a dozen people over
the weekend.

The *San Francisco Examiner* and the *Vallejo Times-Herald*
also received the sinister letter, with very slight variations ("I am
the killer . . .") and one-third of the complete code message.

The papers printed some of the text of the letters, but at police
request did not reproduce the letter itself. This was done so that
there would be preserved certain things that only the killer himself would know about. This is a standard police procedure in
many slayings in order to provide indisputable evidence for the
identification and capture of the criminal.

Each third of the message consisted of eight lines of seventeen
symbols each: Greek symbols, Morse code, weather symbols, alphabet characters, navy semaphore, and astrological symbols.

After making photocopies, the newspapers arranged to have the original letters and cipher delivered to Lynch. The Vallejo P.D. in turn made copies of the code and sent them to Naval Intelligence at Mare Island Naval Shipyard for deciphering.

The *Times-Herald* and *Chronicle* both printed their third of the cipher block in their next editions. On Saturday, the *Chronicle* ran this headline on page four:

> Coded Clue in Murders. This code may conceal
> Vallejo killer's identity.
> This is The Chronicle's portion
> of the complete cryptogram:

See page 51 for the *Times-Herald*'s section of the cipher. The *Examiner* decided not to run their cipher portion until Sunday, possibly because they doubted that the letter was really from the killer.

At Naval Intelligence, the ciphers remained uncrackable. The government codebreaking branches, the National Security Agency and the Central Intelligence Agency, were asked to help.

Vallejo Police Chief Jack E. Stiltz wasn't totally convinced the

letters had been written by the murderer and publicly requested the author to send "a second letter with more facts to prove it." Stiltz admitted that the letters contained details of the crimes that were not public knowledge, but said it was knowledge that could have been obtained from any witness at the death scenes.

Sunday, August 3, 1969

The Sunday *Examiner-Chronicle* printed their third of the weird cipher (see page 52).

Below the *Examiner's* cipher section the paper printed the killer's ciphers to the *Chronicle* and *Times-Herald*. For the first time, the entire message was seen together.

Donald Gene Harden, a forty-one-year-old history and economics teacher at North Salinas High School, one hundred miles south of San Francisco, had a boyhood interest in codesolving, so he read the paper with particular interest.

Since it was a lazy Sunday morning, he decided to fool around

with the cryptogram and went to the shelf and got down his old volume on codebreaking, *Secret and Urgent*, by Fletcher Pratt. Harden cleared off the dining room table, laid out sharp pencils, a ruler, and an eraser and started trying to discover just what kind of cipher it *wasn't*.

The word *cryptography* is derived from the Greek words *kryptos* ("secret") and *graphos* ("writing"), while the word *cipher* is from the Hebrew word *spahar*, meaning "to number." A cipher either systematically rearranges the usual succession of the letters of the plain text or substitutes other characters, letters, or symbols for the normal alphabet.

Harden began to work in neat capital letters, checking the letter frequency of the symbols. Harden knew that E was the most common letter in the English language, followed in order by T, A, O, N, I, R, and S. The most commonly doubled letters in English are L, E, and S. The letters most frequently occurring together are TH, HE, and AN. More than half of all words end in E and more than half of all words begin with T, A, O, S, or W. Harden was aware that the most common three-letter combinations (trigrams) were THE, ING, CON, and ENT. Finally, he decided it was a "substitution cipher," where each letter of the alphabet is replaced by a symbol, letter, or figure. The killer had used so many different symbols that a one-for-one substitution of characters was not possible. The teacher was forced to devise his own procedure, to try and find things that were equal to each other, to search for repeating patterns of symbols. For hours Harden sat at the table working on the same haunting, recurring patterns that danced across his worksheet. If only he could reduce his number of variables!

The real difficulty with deciphering this writing was that Harden didn't know which of the three blocks of cipher came first or where the words were broken.*

At the end of the third hour, Harden's wife joined him in the mystery. Bettye June Harden is the kind of woman who never quits; once she gets her teeth into something, she can't stop. "She has tremendous stick-to-it-iveness," Harden told me. Even though she had never looked at a code in her life, she plunged right in. After all, in theory, anything ever encoded can be decoded.

The couple quickened their methodical pace, worked through the day and into the evening. Then they retired for the night and worried about the solution in their dreams.

Monday, August 4, 1969

Harden was ready to give up on the cryptogram the next morning, but he couldn't convince Bettye to stop. Even though at times she didn't have the slightest idea what she was doing, she kept working; eventually, Harden joined her.

Bettye was of the opinion that the killer was such an egomaniac that he would start out with "I." Intuition told her that he would speak of killing, and while they still didn't know which section of

---

*Actually, as I finally figured out, the killer did mark the order of the ciphers, as a reminder to himself or as a clue. The number of stamps on the letter to the *Examiner* was two, the number of stamps on the *Chronicle*'s letter was three, and the *Vallejo Times-Herald*'s envelope was posted with four stamps.

the cipher came first, she suggested the slayer might start out with a phrase such as "I like killing. . . ."

The answer came like a flash to the two of them. The cryptogram contained a number of double combinations of symbols. According to the frequency table, the most commonly doubled letter in the English language is L. Frequency tables show the comparative frequencies of letters, pairs of letters, groups of letters, and syllables. It's virtually impossible to write a message without repeating words, so the pair looked for four-letter patterns that would fit in with the word "kill." There was a possibility "kill" would be used more than once. (Battlefield cryptoanalysts, for example, scan any captured ciphers for patterns of symbols that might stand for "attack.")

It's a very eerie and exciting thing to see a cipher start to come apart. The killer had used "kill" once, the Hardens eventually discovered. He used "killing" twice and "killed" and "thrilling" once each. Other double-L words such as "will" were used four times, the word "collecting," once.

As the message developed in front of them, the Hardens noted the clever traps the murderer had erected to frustrate them. First he had used the symbol of a backward Q fifteen times to lure the codebreakers into thinking it was the letter E, the most commonly used letter. For the true letter E, he had used seven different symbols.

The killer had employed a check-off system so that alternates were used in order although two different symbols were found to stand for A and S interchangeably. The killer's spelling was poor, probably purposely so, and in some places he had made mistakes in the use of his own cipher. However, both the Hardens agreed that there could be no solution other than the one they eventually found. The decoding had taken them twenty hours of work.

The deciphered code read:

> I LIKE KILLING PEOPLE
> BECAUSE IT IS SO MUCH

FUN IT IS MORE FUN THAN
KILLING WILD GAME IN
THE FORREST BECAUSE
MAN IS THE MOST DANGEROUE
ANAMAL OF ALL TO KILL
SOMETHING GIVES ME THE
MOST THRILLING EXPERENCE
IT IS EVEN BETTER THAN GETTING
YOUR ROCKS OFF WITH A GIRL
THE BEST PART OF IT IS THAE
WHEN I DIE I WILL BE REBORN
IN PARADICE AND THEI HAVE
KILLED WILL BECOME MY SLAVES
I WILL NOT GIVE YOU MY NAME
BECAUSE YOU WILL TRY TO SLOI
DOWN OR ATOP MY COLLECTIOG OF
SLAVES FOR AFTERLIFE
EBEORIETEMETHHPITI

Harden dialed the *Chronicle* night editor long distance and reported solving the puzzle. He received a less than enthusiastic response, since his was only one of hundreds of calls the paper had gotten since the puzzle was printed. Harden was told to mail the solution to the *Chronicle*, and they would put it in the hands of Sergeant Lynch.

It turned out the Salinas couple really had cracked the cipher that had mystified the CIA, FBI, and National Security Agency. Naval Intelligence requested the Hardens' worksheets from Lynch, doublechecked them, and pronounced the answer correct.

Thursday, August 7, 1969

The killer, in response to Chief Stiltz's request, wrote again. This time he gave more details about the two Vallejo attacks. It was a three-page letter.

For the first time he used a name for himself: Zodiac.

Dear Editor
This is the Zodiac speaking.
In answer to your asking for
more details about the good
times I have had in Vallejo,
I shall be very happy to
supply even more material.
By the way, are the police
haveing a good time with the
code? If not, tell them to cheer
up; when they do crack it
they will have me.
On the 4th of July:
I did not open the car door, The
Window was rolled down all ready
The boy was originally sitting in
the front seat when I began
fireing. When I fired the first
shot at his head, he leaped
backwards at the same time
thus spoiling my aim. He ended up on the back seat then
the floor in back thrashing out
very violently with his legs;
that's how I shot him in the
knee. I did not leave the cene
of the killing with squealling tires
& raceing engine as described in the
Vallejo papers.
I drove away slowly so as not to
draw attention to my car. The man
who told the police my car was brown
was a negro about 40-45 rather shabbly
dressed. I was in this phone booth
haveing some fun with the Vallejo
cop when he was walking by.
When I hung the phone up the
dam thing began to ring & that
drew his attention to me & my car.

None of these facts had ever been made public.

> Last Christmass
> In that epasode the police were
> wondering as to how I could -
> shoot & hit my victims in the
> dark. They did not openly state this,
> but implied this by saying it was a
> well lit night & I could see
> silowets on the horizon.
> Bullshit that area is srounded
> by high hills & trees. What
> I did was tape a small pencel flash
> light to the barrel of my gun. If
> you notice, in the center of the beam
> of light if you aim it at a wall or
> ceilling you will see a black or
> darck spot in the center of the
> circle of light about 3 to 6 in.
> across.
> When taped to a gun barrel, the
> bullet will strike exactly in the
> center of the black dot in the light.
> All I had to do was spray them . . .
> No address.

Zodiac had written that when the police cracked the code "they would have him." What the killer didn't know was that the Hardens had already done the deciphering, but that the murderer's identity still remained a mystery.

Tuesday, August 12, 1969

Finally the Hardens' solution was published and amateur code-breakers all over the Bay Area agreed that the remaining letters at the end of the enciphered message, "EBEORIETEMETHHPITI," could be an anagram for the killer's real name. Adding a missing R, M, and P to the dubious anagram they came up with "ROBERT EMMET THE HIPPIE."

Over the next few days inventive readers of the *Chronicle* continued to come up with variations on the anagram: EMMET O. WRIGHT, ROBERT HEMPHILL, VAN M. BLACKMAN, I AM O. RIET, KENNETH O. WRIGHT, LEO BLACKMAN, F. L. BOON, TIMOTHIE E. PHEIBERTE.

One subscriber suggested that the police take the notation "Rush to Editor" that had appeared on the envelopes of all four Zodiac letters and look for a Mr. Rush. One helpful citizen wrote Lynch that the letters at the end of the decoded message stood for "San Benito Mental Hospital." The difficulty with that was that there was no such place.

Lynch was unimpressed with the anagram idea. At most, he felt, the "signature" may have only been the pen name of the slayer. Robert Emmet was the name of an Irish Revolutionary patriot who was executed in 1803. But to be safe Lynch was checking on Robert Emmets, hippie or straight. "The garble might be just that—a garble," he said, "to try and throw us off the track. After all, it says in the cipher, 'I will not give you my name.' We aren't sure 'Robert Emmet' is who we are looking for," he added. "Maybe he'll send another letter and let us know."

Harden felt that the last line was used only in a functional manner to fill out the cipher block and prevent cryptographers from knowing which block was last.

Unlike Dr. D.C.B. Marsh, head of the American Cryptogram Association, I did not think of the murderer as an expert in codes and ciphers. I felt that Zodiac worked only from the example of others. Zodiac was an amateur with codes, as were the Hardens. The hunted and the hunters mirroring each other, feeling their way toward a resolution. We now knew which letter of the alphabet each of the symbols stood for but what I wanted to know was how the killer arrived at his *choice* of symbols.

Fifty-five characters comprise a very complicated cipher. Was this a totally original code or had Zodiac used other sources to build his cipher system? If he had used particular books on code, perhaps these could be traced back to him.

I began by looking for basic books on secret writing. In the preface to *The Codebreakers* by David Kahn a sample cipher alphabet is presented; eight of the twenty-six suggested equivalents had been used by the killer. The Zodiac must have had a copy of this book.

As to the rest of the strange symbols, the almost religious triangles, circles, squares, and crosses, I remembered hearing of a cipher used during the Middle Ages. It was a picture alphabet designed to appear mystical to the uninformed, a cipher alphabet described as "vastly impressive" and "sinister"—just the qualities a man like the Zodiac killer would strive for.

I found it as easily as Kahn's sample code, in a book called *Codes and Ciphers,* by John Laffin. The name of the thirteenth-century alphabet cipher explained for me the choice of the killer's bizarre name. It was called the "Zodiac Alphabet." Zodiac had used many symbols for each letter of the alphabet and arrived at them through the inspiration of this early code.

For example, Zodiac's symbol for "R" is " $\diagdown$ "; the Zodiac Alphabet symbol for "R" is " $\diagdown$." Zodiac's symbol for "T" is " $\mapsto$ "; the alphabet's is " $\rightthreetimes$."

I thought that if these two books had inspired Zodiac's code then they might be found in libraries in the Bay Area, along with records of who had recently checked them out. Because of what appeared to be naval symbols in the Zodiac cipher and because the killer had been described at Blue Rock Springs as having a military-style crewcut, I gave particular attention to army and navy installations in the areas around San Francisco and Vallejo.

I called San Francisco's Presidio and Treasure Island Naval Base (where fire had destroyed part of the library) as well as Oakland's Army Terminal. In these cases the books had either been stolen or were missing. Alameda Naval Air Base never had the books, and Hamilton Air Force Base had "no records of either book." The librarian at Vallejo's Mare Island Naval Shipyard told me the records had recently been purged.

At the JFK Information Center in Vallejo, the librarian told me the book was reported lost some time ago and added that *Codes and Ciphers* was used "for eighth-grade level students as reading material because of its simple language." In the San Francisco Public Library the book was kept in the children's room.

In the letter Zodiac stated that:

> WHEN I DIE I WILL BE REBORN IN PARADICE
> AND ALL I HAVE KILLED WILL BECOME MY SLAVES

Professors at Stanford University recognized this odd mixture of Christian and ancient cult beliefs as having roots in Southeast Asia and some Satan-worshipping devil cults, such as the one run in San Francisco by Anton LeVey. Could Zodiac belong to the ranks of such a cult?

In his cipher Zodiac also spoke of man as the most dangerous game. There was a movie, out of release for many years, called *The Most Dangerous Game.* I went to see it at one of those theaters that show silent films, just outside San Francisco.

The 1932 RKO-Radio Picture, based on Richard Connell's famous 1924 short story, is the tale of a mad hunter, Count Zaroff, who uses fake channel lights to lure passing ships onto the reefs just off his island stronghold. The survivors of the sunken vessels become human game to be hunted in the count's private jungle. Zaroff, as played by Leslie Banks, is a tall, suave Russian with a jagged scar on his forehead. The injury has become a symbol of his madness. "My life has been one glorious hunt," he tells his prisoners. "It would be impossible for me to tell you how many animals I have killed. One night as I lay in my tent with this—this head of mine, a terrible thought crept like a snake into my brain: hunting [animals] was beginning to bore me. . . . when I lost my love for hunting, I lost my love of life, of love. Here on my island I hunt the most dangerous game [humans]." "Only after the kill does man know the true ecstasy of love," says Zaroff. "It is the natural instinct. Kill, *then* love! When you have known that you have known ecstasy!" With his pack of black mastiffs, the count, dressed all in black, his costume's folds gathered and cinched at wrists and ankles, a foot-long knife in a sheath on his left side, a precision rifle in his right hand, races swiftly through the fog in pursuit of a young couple.

After the movie, I stopped in the soft night air outside the theater, looked down the black streets wet with fog, and wondered if the inspiration for the Vallejo murders had been a children's code book and a movie.

The *Los Angeles Times* reported the psychiatric information given to the Vallejo police by the California Medical Facility in Vacaville after the breaking of the cipher.

"He is probably a guy who broods about cut-off feelings, about being cut off from his fellow man. . . . Comparing the thrill of killing to the satisfaction of sex is usually an expression of inadequacy.

"He probably feels his fellow man looks down on him for some reason. The belief that his victims would be his slaves in an afterlife reflects a feeling of omnipotence indicating a paranoid delusion of grandeur—expressed through a belief common among primitive peoples throughout history.

"And the taunting notes and phone calls may be a plea to be found out, exposed, perhaps cornered, in which event a grandiose paranoid quite likely might take his own life, as a grand gesture, to punish the world for its neglect of him in life."

Cecelia Ann Shepard

Saturday, September 27, 1969

For Cecelia Ann Shepard it had been a day of farewell with her friend, Bryan Hartnell, a fellow student at Pacific Union College at Angwin in Napa County on the east rim of the valley. She had known the tall, ruggedly good-looking pre-law student since her first semester at PUC, and the two had once been very close.

After spending the summer vacation with her parents in Loma Linda, Cecelia had come back to PUC for the weekend to pack the few belongings she had left at the school for shipment to Southern California. Having finished her two years at Angwin, she was transferring to UC at Riverside in October to study music.

Hartnell had driven back from Troutdale, Oregon, where he too had been visiting with his parents, in order to give Cecelia a hand with her packing.

The two met at PUC early in the morning, and, after worship, spent an hour putting her property into boxes. The air was exhilarating. They walked to the school cafeteria from Newton Hall among the long, low, modern tan-and-white buildings.

During lunch, Bryan asked, "Are you doing anything special this afternoon?"

"Why?"

"I don't know. We could go out for a walk or go to San Francisco. You know, just because we used to be such good friends, because we used to have such a good friendship."

Bryan opened the door of his white Karmann Ghia for the small, delicate girl with sunlight hair, ran to the driver's side, and the couple sped happily down Howell Mountain Road, past St. Helena Sanitarium, to Highway 29, where they turned left toward Rutherford, home of Inglenook and Beaulieu, old stone wineries with vaulted cellars. At a church charity rummage sale in Napa they picked up an old TV set. Then they stopped in St. Helena for a couple of items, met some friends, and later gave a lift home to a couple of kids. And so it got late.

Instead of going to San Francisco, Bryan suggested Lake Berryessa to Cecelia. "There's this one place, a favorite of mine where I used to go all the time," he told her.

The couple went by way of Pope Valley and Knoxville Road, along the twisting shoreline and inlets of the manmade lake. Berryessa is over twenty-five miles long and three miles wide. It teems with blue gill, German brown, kokanee, and rainbow trout as well as catfish, black bass, and land-locked steelhead.

Earlier in the day, around 2:50 P.M., three twenty-one-year-old women had come the same route as Bryan and Cecelia. As they had pulled into a parking spot near an A&W and stopped, another car, driven by a lone man, pulled in beside them and then backed up so that his rear bumper was even with theirs. The man sat there with his head down as if he were reading something. The women got the feeling he wasn't.

The car was a silver or ice-blue '66 Chevrolet two-door sedan, with California plates. The driver was twenty-five to thirty-five years old, over six feet tall, and weighed about 200 to 230 pounds. He wore no glasses and his dark hair was straight and parted on the side. He had on a black short-sleeved sweat shirt and dark blue pants. A T-shirt hung out of the rear of his trousers but he was fairly clean cut and nice looking. He smoked one cigarette after another.

The girls drove away to the lake. They were sunbathing an hour later when they saw the same man watching them. After twenty minutes, the man drove off.

At 4:00, Bryan parked his '56 black vinyl–topped Ghia on the edge of the road near the lake. There were no other cars there. The pair walked a quarter mile, down to where two large oak trees grew.

"It's an island during the wetter season," said Bryan. "You can see where it was a levee. It's really beautiful out here."

The couple found a cool clearing for their picnic exactly 510 yards from the road on a peninsula of the lake's west shoreline. They laid out a blanket and sat and embraced for an hour.

The lake is surrounded by gentle hills, and the sun flashed off the placid water in front of the couple. Bryan and Celia could see Goat Island before them and to their left an occasional boat. The stretch of beach where they lay was deserted, and the shrubbery covering the bank isolated them even more.

Four-fifths of a mile down the road, a dentist and his young son had earlier parked their car and walked down to the beach. The dentist and his son noticed a man watching them in the still evening. He was within a hundred yards of them, across an inlet. He was a white adult about five feet ten inches tall, with a heavy build, wearing dark trousers and a long-sleeved dark shirt with red coloring. The man wasn't carrying anything and seemed to be just out for a walk along the hillside halfway between the road and the lake.

The man became suddenly aware that the dentist and his son had noticed him and, perhaps, that the boy was carrying a .22 rifle. He turned abruptly and began walking up the hill in a southerly direction, thrusting his hands into his blue windbreaker jacket.

Tire tracks showed the stocky man's car was parked directly behind the dentist's car. The stocky man may have been stalking any cars parked along the route. When he saw the lone auto, he had gone toward the lake to investigate its occupants.

The stranger left the dentist's car and drove south for exactly four-fifths of a mile, where he saw the white Ghia. He pulled in behind it.

Slowly he came down from the highway to a gravel road. About 200 hundred yards from the highway, to his left, was a grove of trees and a marsh. In the distance he saw a long peninsula, devoid of trees and brush, stretching 310 yards into the lake. At the tip of this peninsula were the only other trees outside of the grove, two oak trees. Under these, a boy and a girl were lying on a blanket.

Apparently his plan was to stalk his "game" across a long exposed area and to surprise them. A difficult task. How could he remain invisible and cross an open space kept bare by the lake water during the rainy season?

Cecelia could make out the figure of a man in the distance. He stood far across the wheat-colored clearing of the peninsula but she couldn't focus on his face; it was hazy and indistinct, but he seemed to be watching them. The man was stocky and powerfully built, his hair dark brown. He vanished into a grove of trees about 250 yards away and to Cecelia's right.

Moments later, she glimpsed the stocky man again as he came out of the grove moving toward them. She stopped reminiscing with Bryan to mention that they had company. Bryan was on his back on the blanket, the top of his head pointing directly at the heavy figure advancing slowly across the narrow, rock-strewn expanse. Cecelia was on her stomach facing toward the shore, with her head on Bryan's shoulder. The man was very close now.

The evening breeze blew a bit of dust into Cecelia's eye, and when she raised her head again the dark-garbed figure had disappeared. It was such a balmy evening that Bryan did not even bother to turn around, but Cecelia was alarmed. When she had seen the stranger so close, he was much more menacing than he had appeared from a distance. He had been walking heavily and slowly. How could he have disappeared so quickly and completely?

A few moments later, Bryan heard a rustling of leaves. "Do you have your specs on?" he asked. "Why don't you see what the deal is over there."

"It's that man," she said.

"Is he alone?"

"He just stepped behind a tree." At first Bryan thought she meant a tree in the grove several hundred yards away.

"Well," said Bryan, "keep looking and tell me what happens."

Bryan and Cecelia were under the larger of the two oak trees on the island. The stocky man was behind the second oak to Cecelia's right and twenty feet away.

"My God, he's got a gun!" cried Cecelia, squeezing Bryan's arm. The stocky man had emerged from behind the other tree and Bryan, out of the corner of his eye, instantly became aware of a black, hulking shape over to his left side, silently staring at him. As the couple turned, the figure was walking straight at them.

The man had circled them. Behind the tree he had donned a ceremonial midnight-black hood, square on top, with four corners like a paper sack. He resembled some executioner from the Middle Ages.

The hood hung down over the stocky man's shoulders almost to his waist and was sleeveless; front and back panels came down over his chest. The top was flat, with stitching around the edges. Emblazoned in white on the biblike front was a three-inch square cross placed over a circle. The ends of the cross protruded past the circle. It glowed with an orange tint from the setting sun and had been neatly, almost professionally applied. There were slits for his eyes and mouth cut into the cloth and he wore a pair of clip-on sunglasses over them. Bryan marveled at how ingeniously this mask was devised.

The man's dark sleeves were clamped tight about his wrists, his trousers were tucked above half boots. (Evidently Zodiac was wearing blousing rubbers, used by the military for trousers tucked into boots.) On his left side was a bayonet-type knife, at least a foot long, in a sheath attached to his belt. Around his waist on the right side was a simple black holster with an open flap. Several lengths of common-variety white hollow-core plastic clothesline also hung from beneath the unknown man's jacket.

His feet sank deeply in the shoreline earth; Bryan saw what he thought was the man's stomach hanging over his trousers. However, the stocky man's weight seemed solid, not flabby.

The man's right hand was held outstretched toward the pair as he walked; in it, he carried a blue-steel semiautomatic pistol.

Bryan and Cecelia were frozen in the twilight, watching the bulky man approach. It couldn't be a practical joke by any of their friends; they hadn't told anyone where they were going that day. Had they been followed?

"And so he came out," Bryan told me later. "Of course, there are some things you wouldn't really mind having happened just for the experience of it. I thought, well, I've got only about fifty cents on me. It's worth all of that having it happen. I didn't think of another angle."

The stocky man stood towering over the couple on the blanket.

"I talked to him," said Bryan.

It was a remarkably calm voice that came from beneath the hood, a voice that was not high- or low-pitched, a monotone. The speaker sounded to Bryan to be between twenty and thirty years old.

"That voice . . . it was like a, a student's," he told me later. "But kind of a drawl; not a Southern drawl, though."

"I want your money and your car keys," said the man.

"It's just a robbery," thought Bryan.

The man in the hood continued speaking. The words were even and soft-spoken.

"He didn't seem well educated, but not illiterate," Bryan said later.

"I want your car to go to Mexico," continued the stranger.

Bryan looked up at the black cloth hood with clip-on dark sunglasses covering the eye holes. Beneath the slits of the hood, did he catch the metallic glint of yet another pair of glasses? Bryan could see dark brown, sweaty hair through the slits as well.

The stocky man wore a lightweight blue-black windbreaker over a reddish-black wool shirt. This close, Bryan could see that the crossed circle symbol was sewn on.

The man's hands were hidden by black gloves and he had on baggy, pleated slacks "of the old-fashioned type." Bryan judged him to be between five foot ten inches and six foot one or two inches and to weigh between two hundred and twenty-five and two hundred fifty pounds. Bryan was a poor judge of height, because of his own extraordinary tallness.

He fumbled quickly in his pockets for money and keys. "I've only got a little," he said and handed over the last of the money he had, along with the keys to the V.W. The masked intruder pocketed the change and tossed the keys on the blanket, then put the gun away in the holster.

Bryan thought, Maybe the guy really does need help. Then he said, "There's no strings attached. I don't have any money right now, but if you need help that badly I can help you out in another way maybe."

"No," said the stranger. "Time's running short. I'm an escaped convict from Deer Lodge, Montana. I've killed a prison guard there. I have a stolen car and nothing to lose. I'm flat broke."

"Well, man," said Bryan, "wouldn't you rather be stuck on a stealing charge than a threat of homicide?"

"Just don't start playing hero on me," said the man. "Don't try to grab the gun."

"I didn't really figure the gun was loaded," Bryan told me later. "I always thought it was empty. I heard a lot of times that this is what they do just as a bluff, but I decided not to call his bluff."

Bryan told the man, "You're really wasting time with me. I got a billfold and this much change and that's it."

"I talked all kinds of weird stuff," he told me, "just weird shit. I was taking a sociology class. You're talking about a sophomore in college. Never really run into a real-life criminal. Gee, this guy was nothing to worry about. . . . He wanted just my money. I told him all I had was seventy-six cents and he never ended up taking anything. If I remember right, I gave him the keys and somehow they got left behind. He talked about how the car he had was hot.

I thought he meant he had a very fast car and commented to him about it and he said it was stolen. He talked about being in prison and about contacting me. We talked for quite a while."

The hooded man detached the two-and-one-half to three-foot lengths of clothesline.

The stocky man's knife was even with Bryan's eyes and he stared at it, trying to fix as many details as possible in his mind. The blade was about three-quarters of an inch to one inch wide and eleven to twelve inches long, maybe a bayonet or bread knife, with a hardwood handle decorated with two brass rivets. White surgical cotton tape one inch wide was wrapped around the handle, and the whole knife was fitted into a sheath of wood. The blade was sharpened on both sides.

Had Bryan ever seen *The Most Dangerous Game* he would have recognized it as a good copy of the knife Count Zaroff wore on his black hunting outfit.

"Lie face down on the ground," said the hooded man. "I'm going to have to tie you up."

Bryan defiantly stood up, and was ordered back down on the blanket. "I kid you not, Robert," Bryan said later, "I became really annoyed at the thought of being hogtied. Just really annoyed, and I argued with him about it and thought, not really sensibly but more in the neighborhood of cops and robbers, about getting the gun away. I always felt the way he handled the gun I could have gotten it. The only reason I didn't was I figured it really was a highly optional thing to do and if I screwed up and somebody got hurt I was going to get blamed for being a hero or trying to be a hero."

"You know, I think I can get that gun," Bryan whispered to Cecelia. "Do you mind?"

"And she got kind of fearful about it," Bryan told me, "so I figured since there are two lives involved, not just mine, I wouldn't do it. I thought, Let's just play it safe. This is the way to do it. If somebody robs you, you cooperate. You give them your money. He seemed kind of kooky but was carrying on a fairly logical conversation. All he wanted was the money."

The hooded man turned toward Cecelia.

"You tie the boy up," said the stranger.

Cecelia wound the line around Bryan's hands and feet and tied a couple of loose knots. "She tied me really loose," Bryan said to me, "and I kept my hands apart. Like you see on TV."

While Cecelia was tying Bryan, she reached into his pocket and threw his wallet to the hooded man. He did not pick up the wallet. When she had finished, the stocky man tied her up in a similar fashion. When he touched the girl his hands began to shake, but he bound her very securely. He then found the loose knots on Bryan and double-clinched them (tied them twice as tightly).

"He retied me, extremely tight," said Bryan. "It was that hollow clothesline rope."

"I'm getting nervous," said the man.

Now the two students were helpless, Cecelia on her stomach and Bryan on his left side. "In retrospect," Bryan told me, "why would anyone tie you up after they had robbed you or found out you didn't have any money? Why didn't he have me walk a hundred yards down the way and say, don't turn around. It didn't make sense to hogtie me."

The hooded man talked to them in such a quiet voice that it never occurred to the couple that they would be harmed in any way. Bryan repeated his offers of help, and the three talked for minutes more on the darkening island.

"There was something distinctive about his voice. If I remember correctly, it was not forced. No accent. He had a pronounced way of saying things. He wasn't talking like we're talking now," said Bryan. "Not that I was trying to suck it out of him. He wasn't really trying to talk to me. I was the one asking the questions. He was certainly volunteering nothing. The first time I'm down there laying on my stomach and I'm saying, 'O.K., now that this is all over will you show me if the gun was loaded?' He popped open the end of the gun and he pulled out the cartridges and showed me a bullet. It looked like a .45-caliber.*

"He put it away and I turned my head away."

*The Colt .45 1911A1, used by the U.S. Armed Forces is "similar in design and function" to the Browning High Power but is heavier, longer, and holds only seven cartridges.

The bound couple heard a voice now grown husky say from beneath the hood, "I'm going to have to stab you people."

A shock went through the helpless pair.

"The first time I suspected any iota of trouble was when I saw the knife come out, and then I felt that was it. That was the first hint that things were going to be worse than me getting possibly stuck tied up there overnight."

"Please stab me first," said Bryan, "I'm chicken. I couldn't stand to see her stabbed."

"I'll do just that," said the hooded figure.

He dropped to his knees and ripped the foot-long knife from its sheath and raised it high over Bryan's back. He began stabbing the boy in the back. Spurting blood spotted Cecelia's face until it began to run down it in thin rivulets.

"I'm laying on my stomach," Bryan told me later. "Put yourself in my shoes, someone hits you in the back. What's the first thing you do? You stiffen . . . you just wait for it to stop. There's not a hell of a lot you can do. You're in the most vulnerable position you can be in. For me . . . I was just waiting for it to stop. She's watching all this stuff coming down and screaming for him to stop and all this. She turns on her side so by the time he comes to her she knows precisely what's going to happen and what's the reaction? Try to get away. Try to move out of the way.

"You have these few seconds to recognize what's happening. You're gonna be in a lot different position and that was why she got—she was a fairly frail-bone–type person. She wasn't skinny but she wasn't heavy-boned. When he hit her, he broke ribs."

When Bryan gave a moan and finally seemed to collapse from the intense pain, the black hood turned toward the girl. What was the expression beneath the dark fabric? The heavy breathing of the man spasmodically sucked the cloth in and out.

Still on his knees, the man gave a ghastly, frenzied sound and, letting out a long, low exhalation, began stabbing the girl in the back. Ten times the knife fell. Instinctively, Cecelia rolled over onto her back, and the dark hunter continued thrusting. Once he plunged the knife to its full length into her chest. Once into each breast, once into the groin area, and once into the abdomen.

"Stop, stop, stop, . . ." pleaded the girl. The more she twisted and writhed, the more madly the hooded figure stabbed.

"She's on her side," Bryan told me. "He's stabbing her in the side. I heard later that he had stabbed in the shape of the Zodiac crossed-circle symbol but . . . there was really too much movement for him to do anything that deliberate.

"I think he got her on front and back and sides but that was because she was doing the moving. If I remember right, he was trying to hold her but she . . .

"And I turned away. I looked but then it flashed on me, Hey, look . . . what am I looking at? I can't stand this.

"And I turned away.

"And when I turned away I thought, Smart Hartnell isn't going to move. Obviously I couldn't do anything to save her, but I'm not going to be making any noise or I would die. . . . Freeze."

Sated at last, the stocky man stood up and tossed the money and keys onto the blanket next to his victims. He walked slowly across the open peninsula and was soon lost in the empty twilight.

Back on the road, the stocky man put the hood and bloody knife on the front seat of his car, strode to Bryan's locked Ghia, and knelt by the door on the front passenger side, which was away from the road. He did something to the door and then started up his own car. He had a call to make.

"I don't think I went out," Bryan told me. "If I did black out . . . there is a slight haze in my memory. . . . What I heard him do was walk away in a nonhurried fashion. I quit breathing. I just froze, and then after that there's a little dead spot. But I remember having always contended that I never lost consciousness.

"When you really look at exactly what happened to me, you'll see I was extremely fortunate in that he grazed my heart sac and caused a little bit of the fluid inside to be pink, but he didn't pierce it. Just a fraction of an inch to the right and I would have been dead.

"Cecelia's aorta was cut in several places; mine wasn't. One blade went on one side and one on the other. I really never got hurt. I mean I did, but nothing of any degree of permanency."

Cecelia recovered consciousness and the couple began yelling for help. Bryan's primary concern was "just staying alive" and the next step was getting himself free to go for help. Painfully, he twisted himself into position to get his teeth on the white clothesline around Cecelia's wrists. Blood from the girl's wounds had covered the plastic line and made it slippery; his mouth filled with it. The work was slow and agonizing. Eventually, the girl was free and turned over to untie Bryan's own hands.

"The first trouble we had," Bryan told me, "was he tied me pretty tight. So, gee, I really don't know to this day any reason why she was able to get the cords undone, considering the weakness of her condition. Anyway, when she did get the multiple knots loose, it took awhile for my hands to unnumb 'cause they had been tied for a half hour without really much circulation at all. So that took quite a while to get my hands free enough to move and quit ringing."

Bryan's intention had been to crawl for help, but he had lost so much blood he could barely move.

A Chinese fisherman from San Francisco and his son in a small boat on the lake had heard moans coming from the tip of the peninsula, and they rowed closer for a look. Seeing the terrible sight, they dared not come any farther. They left to search for help. Two miles away at the Rancho Monticello Resort, the fisherman rushed in to tell rangers of the attack. Ranger Dennis Land and Ranger Sergeant William White were in their patrol car three miles away when the call came in over the radio from park headquarters down by the water. "I dropped Bill White off at Rancho Monticello," Land told me, "and he went by boat to the scene and I got enough information from him to know where it was, so I came by car. I didn't know what I was looking for at all. All I knew was that somebody was hurt, that he had cut his foot or . . ."

Back on the peninsula, when he saw the Chinese fisherman and his son row away, Bryan had figured no one would come. He started crawling toward the road. "All I made it up to was the jeep trail when I saw a car coming."

"I found the boy," said Land. "He had crawled about 300 yards from where the initial stabbing had taken place. He was totally untied and en route to the road. I didn't see anybody suspicious. He was lying alongside the dirt road . . . and I got out and looked at him real quickly. He told me his girlfriend was out on the island. As quickly as I could, I got into my car and drove down to where she was."

Two boats carrying Ranger White and the owners of Rancho Monticello arrived, and the rangers wrapped Bryan and Cecelia in blankets until the ambulance could get there. There was no ambulance at the lake; it would have to come all the way from Queen of the Valley Hospital, almost an hour away. While telling the rangers what had happened, the couple kept drifting in and out of consciousness.

As he had crawled, Bryan had kept thinking over and over, "Oh, my God, I don't want to die." Bryan was certain the hooded man had felt they were dead when he left. "I guess I was just afraid to die. I don't remember that much terrible pain. . . . I was mostly in shock," he said. "But she was in pain, just excruciating pain."

"They were suffering so terribly," White later told Dave Smith of the *L.A. Times*. "The girl, she kept pleading with me to give her something to kill the pain or knock her out. She was writhing on the ground in agony and I could barely feel her pulse. I tried to think of something to do. They weren't bleeding anymore, but there were so many stab wounds."

Cecelia had been stabbed twenty-four times.

"I remembered," continued White, "something I'd heard long ago about scratching somewhere away from the pain, that would help to take your mind off it. So I told the girl about that. She tried it and told me it helped for a few minutes but then she started begging me again to put her out of her misery."

The victims, in critical condition, were rushed to the hospital. The girl went into surgery for most of the night.

"Cecelia was in such pain the whole distance," Bryan told me, "until she finally started going out of it, kinda losing it mentally.

I don't know what would have happened if they hadn't come. . . . Clearly she would have been D.O.A., and I don't know, I might have been too. You know, blood loss; even though no vital organs are hit, you die from no juice."

The report of the double stabbing at Berryessa was logged at 7:13 P.M. at the Napa Sheriff's Office. Officer Dave Collins and Deputy Ray Land, Dennis' brother, were sent to the scene.

At 7:40 P.M., one hour and ten minutes after the knifing, the phone rang at Napa P.D. and was answered by the officer-operator.

"Napa police department, Officer Slaight."

The call was on line one. "I want to report a murder—no, a double murder," said the caller. It sounded like the voice of a man in his early twenties to Slaight. The voice was calm.

"They are two miles north of Park Headquarters. They were in a white Volkswagen Karmann Ghia."

There was a long pause.

"Where are you?" asked Slaight.

"I'm the one that did it," said the man in a voice that was "barely audible."

The dispatcher heard the receiver put down, but the connection was not broken. "Is there anyone there? Is there anyone there?" asked Slaight. He could tell that the line was still open because he could hear traffic passing. "For some reason I got the impression," he said later, "there were people near or around because I seem to recall hearing feminine voices in the background . . . however, at the time I was in the process of phoning the Napa Sheriff's Office on another line, so it was hard to tell. I informed the S.O. of the call and then phoned the operator to see if the call could be traced."

Police quickly traced the signal to a pay phone located at 1231 Main Street, the Napa Car-Wash. It was only four and one-half blocks from the police station and exactly twenty-seven miles from the scene of the attack. The police were able to lift a good palm print from the receiver; the print had to be dried with artificial light before they could dust the surface in order to remove it. A print has to be dry or the powder will adhere to all the moisture rather than the acids in the hand as the powder is designed to do.

That the killer thought both students were dead showed he had left the lake immediately.

The awkward one-way streets in Napa and the location of the phone booth caused me to believe that Zodiac was as familiar with Napa as Vallejo. He had taken a right on First Street and gone until he came to the Napa P.D., then taken another right onto Main and made his call to the cops. Afterward the killer had to take Soscol Avenue back onto 121 (which became Highway 29); and since he could not go back in the direction of the lake, he would have been headed south right into Vallejo. Was his home in Vallejo? Or beyond?

The killer liked to call close to the police station, which might explain why he didn't call along the way from Berryessa. And as usual, he had killed or attacked in areas of confused police jurisdiction.

Tough, heavy-set Detective Sergeant Kenneth Narlow of Napa County Sheriff's Office took charge of the investigation and made certain the area of the lakeside attack was canvassed for witnesses who may have seen anyone suspicious. "When I got the call from the office," Narlow told me, "I immediately went to the hospital to talk to the victims. There was no sense in me rushing to Berryessa. Cecelia Shepard was unconscious."

When Narlow finally arrived at the crime scene, his broad, tanned face clouded with anger. Someone had gathered up the multicolored woolen blanket and rope before he got there and put them in a box for him.

Then Narlow looked at the door of the white V.W., and what he saw made the hair on the back of his neck stand on end. The killer had written on the door with a black felt-tip pen:

Vallejo
12-20-68

The numbers meant something to Narlow. They were the dates of the killings in Vallejo and Solano counties.

There was a maniac at large, and he had moved north.

The crime-lab technicians discovered tire tracks from the attacker's car and made plaster casts, "moulages." There were two different-size tires on the front, very worn. Width between the wheels was listed by the police as fifty-seven inches.

A close examination by Deputy Collins revealed an odd footprint leading up to Bryan's car where the writing had been put on the door. The same prints led down to the murder scene and back up the hill to the road. Casts were made of the killer's footprints, size 10½. These prints were very deep. Narlow called for one of the more overweight cops to walk alongside the tracks. He weighed about two hundred and ten pounds but did not sink down as deeply as Zodiac did. "Yes, we took a compaction test in the sand by an officer," Narlow told me, "and in order to put that print so deeply into the sand we figured the Zodiac weighed 220 pounds." It was a heavy man they were dealing with; clear prints at the heel indicated the man was not running when he left.

"I described this guy as being really fat," Hartnell told me later, "I don't know, he could have been moderately heavy and wearing a thickly lined windbreaker. And it's not impossible that the guy was wearing a wig, but the dark hair. I remember kind of a greasy forehead."

Narlow knelt on the sandy rock and looked closely at the shoe prints. Between the heel and the sole there was a strange little circle with printing. "The circle showed, but we couldn't make out the printing. But that's how we identified that particular sole. We were able to determine who the manufacturer was," Narlow told me. He later discovered that they were from a chucker-type boot called the "Wing Walker." "The uppers are manufactured by a company called the Weinbrenner Shoe Company," said Narlow. "They're in Merrill, Wisconsin, which is only about twenty miles from my hometown. The soles are manufactured by Avon—Avon, Massachusetts. That's the printing in the little circle." Over one million of these shoes were manufactured as part of a government contract. 103,700 pairs of "Wing Walkers" had been shipped to Ogden, Utah, and distributed to Air Force and Navy installations on the West Coast.

The government-issue boot pointed to a killer who was involved in some way with the military.

"I don't think [the couple was] really followed, for the simple reason that their plans to go to Berryessa were strictly on the spur of the moment," said Narlow. "Nothing was planned; in fact, they were supposed to go to the city that night. Contrary to some published reports, the wounds weren't in any sadistic shape or form, no pattern to them or anything like that . . . no carving on the breasts to indicate any Zodiac sign.

"Certain type assailants use certain weapons because it gets them closer to their victims. If you wanted to go out and kill for the sheer sake of killing you could use a high-powered rifle and a scope and kill at two hundred, three hundred yards, but you wouldn't achieve a kind of sexual effect. But by plunging a knife into someone it's the most intimate contact you can have with a victim, and there's no question about it, it's where Zodiac gets some of his thrills." Narlow also stressed to me that the knife is a silent killer.

He also discovered that there had been a man acting oddly around the lake earlier in the day, and arranged for Bob McKenzie of the Napa Register to produce an Identi-Kit composite drawing. "This particular sketch," Narlow told me, "was drawn with the assistance of three young girls of Pacific Union College who had seen this particular individual in a car acting suspiciously, but this wasn't even near the scene of the crime. Still, it could easily have been the guy."

"This may not be the killer," said Captain Don Townsend of the Napa County Sheriff's Office, "but we would like to talk with the fellow."

The lab men examined the clothesline and removed the car

door for tests and handwriting analysis and eventually for storage until the slayer was caught.

With a friend, I drove to Berryessa to speak with Ranger Land and take a really close look at the murder site.

Berryessa was practically deserted this time of year and I had no trouble finding Park Headquarters. They reached Land by radio, and within fifteen minutes we were on our way by car to where Bryan and Cecelia were attacked one-half mile away.

"No question about it, Robert," said Land, "it was quite bizarre. The mere fact that somebody had been stabbed up there is not all that uncommon. During the summer months we had different reported stabbings. This was the second murder up here, but the other one's kinda iffy. We don't know if it was a murder or not. Could have been a suicide."

The dusty road was closed off by a chain, but Land got out and undid the combination lock and we drove right out onto the peninsula.

"Watch out for rattlers," he warned.

The day after the murder, Land had been up in a fixed wing plane taking aerial photos of the attack site. The peninsula stuck straight out. I looked at the photos. It was hard to imagine anyone being able to sneak up on someone across a long open area with just two trees at the very end. It wasn't until I sat in the same spot as Bryan and Cecelia and had a friend walk toward me across the peninsula that I realized how the stocky man had disappeared from sight.

To my left, facing shoreward, was a deep depression curving around the light rise of the island with the two oaks on it. At one point my friend just vanished. The depression, over six feet deep, was like a narrow ledge encircling the island. It had enabled the stocky man, without even crouching, to come around them, across a sandy shelf of beach, and to the oak tree, which he climbed up behind and donned his hood.

I looked out at the peaceful lake. In a month the rainy season would swell the lake and engulf the ground on which I stood. I realized that all of Zodiac's killings had been around water. What was the attraction for him?

Monday, September 29, 1969

At 3:45 in the afternoon, Cecelia Ann Shepard, attended by her parents, died from multiple stab wounds to her back, chest, and abdomen.

Townsend had Bryan put under close guard immediately. "With a psychopath on the loose, we can't take any chances with the only living witness," he said.

Bryan was bitter that the ambulance took over an hour to reach them at the lake and then another hour to reach the hospital. "If Cecelia had gotten medical attention when the rangers found us she might have survived. It seemed so long before help arrived."

Thursday, October 2, 1969

On the day the saddened Adventist community attended the funeral for Cecelia at the college church's sanctuary, Townsend told the press, "There are a couple of other things we're still holding back so we'll be able to identify the man if he wants to call again. He can't be anyone but a mentally ill person. He must get his sex gratification from the act of killing."

Townsend admitted the crosshair symbol on the car door was the same one Zodiac used in letters to the newspapers. Napa residents were cautioned to stay out of remote areas, and to travel in groups after dark until the maniac was caught. The fast-food joints and drive-ins became wastelands at night. In Vallejo, parents told their teenagers that if they would stay safely indoors, they could neck with their dates undisturbed.

Narlow's investigation involved Lundblad and Lynch as well as Mel Nicolai of Criminal Identification and Investigation (CI&I). The four worked closely together, exchanging theories and information.

The detectives considered what the Zodiac crimes had in common:

1. The victims were young students, couples.
2. The attacks all occurred on weekends, two near holidays.

3. The murders were at dusk or night.
4. Robbery or sexual molestation was not a motive.
5. A different weapon was used each time.
6. The killer had a compulsion to brag about the murders by phone or letter.
7. Zodiac killed in remote lovers' lanes.
8. The slayings all occurred around and in cars.
9. The victims were always near water.

Townsend believed that the killer had more hatred for the woman victim than the man, since in two cases the man survived the attack while the woman did not. This psychotic executioner seemed to seek out the areas that offered privacy to young couples on weekend nights, when he himself was probably most lonely.

The frightening thing was that now, the killings were coming closer and closer together.

Paul Lee Stine

Saturday, October 11, 1969

It is not easy to park your car at the bottom of a steep San Francisco hill. The stocky man turned his wheels toward the curb, set his handbrake, locked the door, and puffed up the hill to catch a bus to the theater district.

He got off at Post and Powell and stood for a while in Union Square, watching the rows of canary-colored cabs coming and going from in front of the elegant old St. Francis Hotel. This evening he wore a blue-black parka-type jacket to guard against the chill wind off the bay.

Crossing Powell, he began walking up Geary to Mason. Flurries of red taillights passed him and he could see dark couples moving into the brilliant lights of the theater district a block away. It was 9:30 and the audience from the first show of *Hair* poured out of the Geary Theatre. Next door to the Geary was the even more massive and ornate Curren. The stocky man moved back under the red-striped awning of Harold's Books and Magazines and watched the cabs—Luxor, Desoto, Veteran's, City, and Yellow— converge on the theaters.

Paul Lee Stine was parked in the taxi zone in front of the St.

Francis when he received a call for Ninth Avenue. Stine pulled his cab into the Powell Street traffic and turned onto Geary. On the side of his cab were the words "Call 626-2345 Radio Dispatched." The door on the driver's side had been caved in in an accident days earlier.

The crowds slowed Stine down. As he began to edge his cab ahead, passing the Pinecrest Restaurant, a stocky man stepped from beneath a striped awning, placed his hand on the driver's side, near the rearview mirror, and looked down into the cab. Lights behind the man's body silhouetted him, the glare showing through his crew-cut hair revealing the curve of his skull. As he got in the back seat, the stranger requested an address in the Presidio Heights residential district. Stine logged the address on his trip-sheet "Washington Street and Maple" and started the meter.

The cab traveled west up Geary to the corner of Van Ness Avenue, where Stine turned right, then moved along auto row to California, where he took a left. Eleven blocks later, Stine swung onto Divisadero. Another left, and the cab proceeded west on Washington. The night closed in behind them.

Well-lit and wet with fog, Washington Street was lined with stately, expensive homes with great rows of steps and massive quantities of filigree and wrought iron. When the cab slowed at Maple and Washington, the trip sheet destination, the stocky man could dimly make out his own car parked at the foot of the steep hill. After he finished his work in the cab, the stocky man planned to sprint downhill to the auto and disappear into the night.

Suddenly a man appeared in the headlights of Stine's cab, a man out walking his dog. The stocky man leaned forward and told the cabdriver, "Go another block."

There was a soft breeze and the stocky man could hear wind chimes from one of the homes nearby. The cab stopped between two trees on the corner of Washington and Cherry, directly in front of 3898 Washington.

Abruptly, the stocky stranger pressed the muzzle of a gun tightly against the driver's right cheek just in front of his right ear;

with the crook of his left arm he seized Stine's throat. Vainly, Stine tried to raise his left hand over his right shoulder. The stocky man firmly squeezed the trigger; the firearm discharged.

There was little noise. A seal was created between the skin and the muzzle and the blast was expended into the body tissues. Particles of unburned powder exploded about the breech of the weapon, peppering the gloved hands of the attacker. A conical perforation of the skull was created as the projectile was fired. The bullet, twisting and spiraling, particles of molten metal being thrown off as it traveled over a thousand feet per second, created multiple fractures of Stine's skull. The copper-jacketed lead bullet, mashed and fragmented into four segments, penetrated left and laterally toward the midsection of the left zygomatic arch and finally lodged in the left temporalis muscle.

In unison, the barrel and slide of the gun recoiled until the barrel's movement was arrested. Continuing backward, the slide passed over the hammer, cocked it, and slammed against the receiver as the empty casing was seized and ejected onto the floor of the cab. The slide sprung forward again, peeled off the next cartridge from the double-rowed magazine, and forced it into the chamber, then relocked with the barrel. The gun was ready to be fired again.

The killer exited the rear door and entered the right front door. Then he held Stine's head in his lap while he took Stine's wallet and tore off a portion of his shirt.

At 9:55 P.M., a fourteen-year-old girl directly across the street from the taxi looked out of the middle window from the second floor of the building. There was a party going on but she leaned forward, shaded her eyes, and looked down into the misty street below. Abruptly, she called to her sixteen-year-old brother and a younger brother to come to the window. They were almost fifty feet away and their view of the cab was unobstructed.

A stocky man had the head of the cabdriver cradled in his lap. He appeared to be struggling with the driver or searching him. Then he leaned over the cabbie's body to the driver's side and seemed to be wiping down the interior of the taxi.

The stocky man had been doing something to the driver's body but the partygoers, who had now crowded around the upstairs window, could not tell what. The front passenger side of the cab opened, and eventually the heavyset man got out.

He came around the cab, taking with him some sort of rag or towel, and began wiping down the driver's side door, the handle, around the outside mirror and the left passenger side. At one point he opened up the driver's door and leaned forward to wipe off the area of the dashboard again. To steady himself, he leaned his right hand on the rail separating the front and rear windows. The fragment of cloth was still in his left hand. Then he closed the door and walked away.

When he turned the corner, passing close to a mailbox, the children lost sight of him. He was headed north on Cherry in the direction of the Presidio. He did not run.

While all this was happening, the partygoers had called the police communications center. The report was logged by the operator at 9:58 P.M. The operator could tell the caller was under great stress. As he filled out the card with the caller's address, he asked, "Was the crime in progress?"

"Yes."

He tried to get a physical description of the man, and at this point an incredible blunder was made: somehow the assailant was mistakenly described as an NMA—Negro Male Adult. A black man.

"What was the general direction of his departure? Was he armed?"

The operator jotted down the answers. Immediately, the card was handed to the dispatcher, who leaned forward over his lighted panel, consulted a complex map of San Francisco divided into districts and sectors, and broadcast a general call to all police units, cars, and wagons: an APB.

"Caution urged," he added.

A police patrol unit was near Cherry and Washington and raced toward the scene. The patrol reached Jackson and Cherry by 10:00 and saw a stocky man "lumbering" along in the fog toward the Presidio.

The radio unit, Patrolmen Donald Fouke and Eric Zelms,

looking for a black man, shouted to the stranger and asked if he had seen anything unusual in the last minute or so. The stocky man called out he'd seen a man waving a gun running east on Washington, and the patrol car sped off in that direction.

Had the radio unit actually stopped the stocky man, they would have seen that he was drenched in blood where Stine's head had rested in his lap. The stains were hidden by his dark clothes and the deep shadows of the trees along the street. The officers, because of the communications mix-up, had no reason to be looking for a WMA—a White Male Adult. Had the policeman called the stocky man to the side of their car for a few quick questions both officers might well have been gunned down; the killer would have had the advantage of the 9-mm gun hidden in his right hand. The senior patrolman had seen the stocky man's left profile clearly, but it would be some time before the two cops realized they had actually spoken with Stine's killer. They had come within a whisper of capturing him. This was the beginning of the stocky man's pathological obsession with the San Francisco police.

The stocky man stopped in the cool night air. Instead of doubling back to his car right away, he went on into the Presidio and walked to the Julius Kahn Playground. Then, crouching slightly against the stone wall, the man worked south back to his auto.

At 10:55 P.M. Officers Armand Pelissetti and Frank Peda arrived, responding to the alarm simultaneously with Homicide Inspector Walter Kracke, who was nearby, on his way home. Both cars stopped just behind the cab. The men ran from their autos to find Paul Stine shot in the head, his upper torso in the passenger side, his head resting on the floorboard.

When Kracke opened the door, the driver's left hand fell outward, palm up, nearly touching the street. The attacker had not bothered to take his watch and the detective could see the thin black band around the slain man's wrist. A Timex. The attacker had also left Stine his class ring.

The cab meter was still running. The keys to the cab were missing.

The officers called an ambulance, "code three," and broadcast an amended description of the killer as a White Male Adult that the teenagers had given them. More units converged on the scene.

Ambulance #82 arrived at 10:10 P.M. The ambulance steward pronounced Stine dead. Kracke had called out every dog unit available and requested a fire department spotlight vehicle to light up the area. He then notified the San Francisco coroner. Because Inspector Kracke had heard the initial police radio communication and automatically responded, with the help of the two Richmond station cops he was able to preserve a perfect crime scene.

At 10:20 P.M., a call was placed for the on-duty homicide team, the men who would stay on the case until it was solved.

Homicide Inspector Dave Toschi (pronounced Tahs-kee) was exhausted, physically and mentally. He had gone to bed the minute he had gotten home, at eight o'clock. The phone rang at 10:30 P.M.

Toschi answered and heard the voice of the night office police operator, calling from the fourth floor of the Hall of Justice on Bryant Street.

"Dave," the operator said, "Yellow Cab driver's been shot, probably robbed and possibly stabbed."

"Where?" groaned Toschi.

"On Washington Street," said the communications officer, "between Maple and Cherry. Closer to Cherry."

"What the hell is going on," thought Toschi. This would be his fourth murder since the seventh of October. He'd just gotten home from a homicide, a beating death. "Jesus Christ, four homicides in four days!"

The detective reached for his familiar yellow lined tablet and wrote the date, the exact time he had received the information by phone, and the name of the communications operator.

Toschi phoned his partner, Bill Armstrong, and told him that he'd pick him up in ten minutes. Then, Toschi had an afterthought. He dialed the number of the operation's center. "There are a lot of people on a Saturday night wandering by that scene; be sure they try and preserve the scene as much as possible. Tell them to keep as many people as they can away from the cab. And under no conditions let anybody touch the vehicle."

Toschi called the crime lab, stumbled into his small bathroom, and ran his hands through his curly black hair. The detective brushed his teeth and dressed quickly in tan slacks, his second-string set of soft hushpuppies, dark socks, corduroy jacket, and all-weather raincoat. It was cold out and he was often gone for as long as two days. Inspectors work in eight two-man rotating teams. The "on-call team" is responsible for all homicides occurring during their week and have the next seven weeks to work on these cases.

Toschi paused long enough to gulp down a lukewarm cup of Instant Folgers coffee, grabbed his ever present folder, and kissed his wife Carol good-bye. She was used to his being called away at any time and on a moment's notice.

He started up the family car, a red, two-door Borgward, and backed out of the garage. Minutes later, Toschi spotted his partner on the corner, wearing a black turtleneck sweater and black raincoat. Armstrong got in. On the way to the crime scene Toschi notified the military police for help in the search for the killer. The two inspectors arrived at the buzzing murder site at 11:10, precisely the same time as the M.P.s, and just three minutes after the coroner had gotten there.

Red lights, flashing blue lights, klieg lights, blazing yellow lights: Washington Street was glowing like a summer's day. Several hundred people had gathered by the time the detectives parked across from the cab, just under the window where the teenagers' party had been going on. Toschi was glad he had called operations to be sure the cab was really sealed off. But even while isolating the scene from an overcurious crowd, Toschi and Armstrong had to be careful not to drive away any important witnesses or touch or step on anything themselves.

A patrolman filled them in on the details of the murder. It seemed to Armstrong and Toschi that this had begun as one of the many cab robberies that occur in San Francisco every week, but had become a clumsy and inefficient cab robbery gone terribly wrong.

The two partners considered it the work of an amateur: the killer left the scene dripping blood, and most likely did not get much money for his effort. They could estimate from the waybill that Stine had on him at most twenty or twenty-five dollars. The killer had taken Stine's wallet.

In his yellow ledger, Toschi wrote a complete description of the body and its immediate surroundings. On Stine's person the killer had overlooked seven keys, one ring, one checkbook, and some papers: auto and motorcycle registrations. There was exactly $4.12 in the dead man's pocket, all in change.

There was blood all over the cab.

Toschi stayed with the car while Armstrong took the names and addresses of all witnesses.

Toschi leaned down and scrutinized the body, noting any tears in the clothing, whether the blood was fresh or dry, or if there were any weapons in sight. Blood still glistened on the car seat, the dashboard, even the cab meter. It clung and hid in every crevice and crack of the driver's side. "Stine bled profusely," wrote Toschi.

Meanwhile, Armstrong had the uniformed officers checking and rechecking to see if any of the residents had seen or heard anything. Even when the two inspectors were not together, they knew what the other was doing; they avoid overlapping. Usually one man will opt to stay with the body, as did Toschi this night. Toschi has a firm belief that it is the body that will tell you almost all you need to know to solve a case.

Free hand, on a blank sheet of paper, the detective made a sketch of the scene, noting the taxi and buildings and the relationship of the body to them. Even photographs taken from every conceivable angle give a distorted view of the body in respect to its surroundings, so he made exact measurements with his steel tape and added these to the sketch.

When the coroner's office steward pulled the body out of the cab, Stine's bloodied San Francisco street guide came with him and fell into the street. The body was placed in a dark green-black plastic body bag with a long zipper, and then carried to a stretcher. Photographs were taken of anything that may have been underneath Stine.

Toschi bent forward.

Yes, there it was. Almost under the seat and toward the center post of the cab gleamed the copper color of one 9-mm casing. On the corner of the front passenger seat were three streaks that might have been the marks of three fingers printed in blood. Since Stine had fallen to the passenger side palms up, Toschi thought they might belong to the killer.

Just under the dash, Toschi found a pair of dull-black leather gloves. They were soaked with blood but were too small for a man. Later he discovered that they belonged to a woman passenger from earlier in the day.

At 11:30, the crime lab responded, Bob Dagitz from San Rafael and Bill Kirkindal from Pacifica. These were two of the department's best lab men. Both were fingerprint experts. Dagitz and Kirkindal searched the interior of Stine's cab for any latent prints the killer might have left behind.

Latent prints are those which are transferred to surfaces by the natural oils of the hair and face that palms and fingers may have touched. The perspiration from the hands is not lubricative enough to leave impressions. Unless a person has handled grease or dirt, these prints are invisible and must be developed by dusting the surface with a gray or black powder. Once a print is visible, it can be lifted by transparent tape and applied to a three-by-five-inch card with a contrasting background.

The men marked the placement of latent prints, measured the distance of the impressions from the floor and roof, and had the areas photographed by men from the photo lab. Later, prints of all the people who may have ridden in the cab that day, located through the taxi trip sheet, would have to be taken and compared to any clear prints the lab could come up with. The large majority of the prints would be fragmentary or superimposed. Fingerprints of Stine would have to be taken; most likely they would already be on file at Yellow Cab. A detailed inspection of the hands of the victim would also be made for any cuts, bruises, or torn fingernails, as well as an examination of the victim's hair.

Toschi had noticed two long dark marks on Stine's left hand. Perhaps he had thrown up his hand to protect himself from the gun blast.

Then the two lab men discovered the most important clue in the Stine case: the prints of a right hand. The prints had been made in blood. This information and where the prints were found was to be kept totally confidential.

The coroner authorized removal of the victim to the morgue, and Deputies Schultz and Kindred took charge of the body.

Armstrong and Toschi had gotten a rather vague description of the killer from the teenage witnesses, and now they widened the search. "Canvass the area," said Toschi, "and look for anyone who matches this description: dark jacket, crew-cut hair, big guy, kinda stocky, husky . . ."

Dog units began to check the surrounding blocks for anyone hiding in doorways, driveways, or the shadows.

Toschi and Armstrong had made a painstaking search for more shells or bullet holes and found none. The cartridge was labeled and identified with extreme care so that it would not be mutilated in any way. Any recovered spent slug is marked with the officer's special mark on the nose, never on the side, so that the striations on the bullet are not disturbed. Custody of exhibits of evidence are traced from the time of recovery so that a chain of legal evidence can be maintained. The crime lab would need the fatal bullet, fatal shell, any clothing of the victim containing powder burns, and, if possible, the lethal weapon itself.

The Presidio, the present home of the Sixth Army, lies a block and one half north of Cherry and Washington. The base is open around the clock, with virtually no security and with very few restricted sections. The detectives heard from neighbors that a stocky figure was seen dashing across Julius Kahn Public Playground and into the dense undergrowth of the Presidio. Toschi had the high-powered floodlights from the fire department moved into place to illuminate the entire area. A large number of patrolmen began to search tree by tree, shrub by shrub, flashlights slashing lines into the night. In the distance voices called to each other.

Somewhere ahead they hoped their quarry was also pushing his way through the scrub, trying to lose himself in the green expanse of the Presidio. Somewhere ahead hiding in the darkness and silence they hoped to find the killer of Paul Stine.

The dog-patrol units, seven of the best search dogs in the country, gathered at the front entrance to the Presidio and were deployed one at a time in various directions. For more than an hour the dogs moved with swift determination, sniffing the thick undergrowth inside the walls.

Armstrong and Toschi considered the possibilities: Had the killer gone quickly through the dark woods, emerged from the Presidio at Richardson Avenue, taken Highway 101 past Fort Point onto the Golden Gate Bridge, and vanished into Marin County? Could he have cut across Julius Kahn Playground and doubled back southward to Jackson Street?

A call to Stine's boss at Yellow Cab, LeRoy Sweet, revealed that the driver's last dispatch was 9:45 P.M., to 500 9th Avenue. When Stine did not show up, the fare was assigned another cab. The meter of Stine's cab, still running when he was found, read at exactly 10:46 P.M., $6.25. This indicated Stine had picked up another fare, the killer, en route to the 9th Avenue assignment.

Backtracking through the meter reading, Toschi could determine roughly where the killer had flagged Stine down. The city's cabs in 1969 were among the most expensive in the United States; for a two-mile trip Stine would have charged $1.35.

"How had the slayer gotten to the theater district in the first place, and had he gone back to get his car? Was it now parked in the large Downtown Center Parking and Garage?" wondered Toschi.

At 1:00 A.M., the cab was towed across town, to the Hall of Justice, followed by Dagitz and Kirkindal.

At 2:00 A.M., the search was called off. Armstrong and Toschi quit the scene.

A killer had stalked the streets of this rich and elegant neighborhood and then vanished into the fog.

Sunday, October 12, 1969

The police description of the killer was broadcast continuously throughout the night and early morning. By that time, the M.P.s had ceased their search of the Presidio.

At 1:30 A.M., ten minutes after Stine's wife, Claudia, had been notified by phone of his death, Dagitz and Kirkindal began their search of the cab at the Hall of Justice impound room. Yellow Cab #912, California license Y17413, was gone over thoroughly for more casings, slugs, bullet holes, or any other evidence.

Stine's body was the first to be autopsied that morning, at a little after 9:30 A.M.

The coroner's autopsy room, milky-white and cold, is just behind the Hall of Justice and three floors under Toschi's office. The bodies in the storage room are kept on sloping metal tables in drawers, each with its own bus-terminal-lockerlike number. The 38°F. stainless-steel refrigerated alcove is next to the autopsy room, which is kept at 60°F. Bleak fluorescent lighting cools and burns out every shadow. The pathologists dress in green surgical gowns and wear heavy household rubber gloves, the cuffs turned up. Usually the chief medical examiner observes or performs the autopsy himself. An autopsy report will contain, at the very least, the age, sex, race, frame, and distinguishing characteristics of the victim. Signs of death such as rigor mortis, heat loss, lividity, and decomposition, are registered. An external examination of head and trunk and internal scrutiny of the organ systems, stomach contents, neck, spinal cord, head, major vessels, and heart is made. A red manilla tag with a wire looped through one end is twisted around the right big toe of the cadaver.

Before the blood and grime are removed, close-up photos are made of the dead body fully clothed, under the guidance of the pathologist. Any material from the wound is saved for powder granule tests. In order to rule out every possible contributing cause of death, an entire autopsy is done even if the body cavity is not penetrated. "Penetrating" is a term used to indicate an object entering the body but not exiting. When the body is both entered and exited, it is called "perforating."

The autopsy surgeon examined the wound in Stine's head. It was a jagged, star-shaped tear. Gunpowder and soot had created a pocket between the skin and the skull, which had been blackened by the tremendous heat. Charring converged from the outside of the wound toward its center. The "tattooing," embedded powder particles, in the skin adjacent to the ragged wound had been caused by the flare and expanding gases. Both the smudging on Stine's temple and the large, singed wound indicated to the surgeon that the muzzle of the gun had been held in close contact. In such a shooting, the wound of exit is much smaller than the wound of entrance, unlike a non-contact wound in which the reverse is true. In the cabdriver's case, the bullet did not exit but lodged.

Post-mortem lividity, a purplish discoloration of the parts of the body nearest the floor, occurs about two hours after death. This gives an indication of how much time has passed since death occurred. The muscles around Stine's head, neck, jaw, and eyelids had begun to stiffen, the beginning of rigor mortis. It would be two to three days before the rigidity would start to disappear.

While the autopsy was being performed, the police questioned the teenaged witnesses and prepared a composite sketch with a policeman who doubled as an artist. He laid out his ebony pencil, eraser stick, and sixteen-pound Strathmore layout bond.

Tom Macris, the best police artist in the state, once told me, "You've got to tell the witness to believe in himself and in the infinite capacity of the mind to retain details. You conduct a guided interview. You get a feel for the person, their mental range, their free-floating imagery." Like Macris, this artist worked from feeling and intuition. Also like most composite artists, he kept a library of pictures, people with different-shaped faces and hairstyles. The witnesses look through the photos until they find one similar to the suspect. This gives the artist a foundation on which to build. The police artist was doing his drawing full face because that is the way that mug shots are taken and the composite thus can be more easily compared to them. Homicide descriptions are usually the most difficult:

the observer's attention is most likely on the weapon.

"He had a stocky build," the teenagers agreed, "looked like he was about five foot eight inches tall. He was wearing a dark navy-blue or black parka-type jacket and dark trousers."

"What was the shape of the man's head?" asked the artist. "Triangular? Round? Square? Is it like any of these?"

After a half hour, the artist showed the uncompleted sketch to the teenagers and allowed them to look over his shoulder while he was working, letting them help correct and define.

"How about the forehead? The eyes? nose? Large ears? Color of hair? Long or short hair?

"Did you notice if the man had any scars? Is the nose anything like the one I've drawn? Is this close? O.K. Is there anything I should change? Did I make the eyes far enough apart? Have I made him old enough?"

The teenagers had described a white male with reddish or blond crew-cut hair, around twenty-five or thirty years of age, wearing glasses.

Armstrong and Toschi decided to circulate the resulting composite drawing, Bulletin #87–69. They sent one to each cab company in the city. The detectives wanted to alert the taxi drivers that a pattern of cabdriver killings might be developing. Each company got a hundred copies of a wanted circular that described the killer's method of operation:

Suspect takes cab in downtown area at 9:30 P.M. and sits in front seat with driver.

Tells driver destination is Washington and Laurel area or area near Park or Presidio. Upon reaching destination, suspect orders driver to continue on at gunpoint into or near Park, where he then perpetrates robbery.

In one case victim was shot in head at contact.

The weapon was a 9-mm automatic.

Armstrong and Toschi wanted any driver who saw anyone resembling the sketch to get in touch with them. Unknown to both detectives, they did have other witnesses: the two policemen in the radio car who had actually spoken to the killer and been directed on a wild-goose chase.

At this time colorful and soft-spoken Dave Toschi was probably the most dynamic member of the police department's elite corps, the homicide inspectors. He was the city's "Supercop."

A flamboyant dresser, the stylish detective could be found at work in a short-sleeve silk shirt, corduroy jacket, dark brown ankle boots, with large brass buckles, and his ever-present large bowtie. Toschi's shoulder holster, a unique upside-down, quick-draw model, is worn on his left, with a vertical refill row of seven cartridges and a pair of handcuffs. The gun is a .38-caliber Cobra, one of the six variations of the solid-frame .38 Special, with a swing-out cylinder, and is made of aluminum alloy. It's a double/single action revolver weighing just over a pound and measuring seven inches in overall length. Steve McQueen met with Toschi before the filming of his 1968 movie *Bullitt*, which was set in San Francisco. McQueen had a duplicate of Toschi's special holster and gun made up and based much of the character on the Italian, Marina-born sleuth.

Toschi was a compact, muscular man with dark eyes, strong bow-shaped mouth, and cleft chin, all dominated by abundant curly black hair. Over the years he had tried not to bring his case problems home with him. But when the solutions remained elusive, and haunted him, he would drive the length of the Great Highway or take midnight strolls through his Sunset district neighborhood.

And sometimes after a particularly tough day Toschi would come home to Carol and his three pre-teen daughters, and lounge in his big brown leather easychair, put a Big Band record on the stereo, usually *Artie Shaw's Greatest Hits*, and sip a Manhattan while singing along as he'd done at Galileo High and when he was a California Street bartender. He had considered music as a career.

He became a cop instead.

Toschi's senior partner was Bill Armstrong. Tall and handsome, reminiscent of Paul Drake on the old Perry Mason television show, the forty-year-old Armstrong had sharp features and a strong jaw, his face framed by a curly brush of silver hair and the glasses he sometimes wears. His tasteful business suits and short hair are a contrast to the darker, slimmer Toschi. Armstrong was also the father of three girls and tried not to bring his case load home with him.

Lately, this had been pretty hard to achieve.

Stine's blood-stained clothing had been removed, an identification tag wire put on each article, and placed under a drying lamp. When his clothes had dried completely, they were laid flat, with butcher paper between each article to avoid the possibility of any sort of transfer. The clothing was listed on a clothing slip and turned into the property clerk's office to be safeguarded for future lab tests. No piece of apparel is disposed of until the case is terminated. All articles in the pockets are catalogued.

The body is placed on the autopsy table and the surgeon dictates as he examines. The upper half of the sloped metal table on which the body rests has a grated surface: at the foot is a shallow sloping tub that runs beneath the grating. Through the tub streams a continuous flow of water. The arms of the body are at the sides, a wooden block under the shoulder blades thrusts the chest upward and causes the head to fall back. Suspended from the ceiling is a microphone that records every step as dictated by the pathologist, including an accurate description and location of all wounds.

The necropsy surgeon dictated to the coroner, John Lee:

The body is that of a well-developed, well-nourished young adult white male appearing about the stated age. The head is symmetrical and covered with a sparse quantity of dark hair receding at the temples.

There is a large, ragged, irregular-shaped apparent gunshot entry wound over the right side of the head. This wound is located at the superior and anterior attachment of the right ear. The vertical dimensions measure four cm. and transverse dimensions measure two cm.

There is a blackening of the skin over the ventral aspect of this wound, extending for a distance of two cm. When probed, the wound penetrates left laterally toward the midportion of the left zygomatic arch. There is a large quantity of blood present over the face.

The murdered man's wound was removed and examined microscopically for powder residue. The pathologist made notes on preprinted schematic drawings of a male body, shown front and back, with the head shown from above.

In an autopsy a Y-shaped incision is made in the chest and abdomen. A triangular portion of the rib cage is removed. When the throat and neck have been examined, the autopsy surgeon removes the heart and lungs, ligating the large blood vessels. The kidneys, pancreas, liver, spleen, and intestinal tract are taken from the abdominal cavity after the heart has been examined, and dissected on a black dissection board. A sample of blood is taken and blood type is established. Finally, the pelvic contents and genitalia are reviewed.

The cerebellum is fixed by an injection of formaldehyde and the pathologist opens the skull with an electric circular saw, carefully avoiding penetration of the brain. The top is pried off, cranial membrane still clinging. Before the brain is scooped out intact and weighed on a white metal scale, the interior surface of the top of the skull and brain is studied. The brain is then segmented to see if any abnormalities are present.

Then it is up to the attendant to reassemble the form by replacing viscera and organs and putting back in place the triangular piece of rib cage. He stitches up the Y-shaped incision, working from the pubis to midchest. The body is then washed with water and sponged, covered with a black rubber sheet, and returned to its mortuary compartment.

Whenever a physician has to extract a bullet from a body he must use caution, since the impressions of the gun barrel on the bullet link it to the weapon from which it was fired. In most cases, the surgeon scratches his identifying mark on the bullet's nose.

In Stine's instance, a smashed and fragmented copper-jacketed lead bullet was removed. The four fragments of metal were placed in a glassine envelope, which was then sealed and signed by the pathologist. The sealed flap of the envelope also included the location of the found bullet.

Diagnosis: Gunshot wound of skin and subcutaneous tissue, wound of head.
Cause of death: Gunshot wound of the brain.

Stine's cab, impounded in a double-locked room, would be gone over by lab technicians for another two days. The only blood found in the cab was type O-RH Negative, Stine's bloodtype.

Stine would have been thirty in sixty-nine days. He had been attending San Francisco State College and working the night shift for Yellow Cab to pay for his education. He even sold insurance. In January he had planned to complete his post-graduate work for a doctorate in English. He had worked as a reporter for his high school paper and later for the *Turlock Journal*. A powerful man, with a solid 180 pounds spread over a five-foot-nine-inch frame, Stine had lived with his wife in an old green Victorian house divided into multiple apartments at 1842 Fell Street, across from the long, verdant panhandle leading into Golden Gate Park. The couple had no children.

Approximately five weeks earlier Stine had been held up by two gunmen. Twelve days before his murder, on a Tuesday night, another Yellow Cab driver was held up. Could this have been a dry run for the actual killing?

Monday, October 13, 1969

At 9:00 A.M. Stine's file prints were sent over to homicide and compared to the visible prints found in the cab. The bloody prints were not Stine's.

Fingerprints are divided into general types: plain arches, tented arches, plain loops, plain whorls, central pocket loop whorls, radial whorls, double loop whorls, accidental whorls. The fine lines on the fingerprints are called "ridges" and the spaces between are known as "furrows." The average print has about fifty ridge characteristics. The design formed by the ridges is called "patterns." Partial prints often contain twelve characteristic points, but in the case of fragmentary prints they most often can not be positively matched. Anything less than twelve points of similarity would be subject to an expert's "opinion."

Toschi and Armstrong, using the cab trip sheet, went back to the addresses where the passengers were left off, knocked on a lot of doors, and located about a third of the people who had ridden in that particular cab on Saturday. Later on in the day a member of the crime lab would come out to roll a set of their prints to eliminate them positively as murder suspects.

In the crime lab, print man Bob Dagitz classified the visible prints found in the cab. When the killer had leaned forward to wipe the driver's dashboard area, he had held onto the beam separating the front and rear windows and left prints from his right hand.

"Middle finger and third finger of right hand," Dagitz wrote. "8 points on 2 fingers. In blood."

Zodiac

Tuesday, October 14, 1969

At 10:30 A.M., at the *Chronicle*, Letters Editor Carol Fisher had just returned from a long vacation out of the country. She shared a small office on the third floor with the two editorial writers. While the writers, the publisher, and I were in the editorial conference, she would go through the pile of mail that readers showered upon the paper every day. One letter was addressed in blue felt-tip:

> S.F. Chronicle
> San Fran
> Calif.
> Please Rush to Editor
> Please Rush to Editor

The postmark showed the letter had been mailed the previous day and from San Francisco. The return address had been replaced by a symbol.

A crossed circle.

Carefully, Carol slit open the envelope and withdrew a folded letter. As she opened it, a three-by-five-inch piece of gray-and-white cloth, neatly torn, not cut, and spattered with blood, fluttered out onto her desk.

Zodiac had written his fifth letter.

Quickly she scanned the thin blue lines:

> This is the Zodiac speaking
> I am the murderer of the
> taxi driver over by
> Washington St & Maple St last
> night, to prove this here is
> a blood stained piece of his
> shirt. I am the same man
> who did in the people in the
> north bay area.
> The S.F. Police could have caught
> me last night if they had
> searched the park properly
> instead of holding road races ·
> with their motorcicles seeing who
> could make the most noise. The
> car drivers should have just
> parked their cars & sat there
> quietly waiting for me to come
> out of cover.

The letter closed with an incredibly chilling threat. (Though the first portion of this letter has been reproduced before, this is the first time the entire letter has been shown.)

> School children make nice targ-
> ets, I think I shall wipe out
> a school bus some morning. Just
> shoot out the front tire & then
> pick off the kiddies as they come
> bouncing out.

Carol, holding the letter by two fingers, alerted us and raced to the city desk. "I just got this thing in the mail." The city desk immediately telephoned the S.F.P.D. homicide detail.

The letter was first Xeroxed and photographed. We all crowded around to read it while reporter Peter Stack, who was working as a relief for Bob Popp, the regular man at the Hall of Justice, brought the letter and bloody cloth over to Toschi and Armstrong at their office. "I don't know if this has any merits," said Stack. "We got this letter and my boss said to bring it over to you guys and see if it means anything."

Toschi looked up from his desk.

"It's kind of dirty," said Stack. "There's a kind of bloody piece of cloth or shirt." He dropped it on the blotter in front of Toschi and Armstrong.

Toschi saw the fabric and remembered it from Saturday night. "Jesus Christ!" he said. "This looks like Stine's shirt! Bill, I think this is Stine's shirt!"

Armstrong turned to Stack. "We're going to bring this shirt down to the coroner's office. Stine's clothing is being held there."

The detectives had to know how many people had touched the letter and asked Stack to see if he would find out. Before Toschi and Armstrong went down to the coroner's office, they stopped at Chief of Inspectors Marty Lee's office and asked to see him as soon as possible. "We've got something going here," said Toschi.

When they were finally ushered into Lee's office, Armstrong pulled the letter out of its glassine envelope and laid it very carefully on the Chief of Inspector's desk.

"I think we're involved in a heavy case," said Toschi. "I think we're involved with a mass murderer. I think San Francisco is involved. Stack from the *Chronicle* hand carried it over."

"Has this been printed yet?" said Lee, glancing at it without touching it.

"No," said Armstrong.

"I'd better tell the Chief about this," said Lee, reaching for the phone.

Armstrong and Toschi dropped the letter at the photo lab

to have some eight-by-tens made. The crime lab would now make an attempt to bring out any latent prints on the letter. Paper is always the worst surface to work from. Not only is the surface difficult, but most professional criminals wear gloves or put airplane glue, nail polish, or collodion on their fingertips.

Dagitz, the print man, sprayed Zodiac's letter with a highly toxic purplish chemical solution called Ninhydrin. This distorts all printing and turns the paper purple. The chemical reacts on the sweat and amino acids left by the fingers on the paper's surface. Both sides of the Zodiac letter were sprayed and then brought next door to the print-lab darkroom. The letter was placed on a shelf and left to develop. The entire process took from three to four hours.

On the main floor annex, Toschi and Armstrong saw the coroner, Dr. Henry Turkel, who got all of Stine's clothing out of the property clerk's office. They went back upstairs and told Lee that the cloth enclosed with the letter had come from the left lower portion of Stine's shirt.

San Francisco was definitely involved.

Their next step was to compare the printing on the Zodiac letter with printing on other letters Zodiac had sent to the press.

Captain Townsend of Napa agreed to meet with Toschi and Armstrong at his office with his investigator. They also called the Solano County Sheriff's Office, since all of them would probably be working together. Armstrong and Toschi felt stunned. They were involved with an insane killer, one who so far had left five victims dead and two wounded.

Later in the day, Toschi called Paul Avery, the *Chronicle* reporter who had been following the Zodiac case so far. "With the matching of the shirt," said Toschi, "we're pretty definitely up to our ears in the Zodiac murders."

That night Armstrong and Toschi drove to Napa to talk to Townsend and Detective Sergeant Narlow. He agreed that the printing on the letter to the *Chronicle* matched the previous Zodiac printing.

Wednesday, October 15, 1969

Toschi and Armstrong drove to Sacramento to show the actual letter to the head of Questioned Documents for the state, Sherwood Morrill. Even after being chemically treated, an original letter is always better than a copy in making comparisons. Morrill found that the letter matched in every way the earlier communications from the killer.

Zodiac used a bizarre mixture of cursive letters and printing. The killer always used an *r* that was so small it looked like a checkmark and a cursive *d* that seemed about to fall over.

"If this guy keeps this up," said Morrill, "he'll probably concentrate on writing to your department. If he's an ego-nut he'll stay with the larger circulation newspapers."

Toschi looked down at the headlines for that morning's *Chronicle:* "The Boastful 'Slayer' Letter Claims Writer Killed Cabbie, 4 Others." The paper reprinted the composite sketch and ran the top half of the Zodiac letter.

At police request, the threat at the end of the letter was withheld while authorities tried to figure out the best way to handle it.

Friday, October 17, 1969

Publication of Zodiac's threat was finally allowed. The public reacted with panic. There was a flurry of television, radio, wire service, and newspaper reports. An emergency bulletin was issued to police, county, and city school superintendents:

> To all law enforcement agencies. . . .
> A San Francisco cabbie was murdered by an
> unknown psychotic . . . who has threatened to
> "wipe out a school bus . . .
> then pick off the kiddies as
> they come bouncing out."

Advice to school bus drivers on how to handle any sort of violent attack on buses followed:

1. Continue driving the bus on a flat tire. Do not stop.
2. Tell the children to get below the level of the window and lie on the floor.
3. The driver will continue driving and turn on all lights and sound the horn.
4. The school bus shall not be stopped until arriving in a well-populated area.
5. Upon arrival at this location a local law enforcement agency should be notified immediately.

The Napa Valley Unified School District called in all ninety of their full-time and part-time drivers. The drivers were told that "the driver would be the first target in Zodiac's gunsight if there was an attack on the bus." An extra man, a watcher, was assigned to each bus to take over in case of a sniper attack. State law requires that when a school bus driver leaves the bus to escort the children across the street, he must pocket the ignition key. Because of the threat, the driver would leave the key with the back-up driver, who would stay with the busload of children. If the driver were shot, the second driver was to drive away as fast as possible and as far as possible. "Remember," they were told, "attract as much attention as possible by sounding the horn, flashing lights, and erratic driving."

Ten thousand school children in twenty-eight schools rode Napa County's sixty-five yellow-striped buses. The buses traveled four thousand miles, round trip, in a day, much of it around dangerous curves and through blind intersections. In some places the country roads are completely deserted, with as much as two miles separating houses. Toschi could imagine a busload of screaming children careening down an empty gravel road, past orchards and vineyards, horn shrieking, lights furiously flashing, the driver badly wounded behind the wheel. Or perhaps a bus rendered motionless, with Zodiac methodically shooting out each of the tires of its eight wheels and then firing at the forty students inside.

In reaction to the bulletin, seventy units of heavily armed policemen began to ride guard on the Napa school buses. Napa Sheriff's Department and St. Helena P.D. and the Highway Patrol were assigned to guard the children on the buses. Pickup trucks from the forestry department and ranger stations at Lake Berryessa were put into service as well. They were told to follow the buses and to stay one hundred yards behind. Cessna aircraft from the Napa Aero Club and the Sheriff's Department in air patrol planes flew cover over the hundreds of miles of school bus routes. Napa school officials said, "How can you overreact to a threat like that? We are worrying as to whether we've done enough. If a madman could get to President Kennedy, with all the protection he had, then it could happen in Napa even with all we've done."

Because of a bomb threat received in Santa Rosa by a caller who hinted that he might be the Zodiac, a careful check for bombs was made in the morning before the route was begun.

The panic in Napa was no greater than that felt at the Hall of Justice in San Francisco.

At 9:00 A.M., October 16, Fouke and Zelms, the two radio men who had seen the stocky man walking into the Presidio, realized that they must have passed the killer. They filed an initial report with their captain; this was sent as an interdepartmental communication to Armstrong and Toschi. The two patrolmen were "shattered and filled with despair."

With the help of the two patrolmen, a second composite drawing of Zodiac was made. The amended drawing now showed a man thirty-five to forty-five years old, with a thicker jaw. He weighed two hundred pounds or more, was barrel-chested, and wore a navy blue or black waist-length zippered jacket. He was noted as being about five feet eight or nine, with reddish-brown, crew-cut hair, and wearing heavy rimmed glasses.

The patrolmen's report and statement were placed in confidential files; S.F.P.D. officially denied that Zodiac had ever been seen by any policemen. The denial stands to this day. Several sources have told me, "Zodiac had undoubtedly been *almost* captured by the S.F. Police." The police have never been able to explain why a second composite drawing suddenly had to be made.

In the offices of the *Palo Alto Times*, a man had phoned the news desk and claimed, "This is the Zodiac. I had to leave San Francisco because I'm too hot there." The Palo Alto police chief called the anonymous telephone message "extremely serious." It may have been only a crank call, but he preferred to take no chances and got in touch with the district transportation supervisor. Between them, they arranged to have an armed guard ride with each of the system's twenty-five buses.

In almost all Northern California communities, some sort of police protection was provided. In San Francisco, plainclothesmen in twenty-four unmarked cars watched the buses. More than one hundred police vehicles were alerted.

"The interval between attacks has gotten frighteningly short," Armstrong said to the press. "It could come any day. God, I'd hate to speculate."

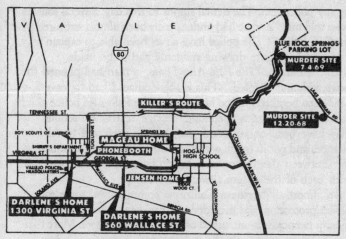

Zodiac's route the night of July 4, 1969, when he followed and attacked
Darlene Ferrin and Michael Mageau. Also shown is the site of the
Jensen-Faraday murders. Map by R. Graysmith.

Dear Editor

This is the murderer of the 2 teenagers last Christmass at Lake Herman & the girl on the 4th of July near the golf course in Vallejo To prove I killed them I shall state some facts which only I & the police know.

Christmass
1 Brand name of ammo Super X
2 10 shots were fired
3 the boy was on his back with his feet to the car
4 the girl was on her right side feet to the west

4th July
1 girl was wearing patowned slacks
2 The boy was also shot in the knee.
3 Brand name of ammo was Western

Over—

Zodiac's first letter to the *San Francisco Chronicle,* August 1, 1969. This letter has never before been reproduced.

ciphen on your front page by Fry. Afternoon Aug 1 ⁻69, If you do not do this I will go on a kill rampage Fry nghte thos will last the whole week end. I will crose aroonl and pick of all stray people on campples that are alone then move on to kill some more untill I have killed over a dozen people.

Threat from letter to the *Vallejo Times-Herald*, August 1, 1969.
The *Chronicle's* letter was phrased slightly differently.

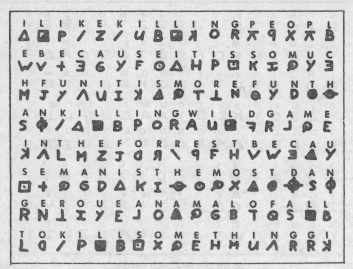

I LIKE KILLING PEOPLE
EBECAUSE IT IS SO MUC
H FUN IT IS MORE FUN TH
AN KILLING WILD GAME
IN THE FORREST BECAU
SE MAN IS THE MOST DAN
GEROUE ANAMAL OF ALL
TO KILL SOMETHING GI

TO THE VALLEJO TIMES-HERALD

VES ME THE MOST THRIL
LING EXPERENCE IT IS
EVEN BETTER THAN GET
TING YOUR ROCKS OFF
IT HA GIRL THE BEST PA
RT OF IT IS THAT WHEN I
DIE I WILL BE REBORN I
N PARADICE AND ALL TH

TO THE SAN FRANCISCO EXAMINER

E I   H A V E   K I L L E D   W I L L B

E   C O M E   M Y   S L A V E S   I   W I L

L   N O T   G I V E   Y O U   M Y   N A M E

B E C A U S E   Y O U   W I L L   T R Y

T O S L O I   D O W N   O R   S T O P M

Y C O L L E C T I N G O F S L A V

E S   F O R   M Y   A F T E R L I F E E

B E O R I E T E M E T H   H P I T I

TO THE SAN FRANCISCO CHRONICLE

The solution to the three-part cipher as decoded by the Hardens.

Dear Editor
This is the Zodiac speaking.
In answer to your asking for
more details about the good
times I have had in Vallejo,
I shall be very happy to
supply even more material.
By the way, are the police
having a good time with the
code? If not, tell them to cheer
up; when they do crack it
they will have me.
On the 4th of July
I did not open the car door, The
window was rolled down all ready.
The boy was originally sitting in
the front seat when I began
fireing. When I fired the first
shot at his head, he leaped
backwards at the same time
thus spoiling my aim. He ended
ed up on the back seat then
the floor in back thashing out
very violently with his legs;
thats how I shot him in the

The first page of the killer's three-page letter to the *Vallejo Times-Herald* on August 7, 1969. This is the first time he used the name "Zodiac." This letter has never before been reproduced.

Zodiac in Costume by Robert Graysmith.
Author's line-cut illustration of Zodiac in costume at Lake Berryessa.

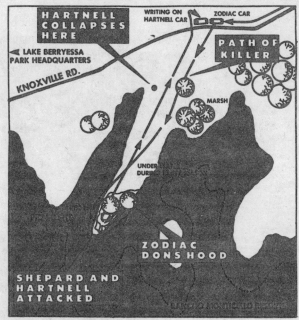

Above: The path Zodiac took at Lake Berryessa, September 27, 1969, when, wearing a garish costume, he stabbed Bryan Hartnell and Cecelia Shepard. Map by R. Graysmith.

Left: Composite sketch done by Robert McKenzie for the Napa police showing suspicious man seen at Lake Berryessa the day of the stabbing attack. The sketch had limited circulation, and may never have been printed—it certainly wasn't in San Francisco.

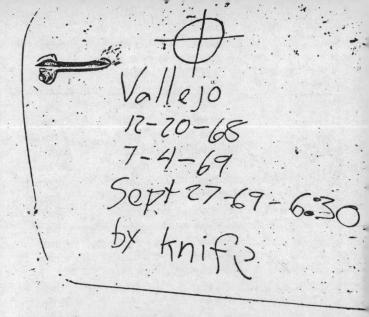

Above: Zodiac's writing in black felt-tip pen on Bryan Hartnell's Karmann Ghia after the stabbing.

Below: Map of the October 11, 1969, Stine killing in San Francisco. Map by R. Graysmith.

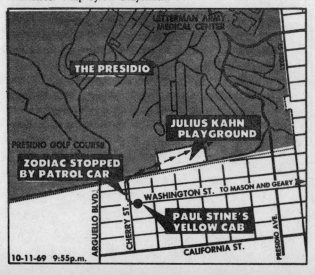

Zodiac's October 13, 1969, letter to the *San Francisco Chronicle*, in which he enclosed a bloody scrap of Paul Stine's shirt.

This is the Zodiac speaking.
I am the murderer of the
taxi driver over by
Washington St + Maple St last
night, to prove this here is
a blood stained piece of his
shirt. I am the same man
who did in the people in the
north bay area.
The S.F. Police could have caught
me last night if they had
searched the park properly
instead of holding road races
with their motor cicles seeing who
could make the most noise. The
cop drivers should have just
parked their cars + sat there
quietly waiting for me to come
out of cover.
School children make nice targets, I think I shall wipe out
a school bus some morning. Just
shoot out the front tire + then
pick off the kiddies as they come
bouncing out.

WANTED

NO. 90-69   WANTED FOR MURDER   OCTOBER 18, 1969

ORIGINAL DRAWING   AMENDED DRAWING

Supplementing our Bulletin 87-69 of October 13, 1969. Additional information has developed the above amended drawing of murder suspect known as "ZODIAC".

WMA, 35-45 Years, approximately 5'8", Heavy Build, Short Brown Hair, possibly with Red Tint, Wears Glasses. Armed with 9 MM Automatic.

Available for comparison: Slugs, Casings, Latents, Handwriting.

ANY INFORMATION:
Inspectors Armstrong & Toschi
Homicide Detail
CASE NO. 696314

THOMAS J. CAHILL
CHIEF OF POLICE

Zodiac's second wanted poster, amended to reflect the more detailed description given S.F.P.D. by the two radio car patrolmen.

Above: Greeting card envelope, overposted by Zodiac as usual.

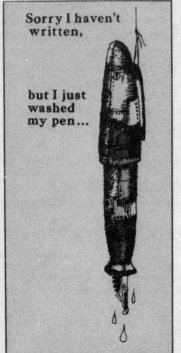

Front portion of Zodiac's November 8, 1969, greeting card to the *San Francisco Chronicle*.

This is the Zodiac speaking,
I though you would need a
good laugh before you
hea- the bad news, and i
you wont got the news
news for a while yet, can't
PS could you print do a
this new cipho- thing
on your fornt page? with
I get awfully lonely it!
when I am ignored,
so lonely I could
do my Thing.!!!!!!

1 Des July Aug
Sept Oct = 7

Inside of the November 8 "dripping pen" greeting card.

The 340-symbol cipher received by Inspector Toschi on November 8, 1969.

This is the Zodiac speaking
up to the end of Oct I have
killed 7 people. I have grown
rather angry with the police
for their telling lies about me.
So I shall change the way the
collecting of slaves. I shall
no longer announce to anyone.
when I comitt my murders,
they shall look like routine
robberies, killings of anger, &
a few fake accidents, etc.

The police shall never catch me,
because I have been too clever-
for them.
1 I look like the description
   passed out only when I do
   my thing, the rest of the time
   I look entirle different. I
   shall not tell you what my
   descise consists of when I kill
2 As of yet I have left no
   finge-prints behind me contrary
   to what the police say

Part of Zodiac's seven-page letter of November 9, 1969, to the *Chronicle,* in which he "changes his way of collecting slaves."

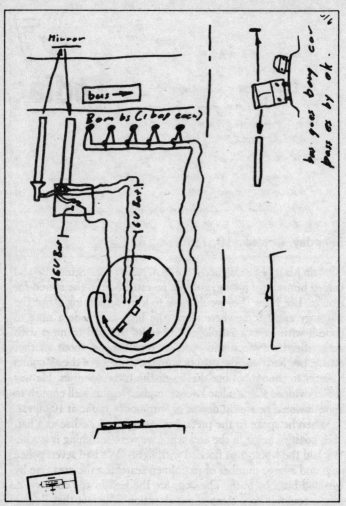

The diagram for the school bus bomb from the November 9 letter.

⊕7
Zodiac

Saturday, October 18, 1969

Captain Marty Lee assigned a ten-man team to the Stine case and braced himself for a long, arduous investigation in the search for Zodiac. Lee knew they would have to learn something about the astrology angle somewhere along the line. He made a note to consult with various astrologers. Lee also planned to meet with authorities from Napa and Vallejo. Apprehensive about another attack, Lee had been the man behind the issuance of the all-points bulletin to the school bus drivers of the three counties. He was also convinced that Zodiac knew Presidio Heights well enough to know it would be almost devoid of automobile traffic at 10:00 PM.

When he spoke to the press, Lee categorized Zodiac as a liar. "His boast of being in the area while we were searching it is a lie. We had the whole area flooded with lights. We had seven police dogs and a large number of patrolmen searching the area tree by tree and bush by bush. The dogs are the best in the country. A mouse couldn't have escaped our attention. The fact that Zodiac failed to mention dogs and floodlights proves he wasn't anywhere in the vicinity."

By mail and phone, literally a thousand tips flooded into

S.F.P.D. from alarmed citizens. The detectives began to sort out the communications that fingered neighbors, fellow employees, and ex-husbands as possible Zodiacs. The police switchboard was inundated with calls. Lee tripled the usual weekend force, who took turns answering phones.

Vallejo Police Captain Wade Bird, who had been looking for Zodiac since July, had his own theories. "I think he'll prove to be a genius who got so far out he went over the edge. He may or may not be a local man. Many—no, thousands—of people lived here during the war and came to know the area, then moved away. He did know about our lovers' lanes, though. They weren't very far apart. Some say he is a commuter; that he commits these murders, then mails letters about them from work in San Francisco. I don't think so. I don't believe a man this disturbed could hold down a steady, regular job. He's too far gone for that."

Dr. Leonti Thompson, a Napa State psychiatrist, told the press that "for some psychotics, the act of killing is a denial of . . . helplessness. Psychosis is the gradual blotting out of the ego, a terrifying loss of one's own image of oneself. He does things, busily, fiercely and then lapses again. Among psychotics, schizophrenics of the paranoid type are usually secretive and guarded in their dealings with the world. They can deal relatively well with the outside world and at the same time carry around their private visions of what the world is really like."

In Napa, Undersheriff Tom Johnson was swamped by hundreds of leads and yet still had not been able to shape them into the image of one solid suspect. "There's no one we want more," Johnson said. "We're not going to let up; he's our top priority."

And yet there was in the air the overriding fear that Zodiac would kill again. And soon.

Sunday, October 19, 1969

State Attorney General Thomas C. Lynch issued an entreaty to Zodiac to turn himself in. At the same time, he quietly called for a seminar on the killer, to include representatives of various jurisdictions so they could exchange information about the earlier killings.

"We will see that he gets help and that all of his rights are protected," Lynch said in his appeal. "He is obviously an intelligent individual. He knows that eventually he will be taken into custody, so it would be best that he give himself up before tragedy is written in blood."

The plea for surrender went unanswered.

Sunday's *Examiner* issued its own plea to the killer. Their message ran across the top of page one:

Five people are dead. Let there be no more killings. Police say you are intelligent. If you are, then listen to reason. You are being hunted everywhere in the state and nation. You are alone in this world. You can share your secrets with no one. No friend can help you.

You are as much a victim of your crimes as those whose lives you snuffed out. You cannot walk the streets a free man. There is no safety for you anywhere. And you will be caught, there is no doubt. You face life as a hunted, tormented animal—unless you help yourself. We ask that you give yourself up, to The Examiner.

We offer you no protection, and no sympathy. But we do offer you fair treatment, the assurance of medical help and the full benefits of your legal rights.

And we offer to tell your story.

Why have you killed? How has life wronged you? Call the City Editor of The Examiner, any time, day or night.

The telephone number is (415) 781-2424. Call collect.

Your call will not be traced.

Zodiac not only ignored this entreaty, but never again wrote to the *Examiner*. Evidently he found their approach insulting.

Monday, October 20, 1969

Nine days after Paul Stine's murder, a Zodiac seminar was convened in San Francisco at the Hall of Justice. Armstrong and Toschi attended, and the sheriff's and police departments of

Napa, Solano, Benicia, Vallejo, San Mateo, and Marin sent investigators. The F.B.I. and Naval Intelligence were present, as well as U.S. Postal Inspectors, the Highway Patrol, and the State Bureau of Criminal Identification and Investigation (CI&I). Napa had asked the state to send one of its agents, and CI&I had provided handwriting experts and arranged for the use of the criminal lab in Sacramento. Attorney General Lynch was still in Colorado attending a meeting of attorneys general of western states and was represented by his number-two man, Arlo Smith.

A large blackboard stood in front of the room. Etched in white chalk on the ebony surface was a large crossed circle—the sign of the Zodiac. One by one the crime scenes were drawn and erased as the detectives exchanged the small scraps of information.

The 9-mm semiautomatic pistol Zodiac had used to murder Stine was relatively rare: only 143 guns of this type had been sold in the Bay Area in the last three years. Toschi's theory was that the 9-mm gun used in the cabdriver's murder was probably a new model Browning, and odds were that it was different from the 9-mm used by Zodiac in the past.

Until the letter to the *Chronicle*, Toschi had investigated the Stine killing as just another big city stick-up. Probably this was what the killer had wanted the police to think. But there was also the possibility that Stine had been chosen for a reason and was not just a random victim.

The most difficult homicide to solve for even an experienced homicide team like Toschi and Armstrong is a holdup and murder of a cabdriver in his cab. Usually the murderer gets the driver to a deserted spot, under the cover of darkness. Most slayings of this type are gun shots to the head, and most are contact wounds. Therefore, no one even hears the report of the gun.

Toschi had learned over the years there is seldom if any physical evidence in the cab. Usually all an assailant will touch is the inner door handle to close the door as he gets in or as he is leaving. All you get are smudge prints, unusable.

Or you get just the opposite. There might be five good usable sets of prints in the cab and on the door posts or the side mirror, mostly left by prior riders or cab company employees.

"In the killing of a cabbie," Toschi told me, "it's either feast or famine. At least in a grocery store slaying the suspect will usually buy or pick up a can of Coke or beer or a box of cookies, a bottle of booze which will leave latent prints. Sometimes in an effort to grab every last penny out of the cash register the suspect will leave a nice area of prints or even touch the counter. In most cabdriver murders the physical evidence is minimal.

"What you really need is a lot of hard work," Toschi told me, "and luck.

In Vallejo later I asked Detective Sergeant Mulanax, who had taken over the Ferrin case, about the cab print.

"So they have a latent print," said Mulanax. "It's my own personal opinion there's a lot of doubt this could be a Zodiac print. You dust a cab you're going to lift some latents off it. Doesn't necessarily mean it's the guy that did the job."

The lab men's investigation had proven that no more than one shot had been fired in Stine's cab. Except for the one 9-mm casing found on the floorboard next to the body, no other bullet hole and no other slug were found.

Through Stine's employers and co-workers, Toschi discovered that the cabbie kept his cab fares either in his wallet or in his pocket, but generally in his pocket. Stine's wife claimed he had only three or four dollars of his own money when he left home for work. He normally kept his fare money and tip money all together and would separate it at the end of the shift.

Captain Lee had made certain that the seminar was a meeting of police professionals only. No psychics, mystics, or astrologists were in attendance, as they sometimes were.

"I couldn't say we're any closer to catching the suspect," he said at the end of the three-hour session.

At the seminar's end, the detectives took note that all of the Zodiac murders had occurred on weekends.

Now would come the back-breaking questioning of gun dealers all over California. In an attempt to match up the handwriting, signatures on gun registration forms would be compared with the

Zodiac letters received so far. New federal gun laws had taken effect earlier that year, but up until then many foreign-made models could be bought through the mail from dozens of outlets that advertised in men's magazines. Perhaps Zodiac had a reason for using a weapon only once.

Meanwhile, in Napa armed guards and volunteers, off-duty teachers, drivers, and firemen, continued to ride the school buses.

Wednesday, October 22, 1969

It was 2:00 A.M. when the phone rang at the Oakland P.D. call room. The police operator picked up the phone and stiffened as a male voice said: "This is the Zodiac speaking.

"I want you to get in touch with F. Lee Bailey. . . . If you can't come up with Bailey I'll settle for Mel Belli. . . . I want one or the other to appear on the Channel Seven talk show. I'll make contact by telephone."

If there was anyone as colorful as attorney F. Lee Bailey, the Boston Strangler's lawyer, it was Melvin Belli, "the King of Torts." Silver-tongued, silver-haired Belli moved in a world of glamour and opulence. Shaken by the call, Oakland got in touch with Marty Lee, and Lee, in turn, with Toschi and Armstrong. Within two hours, Lee phoned Belli at his penthouse at 1228 Montgomery Street, on Telegraph Hill. Belli readily agreed to appear. Arrangements were made with the show's host, Jim Dunbar, for Belli to be on the two-hour program that morning. Dunbar's viewers are invited to call in and discuss the topic of the day, but this particular morning he asked his fans to leave the lines open so that the killer could reach Belli.

Although the show usually started at 7:00 A.M., it began a half hour early that day. Belli and Dunbar sat and faced each other for a period of small talk and soap commercials.

Like thousands of others, I watched the KGO talk show. I wondered if I would finally hear the voice of the Zodiac killer.

At 7:10, the phone finally rang.

It was during a commercial, and the caller hung up almost

immediately. The man had a hesitant and drifting voice.

The next call came at 7:20.

The following conversations are verbatim.

Emotionally, Belli, in his best courtroom fashion, begged the self-styled Zodiac to give him a name less ominous.

"Sam," said the young-sounding voice on the other end of the line.

"How and where can we meet you?" Belli asked him.

"Meet me on top of the Fairmont Hotel," he said. He paused. "Without anyone else or I'll jump!"

Sam hung up, called again, and continued the abrupt conversations for over two hours. Twelve calls were actually heard on the air, out of a total of thirty-five calls made by "Sam." The longest was nine minutes.

"Do you think you need medical care?" asked Belli.

"Yes," answered Sam. "Medical, not mental."

"Do you have a health problem?"

"I'm sick," said Sam. "I have headaches."

"I have headaches too, but a chiropractor stopped them a week ago. I think I can help you. You won't have to talk to a soul in the world but me."

Sam hung up again, evidently fearful of his call being traced.

Lee, watching from his office, said, "We're not trying to trace the call. It's a long, difficult process, and ineffective with these brief calls."

When Sam called back again at 8:25, Belli asked him what his problem was.

"I don't want to go to the gas chamber. I have headaches," he said. "If I kill I don't get them."

"No one has gone to the gas chamber in years," said Belli. "You want to live, don't you? Well, this is your passport. How long have you been having these headaches?"

"Since I killed a kid," answered Sam.

"Can you remember your childhood?"

"Yes."

"Do you have blackouts?"

"Yes."

"Do you have fits?"

"No. I just have headaches."

"Do you take aspirin?"

"Yes."

"Does it do any good?"

"No."

"Did you attempt to call one other time when Mr. Bailey was with us two or three weeks ago?" asked Dunbar.

"Yes."

"Why did you want to talk to Bailey?"

"When do you want to talk to me?" said Belli.

"I don't want to be hurt," said Sam.

"You're not going to be hurt. You're not going to be hurt if you talk to me."

"You're not going to the gas chamber," said Dunbar.

"I wouldn't think that they'd ask for capital punishment. We should ask the district attorney—you want me to do that, Sam? You want me to talk to the district attorney?" asked Belli.

There was a small scream.

"What was that?"

"I did not say anything. That was my headache," said Sam.

"You sound like you're in a great deal of pain," replied Belli. "Your voice sounds muffled. What's the matter?"

"My head aches," he said. "I'm so sick. I'm having one of my headaches."

Another little cry, and a pause.

"I'm going to kill them. I'm going to kill all those kids!" screamed Sam. He hung up.

When Sam called back again, Belli had the call put on a private line so the audience could not hear. "Do you want me to be your lawyer? There is goodness in you. Would you like to tell me anything?"

"Nothing."

"You feel like you're going to flip out? Sam, what do you want us to do?"

"I feel an awful lonesomeness."

"Do you need free medicine or anything else? Wouldn't you

116

like to get rid of those damn headaches?" Belli said he'd try to get a promise from District Attorney John J. Ferdon that Zodiac would not get the gas chamber if he was convicted of murder.

Instead of the Fairmont, Belli suggested the steps of the Old St. Mary's Church in Chinatown as a meeting place. But Sam named another location of his choice: Daly City, in front of the St. Vincent de Paul Thrift Shop, 6726 Mission Street, at 10:30 that morning.

"Take care of yourself," said Belli.

"Yeah," said Sam.

It was probably one of the least secret secret meetings in history. Belli was followed by police, who had monitored the private line; they in turn were followed by television camera crews, radio trucks, reporters, and photographers. Everyone was there. Everyone except Jim Dunbar, who had grown disenchanted with the whole circus. And of course Zodiac—if it was indeed he—who stood everyone up.

After forty-five minutes, Belli gave up and went home to get some sleep.

Sam had said nothing that would help the police catch him. On the other hand, he had said nothing that would prove he was the real Zodiac. At least the mysterious caller's voice had been recorded by Channel 7.

The Oakland patrolman who had received the original 2:00 A.M. call said he was certain he had talked to the real Zodiac and that he did not think it was the same voice he heard on the Dunbar show.

Meanwhile, the three of the four living persons who had heard Zodiac's voice gathered in a tiny room at KGO-TV to hear a transcription of Sam's conversation with Belli. The three were Napa patrolman David Slaight, Vallejo police switchboard operator Nancy Slover, and Bryan Hartnell. For almost an hour they listened intently as the voice of Sam was played over and over. At the end they remained silent and still. Was this the voice of Zodiac?

Bryan spoke first. "I felt that the voice on the tape was not as deep and as old as Zodiac's." The others shrugged their shoulders and shook their heads in agreement.

"It's too young," said the dark-haired, long-jawed patrolman Slaight, "less sure of himself."

"It's too pitiful and pathetic to be Zodiac," said Nancy Slover.

It was only too obvious that the call to Dunbar's show was just someone taking advantage of the opportunity to call into the "Zodiac Telethon"—or, as one sarcastic cop suggested the name of Dunbar's program be changed to, "Son of Zodiac."

"As things stand now, having no idea of the killer's identity, we're willing to try anything," said one detective, "even if it means dealing with kooks."

The mystery of Sam was eventually solved when in subsequent calls to Belli the caller was traced to Napa State Hospital and was discovered to be a mental patient there.

KRON-TV called the press room at the Hall of Justice just before their evening news deadline to check on a story that Zodiac had been captured by the police after he arrived late at the Daly City meeting place. The rumor was that Zodiac was being held quietly until some sort of positive identification could be made. It turned out to be just a rumor, but it created considerable excitement.

Around the same time, the *Chronicle* began to receive calls from readers who saw a connection between Zodiac and the current Dick Tracy comic strip. On August 17, a few weeks after the Cipher Slayer dubbed himself Zodiac, the Zodiac gang, a group of astrological killers, led by a grotesque villain named Scorpio, made their appearance in the strip. The gang polished off an astrology columnist by drowning him, and Tracy found cuff links with a scorpion and a horoscope on his shirt. CI&I agents hoped that somewhere in one of the panels there might be a parallel between the fictional Zodiac Killers and the real life Zodiac. CI&I senior analyst in the crime lab, Earl Bauer, said, "It's just speculation at this point. We really haven't got into it yet. It's just one of those way-out things that you take a look at."

Dick Tracy is written and drawn several weeks ahead of publication to allow for proofreading, the making of matts and proofs, and mailing time. The Tracy-Zodiac sequence did not run until after Zodiac had made his choice of name so it would be impossible for the strip to have influenced him—unless Zodiac was someone who actually worked at a newspaper.

Monday, November 10, 1969

Armstrong and Toschi were notified that the *Chronicle* had received two more pieces of mail from Zodiac, both postmarked San Francisco. In his usual attempt to keep the police from tracing him through his handwriting, the killer had continued to print in tidy, small letters. However, there was no doubt that the mail was genuine: another portion of Stine's gray-and-white shirt had been enclosed.

As before, the envelopes were addressed simply to the *Chronicle*, "Please Rush to Editor." They had been mailed on Saturday, November 8, and Sunday, November 9.

In his new letters Zodiac boasted of two more murders—seven instead of the known five.

The only recent unsolved murders in the Bay Area that Toschi knew of were knife slayings. On August 3, two San Jose teenagers, classmates, left their homes in mid-morning to have a picnic on a hillside in the rugged Alameda Valley section of South San Jose. The girls, Deborah Gay Furlong, fourteen, and Kathy Snoozy, fifteen, locked their bikes to the chain fence at the bottom of the hill and made their way to a sunny knoll overlooking their subdivision homes. When they had not returned by six o'clock, the father of the youngest girl set off to look for them. When he neared the picnic area he saw a large crowd of motorcyclists and police gathered together. Horror-stricken, he ran to the grove of trees. The girls' bodies were lying there. The girls were fully clothed except for a sandal that was found nearby. Detectives felt that they had been slain elsewhere because little blood was in evidence. In the evening dusk, a series of footprints were found in the hillside grove of oaks. The police began making plaster casts of these.

Dr. John E. Hauser, Santa Clara County's chief medical examiner and coroner, was so shaken by the crime that he could scarcely talk.

"I've never seen a case with this many stab wounds," he said. "You know, I've been in this profession a long time and sometimes I think I'm rather callous, but when I saw these girls, believe me, it was terrifying. The Nazi sex mutilations during World War II were nothing compared to what was done to these young girls."

The narrow-bladed knife that took the young children's lives in a blood frenzy had risen and fallen more than three hundred times, all above the waist of the young victims.

Toschi had feared that Zodiac was making good his threat that "children make nice targets."

Meanwhile, Zodiac's threats of murdering children continued to create panic. In San Jose, 475 outraged parents searched for the killer of Furlong and Snoozy in vigilante groups, patrolling the neighborhood in cars marked with white flags. All of the men were armed. The theory was that a tall, thin teenager was the killer and that he lived right in the neighborhood since he had disappeared so quickly after the murders. It would be almost two years until the killer of the children would be caught.

Toschi knew of no other killings, with the exception of an infant that he suspected had been killed by dogs. The detectives turned their attention to Zodiac's November 8 letter. Although, as usual, it had been overposted, the stamps were not placed upside down or vertically but in a normal manner.

The envelope contained a "Jesters" greeting card manufactured by Forget Me Not Cards/American Greeting Cards Co. On the front (reproduced for the first time) was a drawing of dripping wet fountain pen hanging by a string and the caption:

> Sorry I haven't
> written,
> but I just
> washed my pen . . .

120

On the inside was the punchline, written in a splotchy, manic style:

and i can't do a thing with it!

The inscription from the Cipher Slayer read:

> This is the Zodiac speaking
> I though you would nead a
> good laugh before you
> hear the bad news
> you won't get the
> news for a while yet
> PS could you print
> this new cipher
> on your front page?
> I get awfully lonely
> when I am ignored,
> So lonely I could
> do my *Thing*!!!!!!

Five months were listed in abbreviated form at the bottom of the card: "Des July Aug Sept Oct = 7." Victims for all the months but August could be accounted for. It did seem that Zodiac was saying he had killed two people in August. Snoozy and Furlong were the only unsolved murders in August; S.F.P.D. could discover no others.

Within the hour, the Zodiac squad began to check stationery stores that sell greeting cards in hopes that some clerk would remember selling the card Zodiac had sent. In San Francisco alone there were now fifty officers and ten inspectors assigned to the Zodiac case full-time.

Inside the greeting card, Zodiac had also sent his most complex cryptogram yet. The cipher was composed of 340 symbols arranged in a block twenty lines deep and signed with his own personal symbol, a large circle with a cross superimposed over it. Toschi had photocopies made of the new cipher and sent them to the National Security Agency and the CIA in Washington. The NSA said that there was definitely a message in the cipher.

Armstrong and Toschi hoped that when the *Chronicle* ran a photo of the 340-symbol cryptogram, amateur codebreakers might get lucky a second time. "It's just a matter of patience before it pieces itself together. Trial and error," said one cryptographer, "that's what solves cryptograms." A linguistics expert at Massachusetts University ran the code over and over through a computer, but got nowhere.

In the spirit of codebreaking, the *Examiner* ran a cipher challenge to Zodiac from Dr. Marsh of the American Cryptogram Association. Dr. Marsh told the *Examiner* that "the killer wouldn't dare, as he has claimed in his letters, to reveal his [real] name in a cipher to established cryptogram experts. He knows, to quote Edgar Allen Poe, that 'any cipher devised by man can be solved by man.'" Dr. Marsh then printed a message to Zodiac in the killer's own code and dared him to send the ACA his real name encoded. The cryptographer's challenge to Zodiac, when deciphered, was a phone number for the killer to call and give his own cipher.

In the Zodiac letter mailed November 9, his seventh letter, the killer sent the *Chronicle* a seven-page diatribe. The complete text of this letter has never been released before now, and it has never been reproduced. Toschi and Armstrong started with the first page and made notes as they went.

> This is the Zodiac speaking
> up to the end of Oct I have
> killed 7 people. I have grown
> rather angry with the police
> for their telling lies about me.
> So I shall change the way the
> collecting of slaves. I shall
> no longer announce to anyone.
> when I comitt my murders,
> they shall look like routine
> robberies, killings of anger, &

a few fake accidents, etc.
The police shall never catch me,
because I have been too clever
for them.
1   I look like the description
passed out only when I do
my thing, the rest of the time
I look entirle different. I
shall not tell you what my
descise consists of when I kill
2   As of yet I have left no
fingerprints behind me contrary
to what the police say
in my killings I wear transparent finger tip guards. All it
is is 2 coats of airplane cement
coated on my finger tips—quite
unnoticible & very efective.
3   my killing tools have been bought
en through the mail order out-
fits before the ban* went into
efect. except one & it was
bought out of the state.
So as you can see the police don't
have much to work on. If you
wonder why I was wipeing the
cab down I was leaving fake clews
for the police to run all over town
with, as one might say, I gave the
cops som bussy work to do to
keep them happy. I enjoy needling
the blue pigs. Hey blue pig I
was in the park—you were useing
fire trucks to mask the sound
of your cruzeing prowl cars. The
dogs never came with in 2
blocks of me & they were to

*The 1968 Federal Gun Control Act forbade mail-order sales of guns and ammunition and over-the-counter sale to out-of-state residents, mental patients, and convicted felons.

the west & there was only 2
groups of parking about 10 min
apart then the motor cicles
went by about 150 ft away
going from south to north west.
p.s. 2 cops pulled a goof abot 3
min after I left the cab. I was
walking down the hill to the
park when this cop car pulled up
& one of them called me over
& asked if I saw any one
acting supicisous or strange
in the last 5 to 10 min & I said
yes there was this man who
was running by waveing a gun
& the cops peeled rubber &
went around the corner as
I directed them & I dissap
eared into the park a block &
a half away never to be seen
again.

Hey pig doesnt it rile you up
to have your noze rubed in your
booboos?
If you cops think I'm going to take
on a bus the way I stated I was,
you deserve to have holes in your
heads.
Take one bag of ammonium nitrate
fertilizer & 1 gal of stove oil &
dump a few bags of gravel on
top & then set the shit off
& will positivly ventalate any
thing that should be in the way
of the blast.
The death machine is all ready
made. I would have sent you
pictures but you would be nasty
enough to trace them back to

124

developer & then to me, so I
shall describe my masterpiece
to you. Tke nice part of it is
all the parts can be bought on
the open market with no quest
ions asked.
1 bat. pow clock—will run for
approx 1 year
1 photoelectric switch
2 copper leaf springs
2 6V car bat
1 flash light bulb & reflector
1 mirror
2 18″ cardboard tubes black with
shoe polish inside & oute

On the fifth page the killer had drawn a diagram of the inner
workings of the bomb. It was rigged to explode to the height of
buses and to let the lower-carriage automobiles pass by safely.

the system checks out from one
end to the other in my
tests. What you do not know
is whether the death machine
is at the sight or whether
it is being stored in my
basement for future use.

If Zodiac actually did have a basement, then it meant he had
a home of his own, was not an apartment dweller. It limited the
number of places he might reside, since basements are not all that
common in the Bay Area.

I think you do not have the
manpower to stop this one
by continually searching the
road sides looking for this
thing. & it wont do to re roat [reroute]
& re schedule the busses bec

ause the bomb can be adapted
to new conditions.
Have fun!! By the way
it could be rather messy
if you try to bluff me.

At the bottom of the page Zodiac had drawn a large crossed-circle, five x's moving clockwise on the left hemisphere. Were these a symbolic map to the various Zodiac killings, or a map to his doorstep? Most likely, the police decided, they were a calendar showing the dates of the seven murders.

PS. Be shure to
print the part I
marked out on
page 3 [about being stopped by police] or I shall
do my thing
To prove that I am the
Zodiac, Ask the Vallejo
cop about my electric gun
sight which I used to start
my collecting of slaves.

Toschi put the letter down. "Get the Army on the phone and find out if such a Rube Goldberg device could possibly be constructed," ordered Lee.

The army bomb expert said, "Possible? It certainly is."

Later, Chief of Police Al Nelder himself issued orders to the Zodiac squad to keep silent about the bomb details. In cooperation with the police, the *Chronicle* agreed not to print any part of the letter that dealt with the bomb.

Fear of a school bus attack intensified.

Tuesday, November 11, 1969

Officially, detectives were now ruling out Zodiac as the killer of the San Jose girls last August. The contention was that Zodiac's gigantic ego would not let him kill without assuming "credit" for the brutal acts.

"In the press," Marty Lee said, "Zodiac has been made out to be a madman . . . insane. . . . I think the man is legally sane. . . . He has exhibited intelligence by hiding and fleeing from the police. I do not picture him as a man who works with his hands. I guess he has a small job and works with paper. . . . The cryptograms are a work of art. They are meticulously well-aligned. . . . Again a guess. . . . I think he is still in the Bay Area."

Saturday, December 27, 1969

Melvin Belli was in Munich, Germany, for a conference of military trial lawyers, so the barrister's housekeeper sent his unopened mail down to his office to be opened by his secretary. One letter was postmarked December 20, but had been delayed by heavy Christmas mail. There was no doubt who the letter was from. Neatly folded inside the four-by-seven-inch white envelope was yet another portion of Paul Stine's blood-blackened shirt.

This letter, in felt-tip pen, was written in handwriting smaller than the last letter; it contained punctuation and spelling mistakes as usual.

One of Belli's legal associates flew to Munich to give him a photoreproduction of the letter, envelope, and bloody scrap. A card had also been enclosed that said, "Merry Xmass and New Year." The message, printed in block letters, Zodiac's eighth letter, read:

> Dear Melvin, This is the Zodiac speaking
> I wish you a happy Christmass. The one
> thing I ask of you is this,
> please help me. I cannot
> reach out for help because of
> this thing in me won't let me.
> I am finding it extreamly dif-
> icult to hold it in check I am

> afraid I will loose control
> again and take my nineth &
> posibly tenth victom. Please
> help me I am drownding. At
> the moment the children are
> safe from the bomb because
> it is so massive to dig in & the
> triger mech requires much work
> to get it adjusted just right. But
> if I hold back too long from
> no nine I will loose ~~complet~~ all
> controol of my self & set the
> bomb up. Please help me I can
> not remain in control for much
> longer.

Zodiac seemed to be saying that he had taken an eighth victim since his November 8 and 9 letters. There were only two known possible victims: Elaine Davis and Leona Larell Roberts.

Davis had disappeared December 1, 1969, a Monday, and has never been found.

Leona Roberts disappeared on December 10, 1969, a Wednesday, at 6:00 P.M. The body of the sixteen-year-old was found nude on December 28, lying over a roadside embankment near Bolinas Lagoon. She had been kept alive for ten days after her abduction from her boyfriend's apartment in Rodeo. None of her clothing was found, and she had not been sexually molested. But most importantly, she was found near a body of water, as all of Zodiac's victims had been. The killer had taken the keys to her V.W.

Zodiac had also used the phrase "a happy Christmas," which was more common usage in Britain and Canada than in the United States. Zodiac warned of picking off "the kiddies," which is another slang word from Great Britain or Australia. Could Zodiac be British?

Belli was willing to meet in secret with the mass murderer any time, any place. He told the killer through the *Chronicle:* "You have asked me for help and I promise you I will do everything in my power to provide you with whatever help you may need or may want.

"If you want to meet with me alone I will come alone. If you want me to bring a priest or a psychiatrist or a reporter to talk with, I will do so. I will follow your instructions to the letter.

"You say you are 'losing control' and may kill again. Do not make things worse. Let me help you now."

To the reporters, Belli said, "I believe he wants to stop killing. I have carefully studied his letter . . . and feel it was written at a time when he calmly and rationally was considering the future. He knows eventually he will be apprehended and that unless he gets proper legal representation he will most probably be sentenced to die in the gas chamber. That is why he is crying out for help. . . . Why he has come to me? He wants to be saved from the gas chamber."

In a phone call a man claiming to be Zodiac had gotten along so well with Belli's housekeeper that Belli fully expected "when I get home he'll be sitting in the front room with the housekeeper. . . . I think we can do something for him. . . . We might get this guy and save some lives—including his."

The killer never responded to Belli's appeal. It was months before the Cipher Slayer wrote to Belli again.

Joseph DeLouise

Sunday, January 4, 1970

Joseph DeLouise, a Chicago psychic, felt that he had been getting mental transmissions from Zodiac for about a month. He had received impressions that for the killer the excitement of murder was over, and that Zodiac wanted a safe way to surrender to the police. Most amazingly of all, DeLouise had begun to see a mental picture of what Zodiac's true face looked like.

DeLouise had gained national fame two years previously when he predicted the Kennedy family would be touched by tragedy involving a Kennedy around water. Two months later, Senator Edward M. Kennedy's car plunged off a Massachusetts bridge into a canal at Chappaquiddick and a secretary with him, Mary Jo Kopechne, was drowned.

The dark, lean, serious, and almost satanic-looking mystic, aged forty-three, ran a Chicago hair dressing supply business and had been raised in the tough neighborhoods of Chicago after his family came from Italy. Even in Italy, at the age of four, he claimed he had the ability to see the future.

He predicted a major bridge disaster on November 25, 1967, and less than one month later, December 15, the "Silver Bridge" that spanned the Ohio River at Point Pleasant, West Virginia, collapsed. Forty-six people were killed in the catastrophe.

Three and one half months before the arrests in the Sharon Tate murders, the seer pinpointed the hideout in Texas of one of the suspects, accurately described two others who participated in the mass murders, and foretold the number ultimately involved.

In September 1969, he predicted an air crash over Indianapolis and gave the time of the tragedy as 3:30. A month later, an air crash occurred at 3:31.

DeLouise, known as the "prophet of specifics," spoke to Bud Kressin of the *Vallejo Times-Herald* in an exclusive interview and told what he had seen from two thousand miles away.

"I keep getting the word 'Berkeley,'" said DeLouise over the phone. "I don't see him from Vallejo or living there. But I do get strong impressions he is living in Berkeley or recently lived there.

"I feel he is highly nervous inwardly. He doesn't like to drive a car. He'd rather be on foot. I don't know why I get this feeling but I feel he is very mixed up and that he can be helped. I feel he has a little box in which he keeps things. I get an impression about stones. He should get rid of these things. He has a box in which he has certain things he's saving. When he looks at them and runs them through his fingers, it causes him to do hideous things. I feel he should get rid of them as a part of turning himself in.

"Zodiac has done this because he didn't have guidance. At a young age, he spent time in a reform school–type of institution. He didn't have a father's guidance. A big change took place in his life at the age of thirteen because he unjustly was accused of something. I don't feel he was guilty."

Mental pictures of what Zodiac looked like had been flooding the psychic's mind for almost a month, constantly merging and changing. The image that remained clearest to DeLouise was that of a man about twenty-eight years old, approximately five foot eight inches tall, somewhere between 135 to 145 pounds, with a slightly undernourished look. The killer had silky, darkish brown hair that he normally wore in a pompadour, but as a disguise combed forward. "I don't think Zodiac wears glasses," said

131

DeLouise. "He's too vain to wear them even if he needed them. He uses them only as a disguise."

The Chicago seer felt that Zodiac used drugs that had damaged his brain and given him a persecution complex, drugs that kept him high, although in the case of the Berryessa murder he was taking some sort of depressant. DeLouise said "vibrations" he had received told him that Zodiac had resorted to "speed and goof balls," which he took before his murders.

"This man is transmitting," said the psychic. "Only people who deal in this type of extrasensory perception know each other. I hope I can prove to him in some way that I want to help him."

DeLouise planned to meet with Chicago police to help develop some sort of composite drawing of his vision. The seer felt that the killer might be a Scorpio or Aquarian because of the figures "11-2" and "2-11" which he kept receiving, standing for February 11 or November 2.

Because he continued to receive the impression that the killer wanted to turn himself in, DeLouise decided to come to the Bay Area at his own expense to help Zodiac find peace of mind.

Tuesday, January 20, 1970

DeLouise arrived in San Francisco at 7:00 A.M. and was met by his West Coast representative, Christopher Harris, who had flown up from Hollywood. The psychic arrived in Vallejo at two in the afternoon and went directly to V.P.D. Officers took him to the site of the Jensen-Faraday murders, wondering if the months that had lapsed between the attack and his visit would affect his ability to pick up impressions. DeLouise told them there was no time in extrasensory perception and the difference of a year would not weaken his psychic concentration.

Next, DeLouise visited with Napa law enforcement officials, who went over the details of the Lake Berryessa slaying. DeLouise got new feelings about the killer involving horses and a white dog, loneliness, love of flowers, and intense hatred of police. The seer suggested that the killer may have applied for work in law enforcement and been rebuffed or been an outpatient in a mental hospital. The words "roth" and "field" and a picture of a small bridge nine miles south of town flashed into DeLouise's mind, but he was unable to tell what meaning they had in solving the riddle of Zodiac's identity.

He told police, "I will stay until the weekend, but I will stay in San Francisco. I feel it would be more dangerous for me to stay in Vallejo. I can't explain why. I just feel that way."

In San Francisco, DeLouise was not allowed to touch any of the physical evidence from the Stine case and came up with no impressions. "Sometimes just touching these things triggers impressions, brings a name. It's called psychometry," he said. But the police were unmoved.

For three days the psychic pleaded over television and radio for the killer to surrender, but he never did.

The psychic returned to Chicago.

Kathleen Johns

Sunday, March 15, 1970

In Santa Rosa, a man frightened three separate women motorists in an identical manner between 3:00 A.M. and 4:00 A.M. At 5:10, police stopped a man whose auto and license number matched their descriptions.

He was identified as a Vallejo resident in a "1962-64 white Chevrolet." The man, "about twenty-three," was stopped on Fourth Street after he had followed a woman right into the post office parking lot. He claimed that he was lost and looking for a way out of town.

The police let the man go and escorted him out of town.

Tuesday, March 17, 1970

A Vallejo woman was on her way to Travis Air Force Base when a white Chevrolet began to tailgate her. The driver kept looking at her and then began "blinking lights, banging his horn" and tried to get her to stop.

She raced ahead and eventually was able to outdistance the car.

Mrs. Kathleen Johns bundled up her ten-month-old daughter, Jennifer, and left her home in San Bernardino at 7:00 P.M. for the trip to Petaluma, a small dairy-farming community where her sick mother lived. It was easier to travel at night while the baby slept.

Kathleen made her way up dusty Interstate 5 and onto Highway 99 just before Bakersfield, through Fresno, Merced, and Modesto, where she swung left onto Highway 132, a rarely used road. In her rearview mirror she noticed a car she seemed to have picked up on her tail in Modesto. "It wasn't as new as a '68," she told me later. "It was junky."

It was near midnight when Kathleen slowed to let the car pass her. Abruptly, the driver behind began to blink his lights and honk his horn. When Kathleen ignored this, the stranger accelerated and pulled into the lane alongside her 1957 maroon-and-white Chevrolet station wagon. He yelled through his open passenger-side window that her left rear wheel was wobbling.

Kathleen, who was seven months pregnant, was very concerned about stopping on such a lightly traveled road with a stranger.

"It was a two-lane road," she recalled for me later. "The man started flashing his lights off and on. My car was such a clunker I figured something was wrong with it.

"But I didn't stop, because it was dangerous out there. I waited till I got to the freeway, then I stopped by 5."

Kathleen pulled to the edge of Maze Road near Interstate 5, and the light-colored car parked on the shoulder in back of her.

"A clean-shaven and very neatly dressed man" got out with a lug wrench in his left hand and approached her, gesturing toward the back of her station wagon. "He was about thirty," she said later.

"He seemed like a reliable person," Kathleen told me. "Nobody that looked in any way freaky. As a matter of fact, I remember thinking he may have been a service man or something. He was that kind of clean-cut. He had the tire iron when he got out."

"Your left rear wheel is wobbling," he said in a soft voice, leaning on her door and looking down into her car. "I'll tighten your lugs if you'd like."

Kathleen reached over and pulled the blanket over her sleeping baby and then tried to see out the window into the dark where the man pointed.

"Don't worry," he said, walking to the rear of her car. "I'll be glad to fix it for you." Kathleen could hear him working on the wheel, but he was out of her view.

After a while, he stood up and came around to her window. "O.K., that should do it," he said, and waved and returned to his car.

"He went ahead and pulled back on the freeway," Kathleen told me.

She had driven only five or six car lengths before her whole left rear tire spun off, crashing and banging, into the weeds at the side of the road.

She turned off the engine, leaving the keys in the ignition, and got out of the car to see what had happened. Meanwhile, the stranger backed up to the front of Kathleen's car, got out, and ran up to her. For the first time she got a good look at him as he crossed in front of her headlights.

"Oh, no, the trouble's worse than I thought!" he said. "I'll give you a ride to the service station." The stranger stood between her and her car.

Kathleen looked over his shoulder at a light down the road. Not more than a quarter mile away was an ARCO service station, brightly illuminated. ARCO was good because she had a credit card at the time and no money.

"Come on," he pleaded. "I'll give you a drive to the garage. It's O.K."

"I really wouldn't have gotten in his car if I had had any bad vibes about it," she told me. "I remember I told him where I was going, and I think he was going there too."

Kathleen gathered up Jennifer and got into the man's car. Just as they were pulling out, she noticed that the lights to her car were still on and remembered that the keys were still in the ignition. The man smiled, went back to her car, snapped off the lights, and pocketed the keys. Then the stranger drove her away from her car —but not to the ARCO station.

"When he missed it, I really didn't think much about it. I didn't say anything," Kathleen told me. "When he passed the next exit, it dawned on me something wasn't right. As long as he wasn't talking, neither was I. We went several more exits before he got off, and then I just didn't say anything. He was doing the driving."

The man started down a rocky, deserted farm road. Nothing was said for a long time. His windbreaker was open and she could see the white of his shirt glowing dully in the moonlight. The man started to pull over to the roadside and then speeded up. He repeated this several times. Kathleen thought he was going to make a pass at her.

She was the one to break the silence. "Do you always go around helping people on the road like this?" she said sarcastically.

"When I get through with them they don't need any help," said the man, his tone changing as he looked off at the dark woods in the distance.

Kathleen watched the menacing dark shapes of trees and an occasional farmhouse flash by the window of the roving car. After thirty minutes, the stranger turned to look at her and said, "You know you're going to die. You know I'm going to kill you."

"Then he said, 'I'm going to throw the baby out,'" Kathleen told me. "I'm getting past the point of being scared enough to pee in my pants. I'm just thinking, What am I going to do? But real calm and cool. I figured you need an action for a reaction-type thing. Do whatever it is he wanted to do. You know, sometimes you have to cry or beg or whatever. Altogether he drove down those back country roads for two or three hours."

The man drove the frightened woman through a maze of winding lanes, rarely speaking but occasionally looking over at her and repeating either "You know I'm going to kill you" or "You know you're going to die."

Kathleen knew he meant it. "His eyes," she thought; "they're deadpan eyes."

Her head was swimming, but she tried to remember everything

she could about this man during their slow drive. First she noticed that the stranger's shoes had been shined so brightly, "spit-shined," that they reflected the yellow interior lights of the car. "They weren't boot types. They were like Navy shoes. His general appearance, come to think of it, was Navy."

He was dressed in a dark blue-black nylon windbreaker over black woolen bell-bottom pants. The black, thick-rimmed glasses he wore were held firmly in place by a thin band of elastic around his head. His chin was traced with scars of some past acne infection.

"His nose was not especially small," she told me; "his jaw wasn't weak. He wasn't a weak type of person and he didn't have a heavy forehead. His hair was brown, worn like a crew cut. That's probably why I thought of a service man. He wasn't real big, weighed about 166." Kathleen herself was five foot nine inches tall.

"I got the distinct impression that he might not be aware of what he was doing. I think he could even be the man next door and might not know it was himself. Obviously he was sick."

There was a full moon out and it cast a glow on Kathleen's blond hair and gray eyes. She took in everything she could.

His car was an American make, lightly colored, a late-model two-door with old California license plates, the black-and-yellow kind. The car's interior was messy, with papers, books, and clothes strewn about the front and back seats and even on the dashboard. The clothing was mostly a man's, but mixed in were some small T-shirts with patterns such as a child age eight to twelve might wear.

"He is so neatly dressed," thought Kathleen, "and yet the car is so messy." On the dashboard were two colored plastic scouring pads—"house stuff in the car. Stuff that didn't belong there." Next to the pads she could make out a black, four-celled flashlight with a rubber grip.

A sporty console-style auto-transmission gear shift box was between the two black bucket seats, with a special built-in cigarette lighter on its right side and an ashtray at the front end. "It seemed to be part of the car."

The stranger continued speaking in a monotone, with no trace of accent. "No emotion," Kathleen told me. "No anger, no kind of emotion. Nothing. The words just come out. He didn't speak abnormally slow but very precise. It just came out. Period. What he was going to say. It just had no feeling.

"I couldn't handle it anymore, so I decided the next time he came to one of those Hollywood stops—you know, not a complete stop—that he made at the different stop signs, I was going to jump out."

Suddenly the car came to a halt. The man had inadvertently driven up a freeway offramp.

Kathleen scooped up little Jennifer and jumped from the car, dashed across the road, and leapt into an irrigation ditch surrounded by tall grass in the middle of a field.

"It was all wine vineyard with a little gully and I just laid as flat as I could." She held herself on top of Jennifer to keep the baby from making an outcry.

Her heart pounded in her temples, her breath came loudly and rapidly; the car did not move. She could see the man now. He had a flashlight and was playing it about the field, searching for a glimpse of her and the baby. He called out for her to come back. There was silence except for the sound of crickets. The man stepped forward, swinging the light.

"About the same time," Kathleen told me later, "this old semi-truck was going on the freeway, his lights must have flashed on the man because the driver just stopped that big thing on a dime and jumped out and yelled, 'What the hell is going on?' and this guy jumped in his car and split."

The stranger's car accelerated down the black road; a trail of gray dust spiraled behind the vehicle. The driver of the truck came toward Kathleen, and she panicked.

"Not another man! He started coming down the hill toward me and I just started blowing it. I made him wait until a lady came along and I rode with her. But then, when I got to this little one-horse town, she let me off in front of the police station and I went into this dumpy little office where there was just this one old man, a sergeant. I told him my story and he went kind of pale.

I guess things like that don't happen every day around a little town. Well, he got a form and I'm giving him a detailed description of the man and his car."

As she and the policeman talked, Kathleen's gaze wandered up the wall where the cops kept their wanted posters. Her eyes locked on the bulletin board; she gave a start and let out a scream.

"Oh, my God! That's him! That's him right there!"

On the bulletin board was the composite drawing of the murderer of Paul Stine—a composite drawing of Zodiac.

"The sergeant panicked when I told him it was the guy on the wall, and he wanted to get me out of there because he thought the man might come back and try and do us both in. He was the only one on duty and in fact he took me over to a diner that wasn't open. He had the owner open up so I could sit there instead of his office. I was kind of ticked about that. I guess he didn't feel safe with me being there.

"I sat there in the dark cafe and explained to him where my car was," Kathleen said, "by the ARCO station. And I guess the sheriff went out but he radioed back to say there was no car. They kept searching, and then just a while later it came over the radio that the car had been found on this other road, but all burned up."

In order to move Kathleen's car to Byrd Road at Highway 132, it was found the stranger actually had had to put the wheel back on the car.

"The inside was totally burned. I went to the junk yard because all my kid's stuff was in there. I wanted to see if there was anything I could salvage. There wasn't. The inside was just gutted."

In the days following the attack, Toschi sent Kathleen a series of photos of suspects. The ages were twenty-eight to forty-five. I asked her about this later.

"Yeah, he sent them through the Stanislaus County sheriff. But I felt that the suspect was younger and not in those pictures. If I saw him again, though, I would instantly recognize him."

The fact that the murder attempt on Kathleen and her baby

occurred near midnight, on a weekend, at the time of the full moon, and that the man was dressed in Navy garb and wore a crew cut, led me to believe that she had escaped from the Zodiac killer. Added to this was the fact that stranger wore dark-rimmed glasses and spoke in the monotone voice that all the surviving victims have mentioned.

If it was the Zodiac that she had escaped from, then Kathleen had seen him up close and without a disguise longer than any of his victims.

And she had lived to tell about it.

Zodiac

Sunday, April 19, 1970

The man parked in a late-model hardtop at the corner of Bay Street and the Embarcadero seemed to have an obsession about the crime rate in San Francisco. He went on in great detail to list all thirty-five of the city's murders so far that year.

"It's not safe to walk alone," he told Christopher Edwards, a ship's steward, "with all the muggings, murders, rapes, and crime." Edwards had stopped to ask directions while walking to Fisherman's Wharf and he was getting "bad vibrations" from the stranger. The man identified himself as a British engineer who had lived in San Francisco for ten years; he offered the steward a lift. Edwards declined, but listened while the stranger went on with great knowledge about all the murders in the city, save those that were on the minds of most people—the Zodiac killings.

The stranger's reluctance to talk about Zodiac impressed Edwards, and he could not shake the incident from his mind. As soon as he got to the wharf, he called the police. Later, at Central Station, he identified the man from a composite drawing of Zodiac.

Was Zodiac a British engineer?

Sunday, April 19, 1970

The body of renowned lamp designer Robert Salem, forty, was found mutilated and almost decapitated in his elegant workshop-apartment at 754 Stevenson Street, behind the San Franciscan Hotel. The killer (or killers) had tried unsuccessfully to cut Salem's head off with a long, thin-bladed knife; failing that, he cut off the victim's left ear and carried it away with him. On the wall, printed in the designer's own blood, were the words: Satan Saves. Then in larger letters next to a dripping red symbol of a crucified man was the word: ZODIAC. On Salem's stomach was the same crucifixion symbol, also drawn in the victim's blood. Apparently the murderer was covered with blood from his victim and had committed the killing in the nude, leaving trails of blood throughout the studio.

Inspectors Gus Coreris and John Fotinos did not believe that this was the work of the Zodiac killer but that of a "copycat killer."

While detectives continued working on the Salem case, the real Zodiac was busy elsewhere. He was writing on an odd-sized piece of stationery with a blue felt-tip pen, composing another of his letters—the ninth.

The envelope read: "Editor, San Fran. Chronicle, San Francisco, Calif." Two Roosevelt six-cent stamps were turned on their sides on the envelope—twice as much postage as necessary. It was as if the writer could hardly wait for his message to be received. Sometimes the letters were written on expensive Eaton bond paper, but this time the paper was so cheap that it had no sort of watermark that could be traced to any manufacturer.

In a combination of handprinted words and script, the message read simply:

> This is the Zodiac speaking
> By the way have you cracked
> the last ciper I sent you?
> My name is—

Printed after this was a line of thirteen symbols:

This was the most tantalizing clue of all; the string of thirteen characters that Zodiac claimed made up his name.

Everyone tried looking at the thirteen symbols in different ways. Vallejo detectives tried multiplying and adding in various directions using the three circled numeral eights. The numbers looked out of place in the middle of the cipher. Zodiac had not used numbers before. Were they something other than number eights?

The symbols might also be something other than a substitution cipher. Perhaps they could simply be read literally: "KAEN MY NAME." Herb Caen was the *Chronicle's* leading columnist.

AEN ⊕ 8K8M8 ⅄ NAM

AEN K MYENAM

KAEN MYNAME

Or Zodiac could be saying his name was Kane. "Killer Kane"? Was the stocky killer amusing himself, or had he at last told us his real name? Would we be clever enough to extract the answer from the cipher?

The letter continued:

> I am mildly cerous [curious] as to how
> much money you have on my
> head now. I hope you do not
> think that I was the one
> who wiped out that blue
> meannie with a bomb at the
> cop station. Even though I talked
> about killing school children with
> one. It just wouldn't doo to
> move in on someone elses teritory.
> But there is more glory in killing
> a cop than a cid [kid] because a cop
> can shoot back. I have killed

> ten people to date. It would
> have been a lot more except
> that my bus bomb was a dud.
> I was swamped out by the
> rain we had a while back.

Zodiac's reference to killing a cop was an allusion to the dynamite bombing of the Golden Gate Park police station on February 16, which killed Sergeant Brian McDonnell and wounded eight other police officers.

The letter's left margin and printed lines were ruler straight, the size of the letters showing extreme patience. It was the kind of handwriting one would associate with a student or scientist. The capital letter *I* was severe and looked like the Roman numeral *I.*

The second page of the letter began with the words:

> The new bomb is set up like
> this

The rest of the page was taken up with an elaborate blueprint for a new improved school bus killing bomb. At the bottom was a P.S.:

> I hope you have fun trying
> figgure out who I killed

Drawn carefully was the Zodiac symbol and the "score":

> Zodiac-10   SFPD-0

Tuesday, April 21, 1970

The ninth Zodiac letter was received at the *Chronicle* in the morning mail. Toschi was called; he rushed to the paper to see if it was genuine. Although a swatch of Stine's blood-stained shirt was not included, there was enough proof to convince the detective that the taunting message was authentic.

"It's Zodiac." Toschi sighed. "Here we go again."

"Who were the ninth and tenth victims?" he wondered. "If Kathleen Johns was considered by Zodiac to be a victim, who was the other?"

On Friday, March 13, 1970, Marie Antoinette Anstey was taken from the parking lot of the Coronado Inn in Vallejo. Her nude body was discovered in Lake County on March 21, 1970, just off an isolated country road. None of her clothing was ever found. She had been given mescaline, dealt a blow to the head, and then drowned.

The murder fit many of the patterns of the Zodiac killings: it occurred on a weekend, there was no sexual molestation, and it took place near a body of water. The Coronado Inn had been the favorite after-hours club of Darlene Ferrin, the third Vallejo victim of Zodiac. I thought it was strange that the killings so far had taken place in locations that had a form of water in their name: *Lake* Herman Road, Blue Rock *Springs*, *Lake* Berryessa, and *Wash*ington Street, which was quite close to *Lake* Street. Was *Lake* County part of this chain?

The police were most interested in Zodiac's statement that he killed ten people and "it would have been a lot more except *I was swamped out by the rain we had a while back*" (italics mine). He himself was swamped out; he wasn't referring to the fact that driving rain would keep his young victims out of lovers' lanes. Had the rain flooded the basement in which he claimed to have built his bombs? Did he live in a remote area that was cut off from the outside?

Toschi and Armstrong checked suspects who lived in areas that had been recently flooded.

Wednesday, April 29, 1970

The *Chronicle* received the tenth Zodiac letter. It had been mailed just after noon the previous day, in San Francisco. The newspaper held the new letter back a day at the request of Chief

Al Nelder while he made a difficult decision.

Since the first mention of a "death machine" bomb last November (in the seventh Zodiac letter), the papers had voluntarily held back all mention of this device in order to prevent a panic such as the one that had occurred after the death of Stine, when Zodiac had threatened to annihilate a school bus full of children. Now Zodiac was demanding mention of his bomb threats or he *would* below up a school bus.

Toschi and Armstrong studied the new letter, another of those leadenly dull and humorless greeting cards Zodiac was so fond of sending to the papers.

The card (reproduced here for the first time) showed two old prospectors. The first, on a burro, was saying to the second, "Sorry to hear your ass is a dragon." The second miner rode an exhausted fork-tongued dragon.

Above the dragon Zodiac had written:

> I hope you
> enjoy your
> selves
> when I
> have my
> Blast.
> P.S. on
> back

The card was from the International Greetings Co. and was one of the Jolly Roger line. The back of the card read:

> If you dont want me to
> have this blast you must
> do two things. 1 Tell every
> one about the bus bomb with
> all the details. 2 I would like
> to see some nice Zodiac butons
> wandering about town. Every
> one else has these buttons like,
> [peace symbol], black power, melvin eats

bluber, etc. Well it would cheer
me up considerbly if I saw
a lot of people wearing my
buton. Please no nasty ones
like melvin's

Thank you

It seemed that Zodiac had lost his respect for Melvin Belli.

At the end of the letter, the stocky man had boldly drawn his emblem, the second time in the letter. It was the design to be used for the buttons, the seal of the Zodiac.

Chief Nelder felt the bomb blueprint in the ninth letter (April 20) was a ruse, but he called a press conference anyway. "It's not my intention to frighten the public, but this guy has now demanded there be mention of the bomb and has threatened to blow up a school bus if mention wasn't made. I weighed all sides of the question and concluded this information should be made public."

The papers had been printing only portions of the Zodiac letters all along, and now held down any sort of general alarm by describing the bomb plans as dubious. The bomb schematic that Zodiac had drawn was never reproduced.

No buttons were ever made.

Friday, May 8, 1970

In Santa Rosa, a K-Mart department store was evacuated after an anonymous telephone bomb threat by a man identifying himself as Zodiac. A man identifying himself as Zodiac had made a Santa Rosa bomb threat exactly a year earlier.

Friday, May 22, 1970

In a press conference in Los Angeles, Florence E. Douglas, mayor of Vallejo and candidate for the Democratic gubernatorial nomi-

148

nation, said, "I believe some clues were overlooked in the murder of Darlene Ferrin." She pledged to use all her influence to re-open the Ferrin case. She believed that it was a premeditated killing.

Darlene's mother had informed Christopher Harris, Joseph DeLouise's representative, that the night of her death Darlene had told her, "You might read about me in the papers tomorrow." Both Harris and DeLouise felt Darlene knew her killer. Harris was at the news conference with Mayor Douglas and was introduced as a free-lance writer.

I was familiar with Harris. He had been turned in as a Zodiac suspect because of suspicious questions he had been asking Vallejo residents. The police were certain he had absolutely no involvement in the Zodiac crimes.

"The investigation of the death of Darlene Ferrin by the Vallejo Police Department was without question inadequate," Harris said at the conference. "I base this statement on conversations with investigating officers, police authorities in the Vallejo-Napa area, Darlene Ferrin's mother, and Mayor Florence E. Douglas. . . . I observed while in Vallejo that the police disregarded the ridiculous; I am now a firm believer that in the ridiculous, especially in the case of Darlene Ferrin, lies a storehouse of clues. The police should have done a complete character sketch of Darlene Ferrin.

"There are too many questions into her death that have not been properly tied down. The use of the flashlight proves that the killer wanted to make sure he had the right person. I do not agree with the statement that the flashlight was used to make sure he killed his victim. If the Darlene Ferrin case was reopened, it would have a major psychological effect on the Zodiac's deranged mind that would eventually draw him into the open."

In Vallejo, the Ferrin murder investigation continued; the case remained open. There is no statute of limitations on murder. Shake-ups began in the department of police, from the chief on down.

It was two months before Zodiac sent another letter to the *Chronicle* (only small portions of this letter have been reproduced before now). This one was postmarked San Francisco, and mailed on June 26.

The eleventh letter read:

> This is the Zodiac speaking
> I have become very upset with
> the people of San Fran Bay
> Area. They have *not* complied
> with my wishes for them to
> wear some nice ✪ buttons.
> I promised to punish them
> if they did not comply, by
> anilating a full School Buss.
> But now school is out for
> the summer, so I punished
> them in an another way.
> I shot a man sitting in
> a parked car with a .38.
>   ✪-12   SFPD-0
> The Map coupled with this
> code will tell you where the
> bomb is set. You have untill
> next Fall to dig it up. ✪

San Francisco Police Officer Richard Radetich, twenty-five, had been shot to death with a .38 while he was sitting in a parked car on Friday morning in the 600 block of Waller writing out a traffic citation. Homicide detectives vociferously denied that Zodiac could be his killer. "If he's hinting he shot officer Radetich then he's lying. We have already issued an arrest warrant in the case," said one detective.

Zodiac's enclosed map, actually an altered "Phillips 66" service station road map, pinpointed the peak of Mt. Diablo (Devil's Mountain) in Contra Costa County across the bay from San

Francisco. I was intrigued by Zodiac's choice of a road map. For one thing, Phillips was the name of Darlene's first husband.

The new letter now claimed twelve victims for Zodiac. The detectives considered the possibility that the map marked not the site of a new bomb but the burial spot of Zodiac victim number twelve. In imitation of his own crossed-circle symbol, he had drawn a compass symbol radiating from a small square in the center. The Phillips map was not detailed enough to tell what that small square was, so I consulted a larger map and discovered that located at the exact center of his map was the Naval Radio Station, a major relay station on the south peak.

It had been long thought that Zodiac might be a naval man who was out to sea in between murders and letters and thus remained undetected. It was a tantalizing idea. Was the maniac a worker at the station while on shore? Did he stand like a king on top of the double-peaked mountain at night, the Bay Area spread beneath his feet, surrounded by a sky filled with all the actual symbols of astrology? After the Civil War Mt. Diablo was used to plot longitude and latitude for the Bay Area.

Here is the two-line cipher Zodiac included at the end of the letter that was to be used in tandem with the map:

C △ J I ■ ⊙ ⱇ ⅃ ⌄ A M ⅂ △ Ω O R T ⊕
X ⊙ F D V ⌿ ⊡ H C Ɛ L ✦ P W △

Friday, July 24, 1970

The writing of the next two Zodiac letters, I speculated, went like this:

The stocky man began to write with a frenzy. Crouched in the silence of his basement, he donned his gloves and took up his felt-tip pen. Outside the day was bright; here, he was cloaked in gloom, a blackness that clung to every corner of his work area punctuated only by one strange light.

His twelfth letter read:

151

> This is the Zodiac speaking
> I am rather unhappy because
> you people will not wear some
> nice ⊕ buttons. So I now
> have a little list, starting with
> the woeman & her baby that I
> gave a rather interesting ride
> for a coupple howers one
> evening a few months back that
> ended in my burning her
> car where I found them.

The "woeman" could only be Kathleen Johns. Kathleen's terror ride had received scant attention in only one small paper. Zodiac's mention of her would seem to authenticate him as the man who rode with her and her daughter.

The stocky man mailed this letter. Then he began work on the longest letter he was to write to the *Chronicle*.

"This is the Zodiac speaking," he began the thirteenth letter (reprinted completely here for the first time), as usual. Again he mentioned how angry he was that the people of San Francisco weren't wearing Zodiac buttons on their lapels, even "nasty" buttons or "any type" of Zodiac buttons.

He paused. How could he show his displeasure, his boiling fury at being ignored? His blue pen moved across the bond paper as fast as his strange method of writing would allow.

"I" he wrote, and this was a large and bold *I*, second in size only to the Z in Zodiac at the top of the page.

> I shall (on top of every
> thing else) torture all 13
> of my slaves that I have
> wateing for me in Paradice.
> Some I shall tie over ant hills
> and watch them scream & twich
> and squirm. Others shall have
> pine splinters driven under their
> nails & then burned. Others shall
> be placed in cages & fed salt

beef untill they are gorged then
I shall listen to their pleass
for water and I shall laugh at
them. Others will hang by
their thumbs & burn in the
sun then I will rub them down
deep heat to warm
them up. Others I shall
skin them alive & let them
run around screaming. And . . .

Here he began to quote Gilbert and Sullivan, changing the lyrics to fit his own meanings. The stanzas he set down were from *The Mikado*, sung by the Mikado himself. In a spin-off of "The Punishment Fit the Crime," Zodiac wrote:

all billiard players I shall
have them play in a dark
ened dungen all with crooked
cues & Twisted Shoes.
Yes I shall have great
fun inflicting the most
delicious of pain to my
Slaves

The Zodiac symbol had now grown to mammoth proportions and filled the bottom of the page, eclipsing the notation:

SFPD = 0, Zodiac = 13.

The stocky figure hunched over his work and, this time paraphrasing Ko-Ko in *The Mikado*, wrote of a little list of all the people he would like to kill:

As some day it may hapen
that a victom must be found.
I've got a little list. I've
got a little list, of society
offenders who might well be

underground who would never
be missed who would never be
missed. There is the pest-
ulentual nucences who whrite
for autographs, all people who
have flabby hands and irritat-
ing laughs. All children who
are up in dates and implore
you with im platt. All people
who are shakeing hands shake
hands like that. And all third
persons who with unspoiling
take thoes who insist. They'd
none of them be missed. They'd
none of them be missed. There's
the banjo seranader and
the others of his race and
the piano orginast I got him
on the list. All people who
eat pepermint and phomphit [puff it]
in your face, they would
never be missed They would
never be missed And the
Idiout who phraises with in-
thusastic tone of centuries
but this and every country but
his own. And the lady from
the provences who dress like
a guy who doesn't cry and
the singurly abnormily the
girl who never kissed. I don't
think she would be missed
Im shure she wouldn't be
missed. And that nice impriest
that is rather rife the judic-
ial hummerest I've got him on
the list All funny fellows, com-
mic men and clowns of private
life. They'd none of them be
missed. They'd none of them be

missed. And uncompromising
kind such as wachmacallit,
thingmebob, and like wise, well-
nevermind, and tut tut tut tut,
and whashisname, and you know
who, but the task of filling
up the blanks I rather leave
up to you. But it really does-
n't matter whom you place
upon the list, for none of
them be missed, none of
them be missed.

He concluded the Lord High Executioner's aria with another
Zodiac symbol, which took up three-quarters of the last page.
Below this he wrote a hint about the Mt. Diablo map and cipher
of exactly one month earlier:

PS. The Mt. Diablo Code concerns
Radians & # inches along the radians

On Sunday morning, the stocky man printed "S.F. Chronicle"
on the envelope, pushed his chair back, put one six-cent Roosevelt
stamp tilted jauntily to the right on the letter, and went out into
the sunny morning to mail it.

Monday, July 27, 1970

The letters arrived simultaneously at the *Chronicle*.

Late Monday and Tuesday and Wednesday, Zodiac waited to
hear in the media of his latest threats. But there was nothing—
not a word. What had gone wrong? Both letters couldn't have
been lost in the mail.

August and September gave way to early October, almost the
anniversary of Paul Stine's murder. There was still no mention of
the new Zodiac letters. The mass killer had no way of knowing
that on July 27 the police and the *Chronicle* had decided to

conduct an experiment to see how Zodiac would react to the lack of publicity.* It was felt Zodiac's thirst for publicity had become his motive for killing.

Because of the variations from Gilbert's original lyrics, Armstrong and Toschi knew their man wrote the lines from memory rather than copying them directly from the libretto. They began a painstaking search and questioning of onetime Ko-Kos, on the theory that Zodiac may have played the character in his student days. The detectives began with San Francisco's own Gilbert and Sullivan company, The Lamplighters, and questioned all members of the cast, especially the bass-baritones. Handwriting comparisons and obvious differences in physical appearance with Zodiac cleared all present and former Lord High Executioners. Toschi ventured that it was more likely that the killer was just a Gilbert and Sullivan buff.

I discovered that on the night of Paul Stine's murder The Lamplighters at Presentation Theatre were in rehearsal for *The Mikado*, due to open a week later. The theater was roughly thirteen blocks from the site of the cabdriver's murder.

Even more intriguing was the fact that during the entire run of the local *Mikado*, no Zodiac letter was received. The production closed on Friday, November 7. On the following two days, two Zodiac letters were mailed.

Zodiac wrote four letters over a four-month period after the attack on Kathleen Johns, mostly pleas for attention. Only in the fourth letter was the terror ride finally mentioned. Why mention it now? The *Chronicle* was not printing his letters, and the police were openly skeptical that Zodiac was actually killing anyone. Perhaps the killer reached for something concrete that would prove he was active. He had mentioned:

> . . . the woeman & baby that I gave a rather
> interesting ride for a coupple howers one
> evening a few months back that
> ended in my burning her car . . .

*The July letters were finally published on October 12, 1970, by the *Chronicle*.

What, I wondered, made this particular event come into Zodiac's mind if he was not the actual attacker? Only the small circulation Modesto *Bee*, in a story the day after the attack, had mentioned the fact that Kathleen's car had been torched. If Zodiac was only taking credit for the attack, then he had to live close enough to Modesto to have seen the article.

My guess was that Zodiac had held back from claiming this crime because he really was the driver and he had been afraid of what Kathleen might remember and that she might be able to lead police to his door.*

Kathleen Johns at this time went underground. It was not until February 18, 1982, that I was able to find her.

Wednesday, October 6, 1970

In the morning mail the *Chronicle* received a plain, white, three-inch-by-five-inch file card on which the author had composed a message using cut up letters from the previous day's *Chronicle*. He had drawn a cross in blood. The message was dated Monday, October 5, 1970.

It read:

> DEAR EDITOR:
> You'll hate me, but I've got to tell you.
> THE PACE ISN'T ANY SLOWER! IN
> FACT IT'S JUST ONE BIG thirteenth
> 13 'Some of Them Fought
> It was Horrible'

Beneath the "13" was a cross drawn in human blood and a P.S. pasted upside down on the left side of the card:

*Zodiac had a habit of writing letters on the anniversary of his attacks and murders and had written a letter exactly one year from the day of the killings on Lake Herman Road. On March 22, 1971, the one-year anniversary of the attack on Kathleen, Zodiac would write another letter.

> THERE ARE REPORTS
> city police pig cops are
> closeing in on me, F'k
> I'm crackproof, What is
> the price tag now?

The word "Zodiac" in roman type was on the right with a large Zodiac symbol, the cross segment made by strips of tape. The writer had punched thirteen holes in the side of the card to represent victims.

Armstrong and Toschi believed it was a genuine Zodiac letter for almost two days, but eventually they filed it as another copycat effort.

The Zodiac evidence now filled a gunmetal-gray fireproof steel cabinet four drawers high.

Wednesday, October 28, 1970

Paul Avery, the *Chronicle*'s top investigative reporter, had written the bulk of the stories concerning the Zodiac murders. Thus he was not surprised when the next letter from the killer, his fifteenth, was addressed not to the *Chronicle* but to Avery personally.

This time Zodiac had mailed a garish children's Halloween card. On the front was a dancing skeleton with a pumpkin, black and orange, and with white lettering, in boldface, that said:

> FROM YOUR
> <u>SECRET PAL</u>

At the lower left of the card was a verse that began:

> I feel it in
> my bones,
> You ache
> to know
> my name,

> And so
> I'll clue
> you in . . .

Avery's throat went dry. With anxious fumbling fingers he rushed to open the card to read the punchline.

> But then why spoil our game! BOO!
> Happy
> Halloween!

Inside, Zodiac had pasted a totally different skeleton, a portion of another card, and had drawn exaggerated pictures of peering eyes. Some of the eyes were peeking out of slits. Along with the giant Z and the familiar crossed-circle, the killer had drawn a strange new symbol that at first appeared to be composed of meteorological symbols.

Zodiac had lettered on the back, in white ink such as artists and draughtsmen use:

When Toschi and Armstrong were able to get the card away from Avery, they turned their attention to the skeleton that

Zodiac had cut out and pasted inside the card. Carefully, they pulled it up to see if there was a message behind it. There was not.

But on the inner side of the envelope itself there was fine writing. The writing made an X. It said, twice, "sorry no cipher."

"We would check out all the greeting cards as Zodiac sent them just to see how common they were and how easy or difficult it would be for Zodiac to buy one," Toschi told me later. "All the cards sent by Zodiac were common cards that could be purchased in any retail card store. That I checked on my own time, Saturday or Sundays. I just wanted to be sure. Sometimes I did it just to be sure we weren't making it easy for Zodiac to make us look bad."

I obtained a duplicate of the Halloween card in its original unmarked state and realized that Zodiac had added the cutout orange pumpkin to cover the pelvis of the skeleton on the front. Sexual repression?

The card had come originally with only one peering "evil eye." Zodiac had added twelve more, and had given the printed skeleton eyes as well. The cutout skeleton on the inside was portrayed in a posture of mock crucifixion. The card was manufactured by the Gibson card company.

As for the new Zodiac symbol, readers as far away as Detroit wrote to say that it represented a Wide Flange Beam, a structural steel shape used in building construction. Some felt that Zodiac was some sort of civil engineer. The symbol looked like this:

By writing "PEEK-A-BOO—YOU ARE DOOMED!" and "4-TEEN" on the card to Avery, Zodiac was either boasting that he had victim number fourteen already or that Avery was to be next.

The *Chronicle* released the story on page one on Halloween, and it received worldwide attention. The cityroom was filled with television cameras for a while and the light-haired, lanky Avery found himself, for a change, on the other end of an interview.

As a result, there was a flurry of tips, which pleased the police. When asked by reporters if he was concerned about the Halloween death threat, Avery replied that he considered it "just a lot of talk."

As a former war correspondent in Vietnam and a licensed private eye, Avery could handle himself pretty well. But Chief Nelder decided not to take any chances and issued him authority to carry a .38 caliber revolver, and let him work out on the police target range with the gun.

"Chron Newsman Paul Avery is living dangerously," wrote Herb Caen, "His investigative reporting into the activities of the Zodiac killer have won him the accolade of a message from Zodiac, warning 'You are doomed,' as a result of which several Chron newsmen—including Avery—are wearing lapel buttons reading 'I Am Not Paul Avery.' Meanwhile, Avery has applied for personalized license plates reading 'Zodiac,' and that isn't the smartest move I ever heard of. . . ."

"It looks like Zodiac has gotten sore at some of the things I have written about him," said Avery.

In response to a wire service story about the threat on Avery's life, an anonymous letter was mailed to the *Chronicle* from southern California. In the letter was the suggestion that Zodiac may have begun his career of murder in Riverside, California.

The anonymous writer said that he had gone to the Riverside police with his theory but had been ignored. He asked Avery to look into the possibility:

> Please forward the contents of this letter to the detective in charge of "The Zodiac Murder Case."
>
> I hope this information will also help you, as we both would like to see this case solved.
>
> As for myself, I wish to remain anonymous and I know that you will understand why!
>
> A few years ago in Riverside, California, a young girl was murdered, just about, I believe, on "Halloween" evening! I could write a much

longer letter, citing the similarities between Zodiac's case and this murder, which occurred in Riverside but if the police department cannot see said comparative similarities between these two cases, then I will take a "slow boat to China," even if these crimes were committed by two different people! I think, after all the facts are studied, regarding both these cases, if the police have not already investigated these possibilities and are not already aware of the "Riverside case," then, even so perhaps they should look into it. . . .

Letters to newspapers, "similar erratic printing" find out about these two different cases. . . . Give Captain Cross a call on the phone, he knows that "I do not quit."

Mr. Avery, I will give you a call in the near future, please look into this case, the Riverside police have a wealth of information, so does San Francisco, let us hope they are not too proud to work together, and if they already are, let us hope there has been an exchange of information. . . .

Checking with Riverside Police Captain Irv Cross, Avery was able to learn the name of the secret writer. His only address was "general delivery" in an ever changing number of cities. (This man also had written Sergeant Lynch. His handprinting did not match Zodiac's.) Cross said that for some time the man had been trying to convince the Riverside police that Zodiac had murdered a college girl in 1966. Cross outlined the case to the reporter and promised to get an assortment of file material off to him as soon as possible.

Avery was dubious about the connection at first; while there were similarities to the known Zodiac killings, there was no definite link.

This letter was only one of hundreds that Avery had gotten from people who either "knew" who Zodiac was or "knew" how to trap him.

Cheri Jo Bates

Monday, November 9, 1970

Avery finally received the information on the Riverside killing, the only unsolved murder in Riverside history. Among the reports on the girl's murder had been a photograph of a handprinted letter received five months after the killing. The police had considered it only another fraudulent message from some crank; at the time, the signature at the bottom had meant nothing to them.

The author had signed his message with a single letter: Z.

In two hours, Avery was on his way to Riverside, sixty-two miles southeast of Los Angeles. Avery met with Detective Sergeant Dave Bonine, the chief investigator presently assigned to the case, and was allowed access to the files. The victim was Cheri Jo Bates. Since her murder over four years ago, the case file, #352 481, had become voluminous. In conference with Bonine and Captain Cross, Avery began to reconstruct the dead girl's last day in detail. Inwardly, Avery felt that Zodiac had written the penciled note and could be Cheri Jo's slayer.

According to the police reports, Cheri Jo had been an eighteen-year-old college freshman, an honor student, whose main ambition had been to become an airline stewardess. She had been a cheerleader at Ramona High near Riverside City College and was one at RCC. The victim was five foot three inches tall, weighed 110 pounds, had blue eyes, blond hair, and a fair complexion, although at the time of her death she was deeply tanned. She wore glasses, but only for studying. She had lived alone with her father, Joseph, at 4195 Via San Jose in Riverside. Joseph was a machinist at the Corona Naval Ordnance Laboratory. Her mother had left in 1965, and her brother was serving in the Navy in Florida.

The day of the murder, October 30, 1966, Joseph and his daughter attended Mass at St. Catherine's Church on Brockton. At 9:00 A.M., they ate breakfast at Sandy's Restaurant in Hardman Center. At 10:00, Joseph left the house to spend the day at the beach. About 3:00 P.M., Cheri Jo called her friend Stefanie. There was no answer. She called again at 3:45. This time Stefanie was home. Cheri Jo asked if she wanted to go to the college library to get some books and study a little. Stephanie declined, and Cheri Jo left the house somewhere between 4:30 and 5:00. At 4:30, some of her friends had passed Cheri Jo's house and noticed her lime-green Volkswagen still parked in front. At 5:00, Joseph Bates returned home.

When Cheri Jo left the house, she was wearing a pair of faded red capri pants and a long-sleeved pale yellow blouse with a ribbon tie at the throat. She carried an oversize red-and-tan woven straw bag. On her feet were white sandals with straps around the heels and between the first and second toes.

"At 5:00 P.M., Joseph Bates found this note taped to the refrigerator," Captain Cross told Avery. He handed the reporter a plastic-covered note. It read: "Dad—Went to RCC Library."

"Joseph took a phone message for Cheri Jo from Stephanie and went directly out again," said Cross. "At approximately 5:30, Cheri Jo noticed that she had misplaced her term paper bibliography and called a co-worker, Donna, at the Riverside National Bank. Donna hadn't seen it; the two talked for a while."

"Now I'll have to start all over on my note cards," Cheri Jo told her.

"We have a witness report," said Bonine, "that at 6:10 P.M.

one of Cheri Jo's girl friends saw her go by in her V.W. headed over toward RCC on Magnolia. The friend said she waved to her but evidently Cheri Jo didn't see her, she didn't wave back.

"Another report came from an Air Force man who lived near the library. He was passed by a light green V.W. driven by a blond female up an alley parallel to Magnolia and east of the Sherri Lynn Apartments. He recalled that the V.W. was followed closely by a 1965–66 bronze Oldsmobile.

"We figure Cheri Jo arrived at the RCC library annex around six and went into the library. She had friends studying in the library, but none of them recall seeing her. We know she actually entered the library only because of three books on the Electoral College she checked out, which were found on the front seat of her car. Evidently, while she was in the library the assailant gained access to the engine and pulled out the distributor coil and the condensor, and disconnected the middle wire of the distributor. He may have actually gone into the library and waited while she ran the battery down, trying to start the engine.

"He probably came up and offered help, offered her a lift in his car. . . . Then he got her to go down the unlit gravel road to the parking lot, about seventy-five yards east of her car. The killer then placed one hand over her mouth and with the other pressed a knife against her throat.

"He must have begun choking her," said Bonine, "but she was an athletic girl and fought back with such force that we found his paint-spattered wristwatch where she had ripped it off.

"She scratched his face. She must have screamed then. We have a report. . . . A neighbor heard an 'awful scream' between 10:15 and 10:45 P.M., and then about two minutes of silence, and finally the sound of an old car starting up. A man returning to the area at 10:30 told us he heard two screams then."

The medical report said that Cheri Jo had been kicked in the head. A short knife had been plunged into her chest twice. Her left cheek and upper lip were cut, and in three slashes to her throat her jugular was severed as well as her voice box, and she was almost decapitated. She was face down on the ground when the killer plunged the knife into her left shoulder blade. "The churned-up ground where they had struggled looked like a freshly plowed field," read the notation.

Police theorized the killer spent time looking for his watch before taking off for his car.

"It was midnight when Joseph Bates returned home and found a note he had left for Cheri Jo undisturbed. He figured his daughter was out with her girl friends, and went to sleep. Next morning she still wasn't home, so he called Stephanie to see if she was there. He reported his daughter missing at exactly 5:43 A.M. Forty-five minutes later, Halloween morning, Cleophus Martin, the groundskeeper at RCC, turned his sweeping machine onto Terracina. He saw the body, lying face down, her straw purse next to her. He called us. We roped off the area.

"The girl's purse still contained all of her I.D. and fifty-six cents. Ten feet away from the body we found the killer's Timex watch with a seven-inch circumference. The black band was broken away from one side of the face.

"We found a shoe print of a type of shoe sold only in military outlets such as nearby March A.F.B. It was size eight to ten, and produced by Leavenworth prisoners.

"We found debris, scrapings of human skin and hair, under her nails. On the front seat we found the greasy prints of a palm. And on the top of a nearby building," said Bonine, "we found a set of V.W. keys—but these were of no relation to the Bates murder."

Avery scanned the autopsy report, made several notes, shut his notebook, and replaced it in his inside jacket pocket. The earliest the girl could have been killed would have been 9:00 Sunday night, when the library closed. The "awful scream" was heard around 10:30 and is most likely when she was killed. Questions flooded Avery's mind: Did Cheri Jo stand with her killer for nearly two hours in the darkness between the two deserted frame houses? Did they talk and did she know her killer? What was the killer waiting for?

The report said the knife used by the killer had a blade one and one-half inches wide and was three and one-half inches long. Drops of blood led from the murder site to Terracina.

Avery was told that just twenty-four hours after the slaying, Cross and his men had already interrogated seventy-five people and were checking military men from the nearby air base as well as Cheri Jo's fellow students and teachers. The most promising suspect was a local youth who knew the pretty cheerleader. A good case of circumstantial evidence could be built against the local youth, but nothing substantial enough to hold up in court. Cross and Bonine believed that he was guilty. Avery wondered if he could place this man in northern California at the time of the Zodiac killings.

Five days after the attack, Cheri Jo was buried. While hundreds mourned at the funeral, homicide detectives worked their way through the crowd scanning faces for any sign of the killer. "Joseph Bates collapsed at the end of the service," said Cross. "He was crying out, 'My girl! My girl!' "

"Nine days after the funeral," said Bonine, "Captain Cross asked all persons who had been in the library on the night of the murder to recreate their movements. That was sixty-five people.

"We had them wear the same clothes, sit in the same seats, park in the same places. Captain Cross' own car doubled for the Bates auto. We asked them what time they arrived, what people they saw outside, where they parked, and what vehicles they noticed. We asked them to tell us if they recalled seeing anyone who was here the night of the killing and who didn't come in to be questioned. We tape-recorded all interviews. The captain himself took fingerprints and a lock of hair from each man. The FBI got the prints and we sent the hair samples to CI&I.

"We got two missing: a woman and a heavyset young man about five feet eleven inches tall, with a beard. We were out to find any young man with scratches on his face."

Bonine looked down at the file and shook his head.

"We never found either of them, or the '47–'52 tan-gray Studebaker with oxidized paint that was seen that night."

At a second briefing Avery was told about a "confession" the cops received. "We think the killer has a pretty thorough knowledge of identification techniques," said Bonine. "He devised a method that would frustrate the best of experts. It went something like this: First he set his typewriter to all caps. Then he made a book of typewriter paper and carbon, about thirteen pages of paper, twelve of carbon. By sending one of the last copies of the letter, he insured that there would be no prints and that the type would be so blurred that identification of the make of typewriter would be tough."

He opened his top drawer and passed Avery a photocopy. "This has never been printed in its entirety before."*

SHE WAS YOUNG AND BEAUTIFUL
BUT NOW SHE IS BATTERED AND
DEAD. SHE IS NOT THE FIRST
AND SHE WILL NOT BE THE LAST
I LAY AWAKE NIGHTS THINKING ABOUT MY
NEXT VICTIM. MAYBE SHE WILL BE THE
BEAUTIFUL BLOND THAT BABYSITS NEAR
THE LITTLE STORE AND WALKS DOWN THE
DARK ALLEY EACH EVENING ABOUT SEVEN.
OR MAYBE SHE WILL BE THE SHAPELY BLUE
EYED BRUNETT THAT SAID NO WHEN I
ASKED HER FOR A DATE IN HIGH SCHOOL.
BUT MAYBE IT WILL NOT BE EITHER. BUT I
SHALL CUT OFF HER FEMALE PARTS AND
DEPOSIT THEM FOR THE WHOLE CITY TO SEE.
SO DON'T MAKE IT SO EASY FOR ME. KEEP
YOUR SISTERS, DAUGHTERS, AND WIVES OFF
THE STREETS AND ALLEYS.
MISS BATES WAS STUPID. SHE WENT TO
THE SLAUGHTER LIKE A LAMB. SHE DID
NOT PUT UP A STRUGGLE. BUT I DID.
IT WAS A BALL.
I FIRST PULLED THE MIDDLE WIRE
FROM THE DISTRIBUTOR. THEN I WAITED FOR
HER IN THE LIBRARY AND FOLLOWED HER OUT

*I obtained a complete copy only with the use of a magnifying glass and a copy of a photo of a desk at Riverside P.D. on which the confession was propped. Narlow could not show me his copy, but proofread mine and said it was correct.

AFTER ABOUT TWO MINUTES. THE BATTERY MUST
HAVE BEEN ABOUT DEAD BY THEN. I THEN
OFFERED TO HELP. SHE WAS THEN VERY WILLING
TO TALK WITH ME. I TOLD HER THAT MY CAR
WAS DOWN THE STREET AND THAT I WOULD GIVE
HER A LIFT HOME. WHEN WE WERE AWAY FROM
THE LIBRARY WALKING, I SAID IT WAS ABOUT
TIME. SHE ASKED ME, 'ABOUT TIME FOR WHAT?'
I SAID IT WAS ABOUT TIME FOR YOU TO
DIE. I GRABBED HER AROUND THE NECK WITH
MY HAND OVER HER MOUTH AND MY OTHER HAND
WITH A SMALL KNIFE AT HER THROAT. SHE
WENT VERY WILLINGLY.
HER BREAST FELT VERY WARM AND FIRM
UNDER MY HANDS, BUT ONLY ONE THING WAS ON
MY MIND. MAKING HER PAY FOR THE BRUSH OFFS
THAT SHE HAD GIVEN ME DURING THE YEARS PRIOR.
SHE DIED HARD. SHE SQUIRMED AND SHOOK
AS I CHOKED HER, AND HER LIPS TWITCHED.
SHE LET OUT A SCREAM ONCE AND I KICKED
HER HEAD TO SHUT HER UP. I PLUNGED THE KNIFE
INTO HER AND IT BROKE. I THEN FINISHED THE
JOB BY CUTTING HER THROAT. I AM NOT SICK.
I AM INSANE. BUT THAT WILL NOT STOP
THE GAME. THIS LETTER SHOULD BE PUBLISHED
FOR ALL TO READ IT. IT JUST MIGHT SAVE THAT
GIRL IN THE ALLEY. BUT THAT'S UP TO YOU.
IT WILL BE ON YOUR CONSCIENCE. NOT
MINE. YES, I DID MAKE THAT CALL TO YOU
ALSO. IT WAS JUST A WARNING. BEWARE . . . I
AM STALKING YOUR GIRLS NOW.
CC. CHIEF OF POLICE
                    ENTERPRISE

That the killer mentioned "the game," insisted the letter must
be published, and called the police about the crime were all
trademarks of the Zodiac killer.

"The killer mailed this letter from a secluded rural mailbox,
unstamped. We never had any doubt that they were from Cheri

Jo's murderer because of the top secret details he included, principally the ripped-out middle wire of the V.W.'s distributor," said Bonine.

The *Riverside Press-Enterprise* ran an article on the Bates case exactly six months after Cheri Jo's death. The following day, the police received a new letter from the killer. Avery was shown a crudely penciled note on a piece of common three-holed binder paper. In large sprawling letters that tilted downward toward the left was this message:

BATES HAD TO DIE
THERE WILL BE MORE

At the bottom of the blue-lined paper was a small number 2 or the letter Z. The envelope carried two four-cent Lincoln stamps, double the postage. The letter had been placed into Cheri Jo's file but had been considered crank mail and not connected with the confession letter in any way.

Avery was left alone to go through the Bates file. He soon made the discovery that there were two other identical "Bates must die" letters. One was addressed to the *Press-Enterprise* and the other, cruelly, to Joseph Bates.

Avery uncovered a photo of a desk top discovered five months after the murder by a custodian at the RCC library in a storage area. It had been defaced with a gruesome poem (reproduced for the first time), five inches deep by three and seven-eighth inches wide, etched into the varnished surface in blue ballpoint pen:

Sick of living/ unwilling to die
cut.
clean.
if red/
clean.
blood spurting
        dripping,
            spilling;
all *over* her new

dress.
oh well,
it was red
anyway.
life draining into an
uncertain death.
she won't
die.
this *time*
Someone ll find her
just wait till
next time.

This was different from the other sick letters the department had gotten since Cheri Jo's death; this one was signed. At the bottom of the bloody verse were two lower-case letters, *r* and *h*.

In conference with Cross, Avery pointed out that the penciled printing on the "Bates must die" notes was similar to the recent blue felt-tip pen lettering of the Zodiac messages to the *Chronicle*, and that the printing on the notes matched almost exactly the writing on the desk top. The reporter was able to convince Cross and Bonine to activate the Bates investigation in association with the Zodiac case.

It was decided that Avery would hand carry the evidence to Sacramento in sealed envelopes (to maintain the chain of evidence) and deliver it to Sherwood Morrill, expert for the Bureau of Criminal Identification and Investigation, Questioned Documents. Avery phoned Morrill at his home and asked to meet him at the Sacramento airport.

Thursday, November 12, 1970

Avery boarded the plane for Sacramento carrying the actual letters and envelopes from Cheri Jo's killer, and a photo of the desk top poem. Morrill was waiting anxiously for him. He did a preliminary examination on the spot. The carbon copy letters were "very dim" and made identification of the typewriter and typeface next to impossible.*

Avery then produced the handprinted pencil letters he had found in the police file. After a moment, the handprinting expert spoke.

"This doesn't look anything like Zodiac's writing," he said.

The expert then looked at the envelope to the penciled message.

"This begins to look alike now," Morrill said.

He stared at the envelope. "Yes, this is what gives it away. The Riverside letters were by the same person who wrote the Zodiac letters in northern California."

Morrill also took the initial at the bottom of the note to be a Z. He said, "I'll get hold of Armstrong and Toschi on this."

But Avery was excited now and left immediately for San Francisco, notifying Armstrong before Morrill could.

Morrill, a consumate technician, also had the forethought to get samples of Avery's own handprinting to check against the printing on the Riverside letters. Avery checked out clean.

Monday, November 16, 1970

Morrill notified Avery that after four days of study he could say that the printing specimens on the letters discovered in Riverside were "unquestionably the work of Zodiac. The handprinting scratched on the desk is the same as on the three letters, particularly like that on the envelopes, and this handprinting is by the same person who has been preparing the Zodiac letters that have been received by the *Chronicle.*"

Avery wrote an article on the findings of his Riverside trip. It was printed in Tuesday's *Chronicle* under the banner: "Zodiac Link Is Definite."

Cross opened the Bates case on a full-scale basis, but said it was

*Morrill later discovered that the typewriter used was a portable Royal, Canterbury, shaded with Elite type.

possible that the "Zodiac was just trying to capitalize on publicity. After all, the letters were received seven months after the killing.

"A suspect had been in jail, is now out on bail, but there has never been enough evidence to convict him of the Bates murder," said Cross. "I'm not a handwriting expert, but it seems to me altogether possible that whoever this Zodiac is he could have read about the Bates slaying, noted it was unsolved, and could have sent those letters to claim credit for it without having had anything to do with it. Please note the Bates girl was killed in October 1966 and those letters came in April 1967. There was nothing in the letters to indicate that our local boy didn't do it."

Thursday, November 19, 1970

Avery wrote another story for the *Chronicle* about a closed conference in Riverside attended by homicide detectives for San Francisco, Sacramento, and Napa. The nine-hour meeting was a direct result of Avery's discovery of what he called "the Riverside Connection."

When the meeting was over, Cross, Toschi, Narlow, and Inspector Mel Nicolai of CI&I were secretive about what had been discussed. Avery was able to discover that the "consensus of the detectives was that at one time Zodiac had close ties to Riverside." Cecelia Ann Shepard, the Berryessa victim, had been a student at Riverside. The most curious aspect of the Bates murder was the lack of a boast from Zodiac, who in the past never failed to quickly brag about his murders. Did he refuse to take credit for Cheri Jo's murder because he had made some slip-up, left some clue behind that could incriminate him?

Because of the desk-top poem, the police knew that Zodiac was in the RCC library "prior or subsequent to the crime." The most obvious blunder on the part of the mass slayer would be the initials at the bottom of the gory verse. Who was "r. h."? Or did the initials stand for red herring? Or did they stand for the blood factor RH?

Tuesday, November 24, 1970

Twelve days earlier, Morrill had received seven handwriting samples of the man Riverside police believed was the Bates killer. Now, he had finished his examination of them.

There was no match.

Friday, November 27, 1970

Police announced that "a state expert has compared our main suspect's handprinting and ruled that it is not the same as Zodiac's. But that does not mean that our local man did not kill the girl. It merely means that the Riverside man is not the Zodiac."

Zodiac

Monday, March 15, 1971

In the period after Zodiac's death threat against him, Paul Avery had gone on local TV and taunted the killer, reassured by the weight of the .38 in a concealed holster under his jacket. On January 3, 1971, after he had to draw his gun to save a vagrant from a knife attack, he began to have second thoughts. "By carrying a gun I was putting myself in a position, where sooner or later I'd have to use it," he told me. "I finally got rid of it."

Four months after Avery exposed Zodiac's "Riverside Connection," the *Los Angeles Times* received its first letter from the Cipher Slayer.

For the first time, the envelope had a non–San Francisco postmark. It had been mailed from Pleasanton, a small town in nearby Alameda County. Once again there was double postage on the envelope, two six-cent Roosevelts inverted, and the exhortation: Please Rush to Editor. The word "AIR Mail" took up one-third of the envelope. It was his sixteenth letter. He had chosen the paper with the largest circulation in California.

As always, he began: "This is the Zodiac speaking."

Like I have always said
I am crack proof. If the
Blue Meannies are evere
going to catch me, they had
best get off their fat asses
& do something. Because the
longer they fiddle & fart*
around, the more slaves
I will collect for my after
life. I do have to give them
credit for stumbling across
my riverside activity, but
they are only finding the
easy ones, there are a hell
of a lot more down there.
The reason that Im writing
to the Times is this, They
don't bury me on the back pages
like some of the others.
SFPD-O ☉ —17+

Some of the Bay Area psychiatrists Avery spoke with felt that Zodiac was claiming new victims only on paper. "Zodiac's boasts of ever increasing totals of 'slaves,' " said one, "may be just that: boasts."

Boasts or not, Toschi and Armstrong still had to do the same backbreaking amount of work.

Near Pacific Union College, a girl's car had been discovered on the White Cottage Road turnout. Two pieces of her gold-colored jump suit were nearby; her portable radio on the car seat was still going. Groups of twenty-one PUC students, Bryan Hartnell among them, began a foot search. As snow fell and the morning temperatures dropped, a bloodhound was brought in. Because of the very rugged canyon area, it was eight days before the body was found. It was only 225 feet away from the abandoned car, near

---

*This phrase, "fiddle & fart around," is an antiquated one and led investigators to suspect Zodiac was a much older man than they had thought. I learned that it is used in areas of Texas, principally around Lubbock County.

Howell Mountain Road, under a layer of brush and logs and a torn barracks bag. It was wrapped in an American flag. The body was badly bruised, and there was the bloody mark of a blow on the left side of her head next to her long black hair. A wire noose had been twisted tightly around her neck. A bracelet she had used as a key ring was found; all of the keys had been taken by the killer. Like Cecelia Shepard, she'd been killed in an isolated wooded area.

Even though the victim, Lynda Kanes, twenty, was the second PUC coed murdered in the last two years, Sheriff Earl Randol assured the students that they were "not marked for murder." Randol told the students that there was nothing to connect Zodiac to this recent murder.

There was a suspect in St. Helena, a search warrant was issued, the man's house was gone over, a number of unidentified articles were removed for inspection. But nothing came of it.

Monday, March 22, 1971

Only a week later, a common four-cent postcard arrived at the *Chronicle*. It was once again addressed to "Paul Averly" and covered with more newspaper cutouts of pictures and phrases.

The phrases "Sought victim 12," "peek through the pines," "pass LAKE TAHOE areas," "Sierra Club," and "around in the snow" had been cut from the newspaper and glued down. Zodiac had decorated the edges with half-moon cuts made by a conductor's punch. Pasted to the back of the card was an artist's rendering of what was later discovered to be an ad for Forrest Pines, a condominium village currently under development near Incline Village on the north shore of Lake Tahoe, Nevada.

Victim number twelve, therefore, may have been Donna Lass, twenty-five, a pretty nurse with frosted blond hair, who had been missing since September 6, 1970, after she left work at the Sahara Hotel in Stateline, Nevada. The casino nurse's car was found parked near her small apartment, but there was no sign of any struggle and only her purse and the clothes she was wearing were missing. An unidentified male caller had told Donna's landlord and employer on the day she vanished that she would not be returning because of an illness in her family. The police were advised by the family that there was no illness; the call was a lie.

By telephone, detectives in San Francisco and Nevada tried to divine the meaning of the enigmatic "around in the snow." And had Donna been killed and buried near the new development? The ad for the condos had run in the *Chronicle* two days before.

Morrill reported to Toschi that the inked words on the address side of the card "conform and are consistent with all other [Zodiac] writings I have examined."

"Since we haven't any other suspect in the case," said South Lake Tahoe Police Chief Ray Lauritzen, "I suppose the Zodiac theory is as good as any. We most certainly are checking into this possibility because of the postcard sent to the *Chronicle*. From the beginning we have believed Miss Lass was abducted and is dead. It is not her character to 'drop out'—she was, in the true sense of the word, a 'good' girl."

Friday, March 25, 1971

The search for the body was postponed because of snowfall drifts, and it was beginning to snow again. No formal hunt for the young nurse's body was really ever made. Donna Lass has never been found.

Toschi wondered if the phrase "Peek through the pines" was an invitation by the killer to look through the pine trees in the drawing and find where the girl was buried. Ominously, in the foreground was a man digging with a shovel.

"No one ever asked me. I was surprised the police never asked me any questions," Donna Lass' former roommate, Jo Anne, told me years later. I had asked her if Donna had any ties to Riverside. She explained that she and Donna used to go flying with two men from Riverside when they lived in San Francisco. The police had never made a connection with Donna Lass and San Francisco.

"Donna and I worked Letterman General Hospital on the

Presidio. Donna was at the Presidio until June of 1970 and then moved to Lake Tahoe and vanished three months later," she confided.

There was the Presidio connection again. Paul Stine was killed near the Presidio and Zodiac vanished into it. If Zodiac had continued northeast, he would have come to 225 Mallorca Way, where Donna and Jo Anne were to live a few months later. Is this near where the killer was living in 1969? Did he meet Donna here, and then months later follow and kill her in another state?

Wednesday, April 7, 1981

I went to see a low-budget film about Zodiac at the Golden Gate Theater. It played only one week and was seen by fewer than a thousand people. A surly teamster (Bob Jones) is an early suspect in the film, but it is a young man (Hal Reed) who is found to be Zodiac. The film ends by hinting that Zodiac may be the man behind you in the theater.

Since Zodiac was a movie fan and an egotist and since the movie played only to a limited audience in San Francisco, the chances he was in the seat behind you *were* pretty good.

Chronicle reporter Duffy Jennings told me of a contest the producers of the Zodiac movie devised inviting moviegoers to win a new motorcycle by filling out cards telling in twenty-five words or less "I Believe The Zodiac Killed Because . . ."

"Thinking the real Zodiac might be curious and vain enough to see the film, a huge carton was set up in the lobby for deposit of entries," wrote Jennings, "and inside it crouched a man who read each card as it slipped through the slot at the top. Ostensibly, he was to alert theater management via intercom when he spotted a suspicious entry from someone claiming to be the actual killer."

Even though no such message was dropped in the slot, the police studied all cards for any similarities to Zodiac's printing.

The best Zodiac movie was made by Warners in 1971. Called *Dirty Harry,* it starred Clint Eastwood as an Inspector Toschi—

type searching for a hooded sniper, "Scorpio" (Andy Robinson). It is faithful to the facts in the Zodiac case and uses an exact copy of Zodiac's printing in Scorpio's letters to the *Chronicle*.

Sunday, April 11, 1971

Dressed in blue jeans and a white blouse, carrying a paperback book and binoculars, Kathy Bilek, eighteen, took the family car and drove to a county park, Villa Montalvo, just outside the Saratoga city limits. She parked her car in the arboretum parking lot and walked to a small stream where she could read her gothic novel and birdwatch in the remote, heavily wooded and untraveled area. This was the same place where two young girls, Kathy Snoozy and Deborah Furlong, had been stabbed over three hundred times August 3, 1969.

While she read, a figure appeared behind her and moved silently through the tall grass until she was within his reach. With a short-bladed knife, he stabbed her seventeen times in the back. As she fell, he struck her another thirty-two times in her chest and stomach, avoiding her breasts.

When the girl was reported missing, the police found her car but were unable to continue the search because of darkness. The hunt for the blond high school student began again at dawn. Kathy's father, Charles, found her body in the first light of morning while thirty sheriff's deputies searched only yards away. She had been tossed into a shallow gully. When searchers combed the area for clues the next day, they found remnants of her bloody clothing.

Santa Clara autopsy surgeons linked the Easter homicide to the 1969 murders of Snoozy and Furlong, calling it a carbon-copy killing.

Two weeks later, police received a description of a suspicious man who frequented the area where the killing had taken place. This led them to a man, Karl F. Warner, with short blond hair and horn-rimmed glasses, who had once attended Oak Grove High School with Snoozy and Furlong and had lived three blocks from their homes. He had also once been a suspect in a knife assault on a woman.

Armed with a search warrant, detectives surprised Werner, a San Jose City College student, studying for a physics exam. They recovered a knife from him and then took the eighteen-year-old to the scenes of the crimes. In September he pleaded guilty to all three knifings and was given a life sentence.

However, Werner was not the Zodiac. He had been a transfer student from Marlborough, Massachusetts, who had moved to California in early 1969 after the Zodiac murders had begun.

Wednesday, March 22, 1972

Armstrong and Toschi had good reason to sift carefully through their mail this morning: it had been exactly one year since Zodiac had written.

They came up with nothing. Toschi, who by this time was becoming increasingly haunted by the case, considered the possibility that Zodiac had been killed in some accident or in the commission of one of his crimes. Perhaps he had moved out of state; maybe he had worked out his hostility and would kill no more. Or he could be in prison. Or in a mental institution. But Toschi could not believe the supreme braggart could go without leaving behind one last taunting message or some incriminating piece of evidence—a gun, knife, cipher table, or at least the remaining portion of Stine's blood-blackened shirt.

Toschi sensed that Zodiac was still alive and waiting.

Friday, April 7, 1972

At about 9:00 P.M., Isobel Watson, a thirty-three-year-old legal secretary in San Francisco, got off the bus in Tamalpais Valley and began walking up Pine Hill. Out of nowhere, a white Chevy swerved at her. The car stopped and the driver leapt out. "I'm terribly sorry," he said, "Please let me drive you home."

The driver was in his early forties, about five foot nine inches in height, and wore heavy black-rimmed reading glasses.

"No thanks," said Mrs. Watson.

The man repeated his request in a very concerned voice, but Mrs. Watson firmly refused. At this, the man flew into a rage and, pulling a short-bladed knife, began to stab at her back. She let out a series of screams; lights went on in all the nearby houses.

Frozen for a moment in the glare, the man raced back to his car and sped off. Neighbors called an ambulance. The woman was rushed to Marin General, where she was treated for her wounds.

"I think it's a good chance it was the Zodiac," said Ken Narlow at Napa P.D., "a better than fifty-fifty chance. I've been chasing the S.O.B. for two and a half years now, and Mrs. Watson's description seems to fit him to a *T*. And it was a Friday night. Every one of his offenses has been on a Friday or Saturday. We're taking a long look at the case. I kind of hope it is him. If it is, it gives us another eyewitness and lets us know he's still around."

Wednesday, July 12, 1972

"The Police Department still has a Zodiac Squad—Inspectors Dave Toschi and Bill Armstrong," wrote Herb Caen in the *Chronicle*. "But it is sixteen months since there has been any action. Even the kook letters are dying out. 'We used to average ten a week,' says Toschi."

For the next eighteen months there were no sightings of Zodiac or any sort of communication from the killer. In spite of tips from all over the United States and Canada, Toschi and Armstrong were frustrated from the years of false leads and dashed hopes. No real major suspect had ever been developed.

Then, after almost three years, the killer wrote to the *Chronicle* again.

Wednesday, January 30, 1974

The postmark on the new Zodiac letter was "940"; that showed it had been mailed from an adjacent county south of San Francisco early the day before.

Armstrong and Toschi raced to the *Chronicle* and read it at the paper:

> I saw and think "The Exorcist"*
> was the best saterical com-
> idy that I have ever seen.
>   Signed, yours truley:
> He plunged himself into
> the billowy wave
> and an echo arose from
> the suicides grave
>   titwillo   titwillo
>   titwillo
> Ps. if I do not see this
> note in your paper, I
> will do something nasty,
> which you know I'm capable of
> doing
>
> Me–37
> SFPD–0

Zodiac had drawn a strange symbol, across the bottom of the page, perhaps a clue to his real identity, or one last slap at the police:

*A hit movie playing only at the Northpoint in San Francisco at this time.

Looking at the "titwillo" line, Toschi said, "Another Gilbert and Sullivan swipe, and another shot at S.F.P.D. Jeez, why does he single us out every time? What's this grudge?" The aria was that of the Lord High Executioner from the second act of *The Mikado*. There was no explanation for Zodiac's long silence. As to what brought him out again, *The Exorcist* was receiving enormous publicity.*

"Of course," said Toschi, "this guy is a real nut on movies. But I'm willing to bet that it'll turn out to be all the fuss from Monday night."

Tuesday morning's paper had been full of the Monday-night random shootings of whites by religiously motivated blacks, in a series of attacks christened the Zebra killings. The most recent had all occurred within a two-hour period between 8:00 P.M. and 10:00 P.M. This had set off an around-the-clock manhunt involving the entire homicide crew. Members of a fanatical cult hacked and shot twenty-three victims over what was to be a 179-day reign of terror. Fifteen were killed; only eight of the victims survived. Five of the killers were eventually convicted and sentenced to life imprisonment.

Toschi had been forced out of a sick bed to work on the Zebra attacks, and now, on top of that, he had Zodiac back. "His timing's lousy," said Toschi. "But at least now I know that everything we've been doing on this case for the last three years wasn't in vain."

The part that really bothered Armstrong and Toschi was Zodiac's notation of thirty-seven victims. He had said he was going to make his future murders look like accidents. What if this maniac had really killed thirty-seven people?

Toschi was going to think about this a whole lot.

Toschi and Armstrong were unaware of it, but for the last four years agents and investigators in the area around Vallejo had been developing the first major Zodiac suspect. Now, a secret report on the man was being prepared.

*Author-producer William Peter Blatty based his 1983 *Exorcist* sequel, *Legion*, on the Zodiac Killer, calling him the Gemini killer.

184

Andrew Todd Walker

April 1970

It was early in 1970 when the police became aware of Andy Walker. (This name has been changed.)

A highway patrolman had become involved in a cat-and-mouse game with a man in a new green Ford. It was a hot day. The two cars were parked on opposite plateaus facing each other, the freeway traffic passing below and between them. The patrolman could tell the Ford driver in the elevated lot across the freeway was watching him. He decided to check the stranger out.

He backed out of the lot and made his way around to an underpass to take him over to the other side of the highway. When he got there, the lot was deserted. He looked across the freeway to the other side, and there was the green Ford parked where his patrol car had been. While the highway patrolman was on his way over, the man had taken the overpass and reversed places with him.

Two days later, the man was back again. This went on for several weeks. The man had done nothing, but the patrolman was curious. On the long, scorching days, the two cars would park facing each other, a stream of traffic roaring between them. Each

185

time the patrolman would cross over, the green car would trade places with him.

One day, the patrolman parked in the lot on Hunter Hill. Suddenly the new, dark green Ford LTD four-door entered the lot, drove up alongside, and parked so close that the door of neither car could have been opened. The patrolman estimated two inches separated the vehicles.

The patrolman couldn't believe anyone would try to pick a fight with a highway patrolman in full uniform parked in a CHP car. He felt the man was staring at him, but decided to ignore him. Finally, he turned to look right at the other driver.

The stranger's deep, close-set, penetrating, blue eyes radiated a glare of sheer hatred. "I've never had such an experience in my life," he told me later. "He was like in an epileptic seizure. That contorted face. Scary."

And that's how the patrolman met Andy Walker.

Walker was a middle-aged man who had an enormous face like a great owl's, and tight, thin lips. Though his hairline was high, he had an abundant crop of hair, going to gray. He wore dark-rimmed glasses, had a potbelly, weighed over two hundred pounds, and stood six feet tall.

In 1971, Vallejo Sergeant Les Lundblad had him in as one of the suspects in connection with the murder of Darlene Ferrin.

Wednesday May 1, 1974

"I've known for a long time who the Zodiac is," said the Mexican-looking black man. "He's not in his twenties or thirties as the police say. This guy is between forty-four to fifty-four and he's gone from his home two nights a week. He always wears Wing Walker shoes."

Three men stood in the evening shadows of a Vallejo stable. One man was the speaker, a civil worker. The other two men were friends, a Napa bowling alley worker and the highway patrolman.

The patrolman did some checking on Walker. He discovered

Walker lived in a remote area. Since Walker had once been a suspect in the Zodiac case and had exhibited such hatred of the police, the highway patrolman was encouraged and continued his investigation.

At the same time, a pretty young schoolteacher got her fourth anonymous phone call at the apartment complex in Vacaville, just southeast of Vallejo, where she lived. It was the same as the others: just the sound of rushing wind on the other end of the line. Frightened, she decided to visit her boyfriend in Dixon near Sacramento on Silveyville Road. She stayed three days. When she did return home, she took the phone off the hook.

On Monday, she came home to find a letter addressed to her.

From the envelope the teacher could tell it was from someone who didn't know her very well. "It's like it is on my mailbox and in the phone book," she shakily told police much later, "Just my first initial and last name." The letter to her read:

> I watch you a lot and call you a lot. I
> saw you in Davis and Silveyville Road in
> Dixon. I'm pretty angry because your telephone
> doesn't ring at night.
> Bad things will happen if you don't let it ring.

The teacher was mystified. The writer mentioned seeing her everywhere save the place she was employed, the elementary school in Cordelia where she taught seventh and eighth grade.

Badly frightened now, the teacher got in her car and drove all the way to El Sobrante to stay with her parents. In the middle of the night, the phone rang at her parents' house. There was only the same sound of wind on the other end of the line.

Saturday, May 11, 1974

The next unsigned letter the teacher got came to her at her parents' house. It read:

187

It's hard to watch you and call when
you have an unlisted number.
I don't like that.

The writer had crumpled up the letter and then carefully and successfully smoothed it out to get rid of the fingerprints. CI&I in Sacramento said the printing in the letters was "very, very contrived" and that the writer was trying to appear to be an eighth- or ninth-grade student by using poor grammar and printing.

The woman who managed the Vacaville apartment building had seen a "dark-green, four-door Ford parked at the rear of the complex," a sloppily dressed man behind the wheel. He had been there for several afternoons. Once in April, he had come to the manager's door pretending to gather information. He asked a few questions and then drove off. "He was very unkempt and had a potbelly. He did not appear very businesslike," the manager said.

The police were interested because a teacher had been receiving letters matching Zodiac's M.O. and a man resembling their strongest Zodiac suspect had been seen watching the complex. Police decided to find out if the man who spoke to the apartment manager was Walker. In itself this would prove nothing more than the possibility that Walker was misrepresenting himself. It would not prove that Walker was writing anonymous letters to the teacher or was Zodiac. Placing him at the apartment building would at least provide a link.

They arranged for the apartment complex manager to see Walker at a weekly meeting he attended. She identified him from a group of twenty-five people. "He's so neat tonight," she said, "but he's definitely the same man who came to my door."

The Vallejo detectives were excited now. The civil worker had made an accusation against Walker as the Zodiac killer, and here was the suspect possibly involved in a case of anonymous threatening letters similar to the Zodiac letters to the press. In addition, police were studying the report on Walker's suspicious activities in parking lots. Zodiac was always connected to cars and parking areas. Police realized that Walker could conceivably be the man who was asking questions about Darlene at Terry's. On their own time, several investigators began looking into this man. (These detectives, two policemen and a federal investigator, have asked me not to use their names.)

A seventeen-page confidential report on Walker was prepared, entitled "What, another Zodiac suspect?" Over coffee at the home of one of the detectives I was allowed to read and copy their report. Over the years I was to run across this report again and again in such disparate places as Berkeley P.D. and the office of a famous female private detective.

Before I left I discussed their report with them in detail. The investigators told me about the photographs that Linda, Darlene's sister, had been shown in San Jose. "She picked out Walker," they said, "The way she put it was that 'He was most likely the same man who was terrorizing Darlene in the months before her death.

"She told us she had seen this man twice. Once in February 1969 (at Terry's) and once in May 1969 (the painting party)."

The detectives were heartened by this.*

I spoke with Linda much later about it. Vallejo policeman Steve Baldino, a close friend of Darlene's, had been at the party and picked out Walker as having been there. "Steve was pretty shook up over all this," Linda said. "He knew the family. . . . He was a really good cop and when Darlene died he went overboard a little bit trying to find her killer."

The detectives had gotten their hands on an NSA cipher computer printout of one of Zodiac's codes and claimed that words that approximated Walker's name were repeated several times in the cryptogram. This evidently was the last line of the Zodiac cipher of July 31, 1969.

"I was swamped out by the rain we had a while back," Zodiac had written. The area of Walker's house was flooded at the time of Zodiac's letter, and the detectives had secured photos to prove it. "Peek through the pines" said a Zodiac card. One of the

*I later learned that others were skeptical that this man was Walker. Darlene's friend, Bobbie Ramos, said she did not believe it was Walker. Lynch told me he did not believe it was Walker either. Finally, Darlene's sister, Pam, expressed doubts that he was the man.

detectives explained to me that Walker lived in a grove of pine trees in an isolated section. "You can't even see the house until you get up close enough to peer through the pine trees which are in long rows."

I looked at the photos of Walker's house that they had taken and saw that the water had come up over the road and had piled banks of mud near the center. The entire area had, I found out when I visited it, in spite of the green pines, a desolate chill to it.

They then began to mention a long list of connections between Walker and the Zodiac murders and letters. "We can connect him to the Sierra Club." Zodiac had mentioned the Sierra Club on the same card he mentioned peeking through the pines.

The investigators had done extensive work on developing a Lake Berryessa connection. On the same day Bryan Hartnell and Cecelia Shepard were attacked at the lake, a stocky man came into Moskowite Corners General Store, across from Pearce's Chevron Service near the lake. He was nervous and was frantically asking anyone who would listen what was the quickest way to leave the lake.

The detectives had located a witness who was having lunch at the general store at the time and who felt the man was acting highly unusual. He had even followed him out of the store and watched him get into a white automobile and drive away from the lake. "He matched the description," they told me, "of a man who had been watching some girls taking a sunbath near where Hartnell and Shepard were knifed. The police never found such a man or the car he was in." I told them I recalled the man seen at the lake was thought to be much younger than Walker.

"We brought our witness an assortment of photos," they continued, "and bang!—he picked our man out. He was the one he had seen at Moskowite Corners. The following Tuesday we took him to a group meeting so he could see Walker in the flesh. He wasn't totally certain that Walker was the same man. Our witness thought that Walker had dyed his hair. He did tell us that Walker's voice was almost exactly the same as the man asking directions the day of the Berryessa murder. And this was about five years after the death of Shepard.

"Unfortunately we lost our witness ten days after he was taken to see Walker. This was in an explosion. The witness' death was ruled an accident."

We all agreed that Walker met the general description of the Zodiac with the exception of age. The detectives had seen an employment form filled out by Walker and noted that their suspect had in the years 1942 through 1945 taught code in the military service. "He taught code for two years. He went right from a seven-month stint in code school to being one of the teachers. He'd have to be pretty bright to do that."

The detectives had checked Walker's records at Social Security and discovered that he had a card not only under his own name but three others. "All of the Zodiac murders and letters were done while Walker was not working and none during the periods of his employment. He is ambidextrous. I've seen this myself," I was told.

The investigators also stressed, "Walker spent considerable time at Terry's Restaurant during the time Darlene was a waitress there. This was just before she was killed. Officer Steve Baldino verified this. We know from DMV that Walker owned a 1961 four-door white Biscayne in 1968. As you know this is a like design to the Impala.

"We know he's actively hostile toward law enforcement." They then told me about the incident with the highway patrolman. "We know that he's altered the way he looks while at the apartment building of a teacher receiving threatening letters. We can connect him with at least two of the murders, he knew Ferrin and may have been at Berryessa.

"Walker is a hot-tempered guy, suffers from painful headaches and has always had trouble working with women on the job. We were told this by his former supervisors."

Walker finally admitted to "spending many hours at Terry's," which of course was no proof that he had been the man harassing Darlene. The detectives then embarked on a series of schemes to get more evidence against the suspect, palm prints.

The investigators had an associate wait near Walker's work place. They had put casts on both of their friend's arms and placed a small and a large goldfish bowl on a storefront ledge.

As Walker approached on the way to work, the associate stepped forward and said, "Excuse me, sir. Can you give me a hand with these fishbowls. My car is just down the street."

Walker looked the man up and down. Then he looked at the two water-filled fishbowls. "I guess so," he said, picking up the large bowl.

Walker hadn't held the fishbowl more than a few seconds when the man shouted, "No. No. I meant the small one." The associate lunged forward, thrust the ends of both casts around the outer surface of the bowl (as to not smudge the prints) and went sprinting off, splashing as he went, and leaving behind a very perplexed Walker.

Unfortunately, because of the water, no part of any print adhered to the glass surface.

The three detectives' next scheme involved tailing Walker. Each weekend night they waited in two autos in a grove near Walker's ranch house. One Friday, as they watched, one of Walker's cars, a '72 Dodge, shot out of the tree-lined driveway, turned right and roared off into the night trailing a column of dust.

Instantly the investigators raced after the bronze car, lights off.

"He knows we're here. Give it the gun. Go as fast as you can." However Walker quickly outdistanced and then lost his pursuers. A half hour later the investigators returned and saw the Dodge parked in the driveway. Walker was leaning against the rear fender, smoking.

The following week the police arranged for Social Security to call Walker in on a pretext in order to gather handwriting samples. When he returned home Walker told his wife about the visit and that he believed that they were trying "to get some sort of evidence" against me. He then told his wife about the ill-fated tailing incident. She reported this to the authorities.

The next morning the detectives were ordered by the judge to "cease their harassment of Andrew Walker" and "close the case against him."

The two investigators felt the odds were excellent that Walker was Zodiac. As they stressed at the conclusion of their report there were only two good reasons why Walker had been refused as a suspect by the authorities up to this point. The first, they told me, was that his handwriting did not match the printing on the Zodiac letters. The detectives felt that not enough exemplars of handwriting had been compared and that the check should be redone. Secondly, Walker's fingerprints did not match the bloody print on the outside of Paul Stine's cab in San Francisco.

The explanation advanced by the investigators was fairly far-fetched but since they felt that Zodiac was a highly demented and warped individual it would not be beyond his method of planning.

"He intended to leave fingerprints," they said. "They were fingerprints but not his own. I can't tell you how he accomplished this. We think it may have been with the use of reverse image prints or with the use of severed fingers from some victim we don't even know about—whatever. He wanted to thumb his nose at the police. He has a special hatred of San Francisco's department. Think about it. In the murder of the San Francisco cabbie he had worked out a meticulous plan. He carried off the killing, ripped off a piece of Stine's shirt to prove he was the killer, wiped down the vehicle, placed a get-away car within walking distance —I can't believe he would slip up and leave prints unless he had planned to."

There was one last bizarre note. The detectives discovered on the posts and poles around the suspect's rural house and on his ranch's back gate hand-painted symbols in color. These were photographed by Polaroid camera and sent to the Department of Justice:

"Enclosed are five photos of various signs photographed in a rural area. Please determine if the enclosed photographs represent signs in witchcraft. If so, please determine what each individual sign's significance is in witchcraft."

193

Experts could not connect them to any known witchcraft symbols.

I showed Walker's photo to the three teenagers who had witnessed the Stine murder. They thought that he was too old to be the killer.

I now believe that Walker is not the Zodiac killer. But up to this point, almost six years after the Lake Herman Road murders, he was the best anyone had come up with.

Zodiac

Wednesday, July 10, 1974

Toschi referred to two new Zodiac letters:

"He's not fooling anybody—no matter what his game is. There's no doubt in my mind about either one. I took them to a documents expert and in less than five minutes he told me positively they were in fact written by the Zodiac. He's trying to slip letters and cards into the *Chronicle* without being detected."

The new messages were handprinted as always, but the spelling and punctuation were correct and no new claims of victims were made.

The first was a postcard that had been mailed in Alameda County on May 8 and had not arrived at the paper until June 4.

> Sirs—I would like to
> express my consternation concerning
> your poor taste & lack of
> sympathy for the public, as
> evidenced by your running
> of ads for the movie
> 'Badlands' featuring the

blurb 'In 1959 most people
were killing time. Kit & Holly
were killing people.' In
light of recent events, this
kind of murder-glorification
can only be deplorable at
best (not that glorification of
violence was *ever* justifiable)
why don't you show some
concern for public sensibilities
& cut the ad?

                    (signed) A citizen

The second letter was mailed July 8, a Monday, from a San
Rafael postbox. Of all the letters this was one of the oddest, a
concoction of neat letters written painstakenly with long, swoop-
ing tails and flowing lines.

Editor—
Put Marco back in the hell-hole
from whence it came—he has
a serious psychological disorder—
always needs to feel superior. I
suggest you refer him to a shrink.
Meanwhile, cancel the Count Marco
column. Since the Count can
write anonymously, so can I—
(signed) the Red Phantom
                    (red with rage)

Anti-feminist columnist Count Marco Spinelli, a former hair-
dresser, quit the *Chronicle* after fifteen years because of this
threat and moved to Hawaii for a life of leisure. He has since
returned.

The only film with a "Red Phantom" in it was currently being
shown at a silent film palace, a theater with a domed ceiling
decorated with a gigantic design of the zodiac. This film was *The
Phantom of the Opera* (1924), starring Lon Chaney.

S.F.P.D. still had not developed a major suspect in the case.

Saturday, July 24, 1976

Armstrong looked down at the body sprawled on the sidewalk on Van Ness, and suddenly all the grueling years of homicide work caught up with him. He quit homicide for good on the spot. The next day, he transferred to the Bunco division. Sherwood Morrill heard there was some friction or dispute with Toschi that has lasted to this day. Both men refuse to discuss it. But basically it had been just one murder too many for the sensitive, intelligent Armstrong.

In Vallejo, Sergeant Lynch told me, "Armstrong seemed to me to be just worn out. He could never sit down and talk to you like this. You had to be walking some place or going upstairs. The guy was just like ready to erupt."

Thursday, July 29, 1976

Herb Caen in his daily column in the *Chronicle:*

> ONWARD: Homicide Inspector Dave (Trenchcoat) Toschi is the only S.F. cop now working on the Zodiac case. He heard last from the killer a couple of years ago when Zodiac criticized "The Exorcist" as "a bad comedy," ending his note with his alleged score as a slayer: ME 37, SFPD 0." Maybe "The Omen" will smoke him out again.

Now that Armstrong had transferred, Toschi was the only San Francisco detective working on one of the most baffling cases in the history of American crime.

"It's quite a challenge. I never let a day go by without remembering Zodiac. Now that I'm the only one working on it," said Toschi, "it's gotten to be more personal. I've got eight filing cabinet drawers filled with Zodiac data—including the names of more than 2,000 potential suspects. I don't know if I'll ever get the case solved, but I'm sure as hell trying. I feel he's out there. I feel he's going to surface."

Toschi's health would suffer from the strain of following an endless maze in search of a pathological killer. Along the way, he would gather fame and the admiration of a great city, and make many powerful and jealous enemies.

Tuesday, May 31, 1977

On March 3, the FBI had requested copies of all the Zodiac letters. Even in 1977, the bureau was still poking about in the Zodiac case.

The top psycholinguistics expert in the country, Dr. Murray S. Miron, working from nineteen of the killer's letters, came to these conclusions about Zodiac in a secret Syracuse Research Institute report: Zodiac "has had some exposure to our training in elementary cryptography" and "is a Caucasian unmarried male in his twenties. He is no more than high school educated, reads little, is isolated, withdrawn, and unrelated in his habits, quiet and unprepossessing in disposition." Miron felt the killer had good eyesight and was "a discretionary illiterate," someone who prefers "the passiveness of pictures, TV, and the movies" and does not even have a library of "cheap pocket books." Zodiac, in Miron's opinion, "would have spent much of his time in movie houses specializing in sado-masochistic and occult eroticism" and was "a borderline psychotic. . . . His communications display the characteristic signs of magical thinking, and narcissistic infantilism typical of the schizophrenic.

"Zodiac rather well fits the pattern of what might be called pseudoreactive schizophrenia. . . . Such individuals engage in their bizarre behavior as sort of a cover-up for their underlying and more hidden psychosis. They can be expected to display wide swings of emotion from intense euphoria to deepest depression.

"He lives the secret life of seclusion and presents to the world a mask of containment, pleasantness and ordinariness."

Miron thought the December 1969 letter to Belli contained hints of the depression that "frequently overtakes him. . . . It is not entirely unlikely that in one of these virulent depressions, such individuals could commit suicide." Because of Zodiac's concern with control, Miron felt he would shun the "disinhibiting effects of alcohol," and would avoid "normal sexual contacts with women."

The "moralism" expressed in Zodiac's letter of 1974 contained "no explicit threat," no "braggadocio," and "uses none of his identifying symbolism. The moralism expressed in that communication is consistant with motivation which could precede a suicide. There is an alternate interpretation of this progressive change in Zodiac. It is possible that the suicide he references is the symbolic death of Zodiac. . . . The sociopathic personality eventually 'burns out' . . . as he ages."

Friday, June 10, 1977

At around ten A.M., a federal investigator was talking to a young woman named Karen at her home in Vallejo. She had been Darlene Ferrin's babysitter in February 1969 and had been the first to see the man in the white car who parked outside Darlene's home on Wallace. Friends had talked her into coming to the police with the information at last.

The investigator and Karen talked over coffee in her living room. Finally the investigator took out his tape recorder, placed it on the glass coffee table, and took out his pen and yellow pad. Even though the conversation was being taped the investigator wrote down every word.

She carefully explained the events of February 26, 1969.

A white American-made sedan had been parked outside the house since 10:00 P.M. A man had been watching the house. Around midnight, he lit a match and she was able to see his face. But only briefly.

"He was heavy-set with a very round face," she told him. "He had wavy dark brown hair. I think he was middle-aged."

Karen said that the next day she mentioned the man to Darlene. "She seemed to know who he was. Darlene told me, 'I guess he's checking up on me again. I heard he was back from out of state.' Darlene told me she had seen him murder someone.

"Darlene mentioned the man's name, but all I know is that his first name was very short, three or four letters, and his second name was just slightly longer.

"The name was quite common. I have a very good mind for names. It's . . . it's . . ."

This is it! the investigator thought. "Take your time, Karen," he said. "We've got all the time in the world."

The investigator waited. He traced over the letters on his pad, shifted his weight in the chair, gazed at the clock ticking on the mantle.

Finally Karen shrugged. "I'm sorry. I just can't remember."

"I've got an idea," said the investigator. "Let me use your phone for a minute." The investigator got in touch with Lieutenant James Husted of Vallejo P.D. to see if a hypnosis session with Karen could be arranged. It would help her remember everything that happened that evening in 1969. Husted said that would be agreeable with him and that he would set it up soon.

The investigator got Karen's permission for the session, and drove slowly back to San Francisco.

Wednesday, June 15, 1977

Lieutenant Husted contacted Lieutenant Larry Haynes, of the Concord, California, P.D., who agreed to help with Karen. Haynes had been trained by the L.A.P.D.'s Law Enforcement Hypnotic Institute. He said the number of years that had passed since the killing didn't matter.

Thursday, June 16, 1977

Karen met Husted at the Vallejo P.D., and at 1:00 P.M. they met Haynes for the hypnotism session in Concord. The session was taped by both audio and video equipment.

"Lieutenant Haynes, after inducing a hypnotic trance," read Husted's report, "explored certain areas of concern, particularly the discussion Karen had with Darlene Ferrin . . . in regard to a person she said that she had once seen murder someone. From that particular questioning, Karen was able to recall a general description of the male in the vehicle. . . .

"The name of the individual was not recalled, although she remembers clearly the conversation with Darlene," continued the report. "She did relate that a phone was ringing. It's felt that this phone ringing is offsetting her subconscience and possibly she's trying to subconsciously suppress the information due to her fears about having to testify in court over this matter."

The federal investigator had his own feelings about this. Husted was a good detective but a brusque man, and the investigator was sure that Karen was unable to recall the name because she was nervous in Husted's presence.

"She was also given instructions that she would remember the face that she perceived in the trance, and that she would assist in producing a composite with a police artist," ended the report.

This was never done.

As head of the Questioned Documents Section of CI&I in Sacramento, Sherwood Morrill was with the Zodiac case from the beginning and remained so even after his retirement. Morrill was the foremost handwriting expert in California, handling up to a hundred cases a month; it was his job to authenticate or reject each Zodiac letter as it arrived over the years. The expert lived for the day he would find a match with Zodiac's distinctive writing. I met often with the tall, dignified, fit student of science and psychology in his south Sacramento office, and we became friends. After thirty-nine years as the state's top handwriting examiner, he retired in December 1972. He had testified in court 2500 times. He was in on the Juan Corona, Angela Davis, and "San Quentin Six" cases. But to him they all paled beside Zodiac.

"Do you think," I asked Morrill, "that the cursive letter *d*'s and checkmark *r*'s are part of Zodiac's real handwriting?"

"I think so. He's been consistent."

"What about that unusual *k*?"

"At first we thought that was consistent, but he got away from it. He made it in three separate strokes instead of the more usual two," said Morrill.

"I've heard that you said if you were standing next to Zodiac at the bank and he were filling out a deposit slip you could recognize him."

"I really believe it. If he printed enough on the deposit slip, I think I'd spot him right away."

"I've heard the paper size on the letters was seven and a half by ten," I said.

"Seven and a half by ten inches," said Morrill thoughtfully. "That's an odd size. That doesn't make sense. Eight and one half is the norm."

I decided to check into that.

The Riverside Zodiac letters were written on teletype paper. Was Zodiac unrolling the stationery like so many kitchen paper towels and then trimming it to size? There were rolls of teletype paper (TTS paper) used in the late sixties for pre-edited copy on newspapers. It is not made anymore. I recalled it as being quite narrow, but a call to AP and UPI told me it wasn't narrow enough to fit the Zodiac letters unless the killer had trimmed the sides as well. TTS paper would point once again to someone connected with a newspaper.

I wondered if the Zodiac could be a printer utilizing odd sizes of leftover paper stock. I called several stationery stores and they told me the letters had been written on a style of paper called "Monarch size"; if I wanted some I had to order a minimum of five hundred sheets that they would cut out of the center of five hundred sheets of regular-size bond paper.

The edges of the Zodiac letters were sharp, clean, and even, and had been cut by a machine at a store or at a factory and not by hand. But each of them was slightly different in size and varied as much as one-eighth of an inch in width or length. No factory put out paper that imperfect, so I had limited the paper to custom-cut stock. The different sizes meant that Zodiac had put in many special orders of five hundred sheets each and used pages from each order.

Somewhere there might be a printer who would remember the man who bought so much Monarch-size bond paper.

Monday, January 30, 1978

"I think he's alive," said Dave Toschi in a *San Francisco Examiner* front-page recap of the Zodiac case. "It's almost a gut feeling. But, if he had been killed in an accident or committed suicide or been murdered, I believe someone would have gone into his room. And I think he would leave something for us to find.

"He got his pleasure by telling us about the murders," said the detective. "My guess is that he hasn't been killing. Ego is what forced him to kill and write letters, knowing the media would broadcast and print it. I think he is in a period of remission and that some symptoms abated. Perhaps during this period, he had no desire to kill."

Tuesday, March 28, 1978

All through the month of March there had been strange stirrings of movement, odd activities that were attributed to cranks.

Toschi looked down at a S.F.P.D. Initial Incident Report, Code 64070: Suspicious occurrence:

TIME OF OCCURRENCE: MON/03/13/78 0700HRS TO TUE 03/14/78 0030HRS
DISTRICT OF OCCURRENCE: TARAVAL   UNIT REPORTING: 311
REPORTING AREA: 422
TYPE PREMISE: HOUSE-SINGLE DWELLING
SUSPECT-1 NOT/KNOWN
ARTICLE-1 (PROPERTY FOR ID): NOTE

NUMBER:1   CATEGORY:30

NARRATIVE
REPORTEE———STATED UPON ARRIVING HOME FROM BABY SITTING SHE DISCOVERED THE ABOVE NOTE *PINNED* ON THE

FRONT GATE WITH A FLOWER. THE NOTE READ "YOU'RE NEXT" (THE ZODIAC KILLERS).
REPORTING OFFICERS: KAWAGUCHI/TODD/L/PTL/1099

Toschi called the woman and reassured her that the note was not from Zodiac because the handprinting was not that of the killer. He advised her to think back on any co-workers or neighbors who might play such a cruel prank on her, tell her landlord about the incident, and to contact him at the HOJ if it should happen again.

Toschi studied another suspicious occurrence from the Mission District.

TIME OF OCCURENCE: MPN 03/13/78 2300HRS
NARRATIVE
REPORTEE———STATED TO OFFICERS THAT UPON PLAYING HIS PHONE MESSAGE RECORDER THIS MORNING, THE MESSAGE WAS AS FOLLOWS: "THIS IS THE ZODIAC, TELL THE PRESS THAT I AM BACK IN SAN FRANCISCO." THE REPORTEE STATED THAT HE HAS NO IDEA WHY THE CALL CAME TO HIM. HE FURTHER STATED THAT HE HAS OFTEN TIMES RECEIVED SUSPICIOUS PHONE CALLS. HE BELIEVES THE CALLS ARE FROM JUVENILES.

Even into April the reports continued to pour in.

TIME OF OCCURRENCE: FRI 05/05/78 0700HRS
LOCATION OF OCCURRENCE: 600 MONTGOMERY ST
NARRATIVE
OFFICERS KELLY AND SIMPSON SENT TO THE TRANSAMERICA BUILDING ON A REPORTED BOMB THREAT. WE WERE TOLD THAT THE SAN MATEO POLICE DEPT. OPERATOR HAD RECEIVED A CALL AT APPROX 1700 HOURS, FROM A MALE CLAIMING TO BE "THE ZODIAC." THE CALLER STATED THAT A BOMB WAS IN THE TRANSAMERICA BUILDING AND WOULD DETONATE.

HEAD OF SECURITY INFORMED ME THAT HE HAD PREVIOUSLY BEEN ADVISED OF THREAT. THE BUILDING HAD BEEN SEARCHED AND FOUND SECURE AT 1730 HOURS. CONTINUING

OBSERVATION OF ALL PUBLIC AREAS, SINCE THAT TIME HAS REVEALED NO SUSPECTED DEVICES.
COPY SENT TO CHIEF OFFICE AND TASK FORCE.

Toschi circled an ad for a performance of *The Mikado* on May 30 and sent it to me. "I wondered if this ad might be noticed by Zodiac, since *The Mikado* hasn't played SF for almost ten years," wrote the detective. "We'll have to watch our mail during that time!" The G & S production would be at the Curran Theatre, 445 Geary Street—only a few feet away from where Zodiac hailed Paul Stine's cab that foggy night so long ago.

I attended all four performances of *The Mikado*, which was playing in tandem with two other G & S productions. Since the cast was British and had never played San Francisco before, I went primarily to scan the audience in search of any of the suspects. I saw none.

I wondered if the return of "The Lord High Executioner" would elicit any sort of response from Zodiac.

Tuesday, April 25, 1978

"See Sergeant Ralph Wilson," said Captain Vince Murphy. "He'll help you out." I was in the sheriff's office just above the jail in Fairfield, California. Murphy was setting up an appointment for me to see the exact site of the Faraday and Jensen murders.

Sergeant Wilson motioned me into his office. He had been thirteen years with the sheriff's department and four with the Vallejo P.D. He was a sturdy, craggy man who reminded me a great deal of the actor Ben Johnson. He radiated a kind of likable authority. He walked me out to his squad car.

We drove down narrow, two-lane Lake Herman Road, past black wood fence posts strung with barb wire. Around each of the curves in the road were cows grazing and scrub and trees casting dappled shadows on the gravel. At night there would be no light at all. We pulled into a rocky clearing in front of a bent steel meshed fence that separated us from a rolling hill, with two triple-decked high tension towers and an observation building small in the distance.

Sergeant Wilson re-enacted for me exactly what had happened almost ten years ago when David and Betty Lou parked in this dark and lonely place, exactly where Sergeant Wilson parked now. Beside the police car was an empty space where Zodiac had pulled his car close to the Jensen station wagon. Wilson showed me exactly where David Faraday's body had fallen outside the right front door of the Rambler.

Getting out my camera, I took ten pictures of the death site. The sun seemed bright and there was a slight breeze. At two in the afternoon the area was not threatening at all. Later, when I developed my pictures, the scene appeared overcast, dark clouds boiling up in the distance and long black shadows on the ground.

Wilson drove me to the Blue Rock Springs parking lot and showed me where Ferrin and Mageau were attacked on July 4, 1969. Then he took me back to his office. I thanked the sergeant and drove back to San Francisco.

Later that evening, as I was preparing to eat dinner and was jotting down some notes, I was startled to hear an excited announcer on Channel 2 talking about Zodiac.

"Good evening! After four years of self-imposed silence the elusive, boastful killer known as Zodiac wrote a letter to the *San Francisco Chronicle* today."

I got in my car and made the ten-minute drive to the *Chronicle*. The photo of the letter was being processed in the art department and a banner headline pasted up.

The headline read: "Zodiac Ends Silence—'I Am Back With You.'"

Dear Melvin

This is the Zodiac speaking I wish you a happy Christmass. The one thing I ask of you is this, please help me. I cannot reach out for help because of this thing in me wont let me. I am finding it extreamly difficult to hold it in check I am afraid I will loose control again and take my nineth & posibly tenth victom. Please help me I am drownding. At the moment the children are safe from the bomb because it is so massive to dig in & the triger mech requires much work to get it adjusted just right. But if I hold back too long from no nine I will loose ~~complet~~ all controol of my self & set the bomb up. Please help me I can not remain in control for much longer.

December 20, 1969, letter from the killer to attorney Melvin Belli. This also contained another swatch of Paul Stine's bloody shirt.

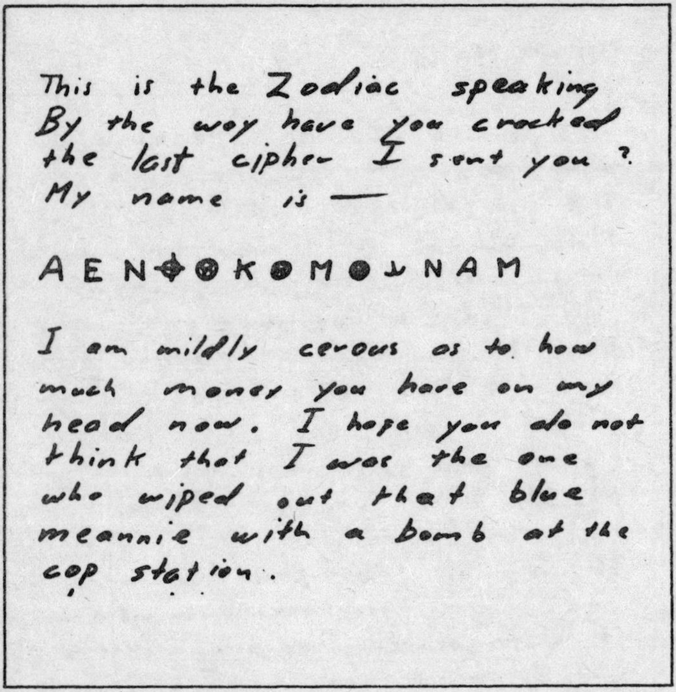

This is the Zodiac speaking
By the way have you cracked
the last cipher I sent you ?
My name is —

AEN⊕⊗K●M●⊥NAM

I am mildly cerous as to how
much money you have on my
head now. I hope you do not
think that I was the one
who wiped out that blue
meannie with a bomb at the
cop station.

Zodiac's name in cipher in an April 20, 1970, letter to the *Chronicle*.

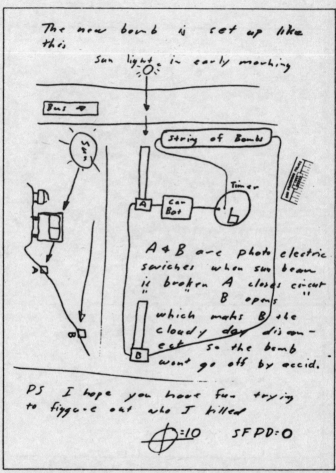

Another bomb diagram enclosed in the April 20 letter. This diagram has never before been reproduced.

April 28, 1970, "dragon" greeting card from Zodiac to the *Chronicle*.

If you dont want me to
have this blast you must
do two things. Tell every
one about the bus bomb with
all the details. & I would like
to see some nice Zodiac butons
wandering about town. Every
one else has those butons like,
, black power, melvin eats
bluber, etc. Well it would cheer
me up considerably if I saw
a lot of people wearing my
buton. Please no nasty ones
like melvin's

Thank you

Letter on the back of the greeting card.

This is the Zodiac speaking

I have become very upset with the people of San Fran Bay Area. They have <u>not</u> complied with my wishes for them to wear some nice ⊕ buttons. I promiced to punish them if they didnot comply, by anilating a full School Buss. But now school is out for the summer, so I punished them in an another way.

I shot a man sitting in a parked car with a .38.

⊕-12   SFPD-0

The Map coupled with this code will tell you who-e the bomb is set. You have antill next Fall to dig it up. ⊕

C △ J I ⬛ O K ⅃ A M F ◢ Ω O R T G
X ⊙ F D V ⅂ ⬛ H C E L ⬥ P W △

Zodiac letter of June 26, 1970, to the *Chronicle*. This included a map of Mt. Diablo.

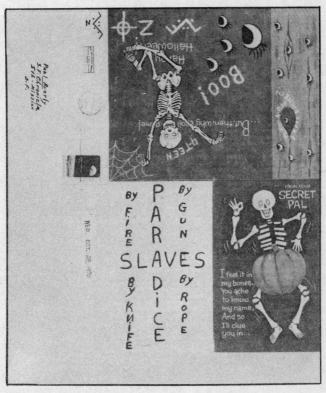

Zodiac death threat card to *Chronicle* reporter Paul Avery on October 27, 1970.

BATES HAD
TO DIE
THERE WILL
BE MORE

2

April 30, 1967, penciled note from Zodiac to Joseph Bates, the father of victim Cheri Jo Bates, in Riverside, California. This has never before been reproduced.

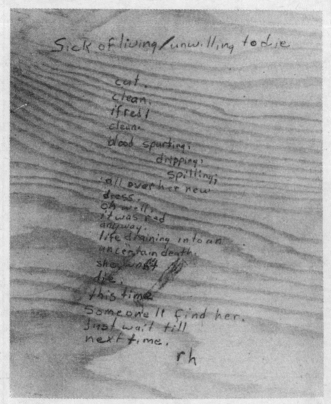

Sick of living/unwilling to die

cut.
clean.
ifresh
clean.
blood spurting;
      dripping;
         spilling;
all over her new
dress.
oh well;
it was red
anyway.
life draining into an
uncertain death.
she won't
die.
this time
someone'll find her.
Just wait till
next time.

rh

Desktop poem (scratched in ballpoint pen) in Riverside City College library, discovered shortly after Joseph Bates received his letter from Zodiac.

April 30, 1967, Zodiac envelopes addressed to Joseph Bates and the Riverside police department. Note the double postage.

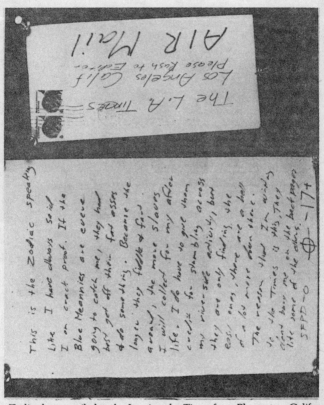

Zodiac letter mailed to the *Los Angeles Times* from Pleasanton, California, on March 13, 1971.

The March 22, 1971, postcard to Paul Avery that linked Zodiac to the disappearance of Lake Tahoe nurse Donna Lass.

I saw + think "The Exorcist"
was the best saterical com-
idy that I have ever seen.

  Signed, yours traley :

He plunged him self into
the billowy wave
and an echo arose from
the sucides grove
    tit willo   tit willo
        tit willo

Ps. if I do not see this
  note in your pape-. I
  will do something nasty,
  which you know I'm capable of
  doing

          Me - 37
          SFPD - 0

The *Exorcist* letter to the *Chronicle*, January 29, 1974.

Sirs - I would like to express my consternation concerning your poor taste & lack of sympathy for the public, as evidenced by your running of the ads for the movie "Badlands," featuring the blurb: "In 1959 most people were killing time. Kit & Holly were killing people." In light of recent events, this kind of murder-glorification can only be deplorable at best (not that glorification of violence was ever justifiable) why don't you show some concern for public sensibilities & cut the ad?

A citizen

May 8, 1974, *Badlands* letter to the *Chronicle*.

Dear Editor
   This is the Zodiac speaking I
am back with you. Tell herb caen
I am here, I have always been here.
That city pig toschi is good but
I am ~~bu~~ smarter and better he
will get tired then leave me
alone. I am waiting for a good
movie about me. who will play
me. I am now in control of all
things.
            Yours truly :

   ⊕ - guess

   SFPD - O

Zodiac returns with his letter of April 24, 1978, to the *Chronicle*.

OKEN	ZODIAC	ASTROLOGICAL MEANING
△	△	TRINE
∟	∟	SEMI-SQUARE
>	>	SEMI-SEXTILE
⊼	⊼	INCONJUNCTION (OKEN'S)
∨	∨	SEMI-SEXTILE (OKEN'S)
☉	☉	SUN
+	+	THE CROSS (MATTER)
O	O	THE CIRCLE (SPIRIT)
·	·	THE DOT
ℭ	ℭ	THE SEMI-CIRCLE (SOUL)
⊥	⊥	THE ROD (FORCE)
<	<	QUINCUNX
∧	∧	QUINCUNX
□	□	SQUARE
♎	♎	LIBRA (BALANCE)
♈	♈	ARIES
♂	♂	CONJUNCTION
P	P	PARALLEL OF DECLINATION
⊕	⊕	PART OF FORTUNE
△	△	
-	-	
●	●	NEW MOON
◑	◑	FIRST QUARTER
O	O	FULL MOON
Φ	Φ	LAST QUARTER
Q	Q	QUINTILE (OKEN'S)

Comparison between horoscope book and Zodiac's cipher symbols. Chart by R. Graysmith.

Zodiac

I looked down at the first Zodiac letter in four years.

> Dear Editor
>   This is the Zodiac speaking I
> am back with you. Tell herb caen
> I am here, I have always been here.
> That city pig toschi is good. but
> I am smarter and better he
> will get tired then leave me
> alone. I am waiting for a good
> movie about me. who will play
> me. I am now in control of all
> things.
>
> > yours truly:
> > ❀ - guess
> > SFPD - 0

The new letter had been mailed on Monday, April 24. Although it bore a San Francisco postmark, notations on the cancellation mark designated a Santa Clara or San Mateo county origin. It may only have been processed in San Francisco and mailed from elsewhere.

It was the killer's twenty-first letter since 1969. Taking into account the carved desk, car door, and Riverside letters, the killer had provided the police with twenty-seven separate written communications.

As usual, it had too much postage, a subconscious attempt by the killer to rush his message. It was received at the *Chronicle* about 2:15 P.M., the same time I was on Lake Herman Road with Sergeant Wilson.

Brant Parker, a copyperson who had only recently returned to the paper, recognized the printing. He gave the letter to Mike Duncan, his boss, and told him it was a new Zodiac letter, the first in fifty-one months. Duncan opened it anyway and screamed for Duffy Jennings, a few desks away. Jennings had taken over the case after Avery had left the *Chronicle*.

Jennings immediately had the letter and envelope photographed by the photo department. He was in the habit of saving up a number of possible Zodiac letters that would trickle into the newspaper and then dropping them off in a bundle to Toschi at Homicide. But Jennings was positive that this letter was authentic, so after trying unsuccessfully to reach Toschi by phone he took the bus the short distance to the Hall of Justice.

Toschi was with his partner, Frank Falzon, trying to serve subpoenas on three bikers who had witnessed a double murder in front of the Jack In The Box restaurant on Seventh and Market Streets, when he heard his code number on the radio and the message to call his office. There was a police call box at Valencia and Twenty-Second, and Toschi got his secretary; Jennings was standing there waiting to talk to him.

"This is the real thing, Dave!" said Jennings. "You'll just go nuts when you see it."

"See what, Duffy?" said Toschi.

"You'll have to come in. I've got to get back to the paper. I'm going to do a story on it. It's very important."

Toschi had a pretty good idea of what was waiting, just from the excitement in the young reporter's voice. He rushed back to his office.

"Deputy Chief DeAmicis wants you in his office," said Toschi's secretary. It was now 3:00 P.M.

The detective saw the familiar plastic evidence envelope on the Deputy Chief's desk and the blue printed letter inside.

"I want you to see this," said DeAmicis. "What do you think?"

Toschi was so excited that he could only see a word here and there. The detective was having a hard time focusing on the message as a whole.

"This looks real good," said Toschi.

DeAmicis hadn't been with Homicide in the late sixties when Zodiac had kept the city in terror. This excitement over a single letter was new to him.

Toschi got on the phone to John Shimoda, head of the Postal Service crime lab in San Bruno.

"John, I've got a possible Zodiac letter. How much longer are you going to be there?"

"Only 'til about four-thirty."

"Give me twenty minutes. I'll be right there."

With the letter still in its plastic envelope, Toschi made six Xerox copies, three for himself and three for DeAmicis. There was always the possibility Shimoda would want to keep the letter overnight.

As Toschi swept past a desk, he shook out a Pall Mall from a package, and lit it. Halfway down the elevator he snatched it out of his mouth. "What the hell, I don't smoke anymore!"

He got to Shimoda by 4:10 P.M.

Using tweezers to carry the letter, the handwriting expert walked to the center of the room, where he had a box of eight-by-ten-inch photos of Zodiac letters written up to 1973. After thirty minutes, he looked up.

"I'd say he's back."

"Are you sure?"

"That's your man," said Shimoda. "He's back."

"I'll need a note from you saying so. The *Chronicle* will be running a story no matter what," said Toschi.

"It's sure enough his writing."

Toschi called DeAmicis from Shimoda's private office and told him the letter had been authenticated. When he got back, he called Duffy Jennings directly from the police garage and told him, "Yes."

"It had been a long four years," said Toschi. "I could feel the excitement in my body."

Even though the *Chronicle* had photos of the letter and envelope, they held back from printing an actual picture of the message, in order to cooperate with the police. S.F.P.D. did not want to reveal how little of the letter they were holding back—the closing line.

Toschi went directly to DeAmicis' office. "What are you going to do with the original now?" asked DeAmicis.

"I'm going to take it down to the photo lab."

The letter was photographed in Toschi's presence. "I wasn't about to leave it," he told me later.

Ten photocopies were also made for other law enforcement agencies. Then Toschi personally took the letter to the crime lab, gave it to print expert Ken Moses, told him it was an authenticated letter from Zodiac, and asked if he could try and get some prints off it. Moses sprayed it with Ninhydrin, but nothing usuable appeared. "I'm going to wait until morning and use a silver nitrate solution to bring out anything the Ninhydrin might have missed," he said. The tests all proved negative. The letter was booked into the property clerk's office the next day.

Nine-thirty found DeAmicis at a televised press conference reading the new letter, written on the blackboard behind him. "It doesn't appear to be threatening in its context. . . . The tone is very, very different from the letters that have been received in the past," said DeAmicis.

The newspeople were on Toschi the minute the official press conference was over. He told them that the police would be sending copies of the new Zodiac communication to all counties involved, and that tests made so far showed no prints or clues on the letter and envelope.

Saturday, April 29, 1978

Analysis of the killer's letter and speculation about his whereabouts for the last four years saturated the news for days, but Toschi was aware that a very tight rein was being held on him. He was assigned a captain to monitor his interviews with the media. Toschi was puzzled by this. I had my own theories on the subject. Toschi had been asked by the city's Italian community to run for sheriff, and one city supervisor, planning on a bid for the mayor's seat, had him down as her choice for police chief. Intelligent and successful, Toschi was now focused in the public eye since the new letter had singled him out.

DeAmicis, in reaction to the new Zodiac letter, pulled Inspector Tedesco from Special Investigations and Inspector James Deasy from the gang task force and assigned them to the case. "Tedesco will coordinate the effort," said DeAmicis, "Toschi will continue to be chief field investigator, while Deasy will analyze the data police have assembled." By taking control of the investigation from him, Police Chief Charles Gain, through DeAmicis, could control Toschi's access to the media.

Toschi was also aware that someone was going through his papers. Was this an effort to get something to use against Toschi should he prove a political threat?

When reporters asked why Toschi was not put in charge of the effort, DeAmicis said, "It's impossible for a detective to administrate and investigate at the same time."

Toschi was uneasy. He was a sensitive and observant man, and he felt that something was wrong.

Friday, May 5, 1978

"That city pig toschi is good but I am smarter and better he will get tired and leave me alone," Zodiac had written in his new letter. Why had the killer singled him out of all the counties and policemen involved? Had he seen the detective on TV, or read something about Toschi that aroused him or frightened him? Had the investigator come close to discovering the maniac? Was Zodiac's true name in one of the manila envelopes in Toschi's filing drawers, a man already cleared or questioned?

"Do you think I should be concerned he mentioned me?" Toschi asked me.

"Be careful," I said.

Wednesday, June 14, 1978

Duffy Jennings came over to my desk while I was drawing the next day's editorial cartoon and told me that a confidential meeting had been arranged with Ron Pimentel of Oakland's Roper Detective Agency and an Oakland policeman versed in handwriting identification. They had what they thought was a hot piece of handprinting relating to Zodiac and wanted our opinion on the sample, as well as a peek at the *Chronicle*'s copies of the letters.

There was only one proviso for the meeting: "Don't tell Toschi." The Oakland cop wanted to keep his theory secret from his boss.

Thursday, June 15, 1978

Over the phone, the Oakland men would give us only the suspect's first name. He promised to give us the last name only after we gave him our opinion of the seven pages of writing samples they were to bring with them. The meeting had already been delayed three times, and Duffy was getting disgusted.

The Roper detective had gotten onto the man's trail after the suspect attended the Zodiac movie three times and the theater management had caught him masturbating in the john after the most violent scenes. The Oakland men were able to get a fix on him because he dropped his name and address in the box at the Golden Gate Theatre to win a motorcycle by telling in twenty-five words why Zodiac kills. Tom Hansen, the movie producer, had pledged $100,000 to the Roper Agency if they caught Zodiac, the reward to come from the profits the Zodiac movie would make from the capture. The major motive for the Oakland policeman's involvement was not the money, however, but the credit for the arrest of Zodiac.

Inspector Toschi's theory had always been that Zodiac got his sexual satisfaction from masturbating while he wrote.

After the meeting was postponed again, I decided to find out who their suspect was, based on the information we had already gotten from them. From their conversations, I knew he lived somewhere in Santa Rosa, kept a locker in San Francisco, was a Vietnam vet, worked as a mechanic, and was from St. Louis.

I found him in my file of suspects.

He had been checked and cleared by Toschi and Armstrong.

The next day I finally saw the handprinting samples. They were not like Zodiac's writing.

Monday, July 10, 1978

One day before Dave Toschi's forty-seventh birthday, after twenty-five years with the department, eighteen of them as a star of the elite homicide bureau and nine of them chasing the elusive Zodiac, his entire world fell apart.

"Shocker in S.F. Zodiac Case" read the headlines in the *Oakland Tribune*.

At 4:55 P.M., Chief Gain issued not only a press release announcing Toschi's transfer from Homicide to Pawn Shop Detail, but also a second press release doubting the authenticity of the new Zodiac letter, stating that other experts would now examine it.

A complaint, dated June 6, 1978, had been filed by Armistead Maupin, a *Chronicle* columnist, and his public relations man, Kenneth Maley, against Toschi. Maupin and Maley felt that the latest Zodiac was similar in "tone" to some anonymous fan letters Maupin had received praising Toschi, and they thought Toschi had written them. In Maupin's popular serial, "Tales of the City," Toschi was featured as an adviser to the ficticious character, "Inspector Tandy," whom Toschi eventually arrests as the infamous Zodiac-like mass slayer "Tinkerbell."

The evening television news spoke of "a big political battle with a veteran cop in the middle." Governor Jerry Brown's office offered "ex-Homicide Inspector Toschi any assistance he may need in his case."

Duffy Jennings reached Toschi at home. The detective freely admitted writing three letters praising himself to Maupin in 1976.

"It was a silly mistake," said Toschi. "He made me the hero of the story and it was fun for me and my family. So I sent some notes, three or four, saying how good it was that he put a real-life homicide inspector in the column. It was kind of like sending fan mail to myself. It was done in a harmless way. I didn't think anyone was going to be hurt by it. Any suggestions that I faked a Zodiac letter are absolutely absurd.

"When Chief Gain told me that state documents experts had checked my handwriting against that of Zodiac's over the weekend, I was shocked. I wrote no Zodiac letter. The fact that Zodiac mentioned me by name for the first time disturbed me and my family very much. I was very unnerved by it."

Sherwood Morrill, who had formally held the post of state handwriting examiner for CI&I, was enraged by the treatment of Toschi. "The last letter was by the real Zodiac. There is no question in my mind. I've heard they're accusing Toschi of writing them. If Toschi wrote the last one, he's the Zodiac. He wrote them all."

John Shimoda, David DeGarmo, Pleasant Hill handwriting expert, and Morrill had all agreed the new Zodiac letter was real.

"I won't work on any Zodiac matters for the San Francisco department from now on," Morrill said. "Armstrong and Toschi made the first contact with me and I was doing it for them. I think Toschi's had too much publicity and some people may not like it."

A silence descended over the Hall of Justice as furtive officials and Toschi's jittery colleagues in Homicide were barred by Chief Gain from discussing the Zodiac controversy.

Carol Toschi showed me into their living room. I saw Dave in a maroon bathrobe just getting up from his chair. It looked as if every bone in his body ached. He was completely exhausted, almost trancelike, with dark circles under his eyes, a shadow of a beard giving his face a bleak look. He had been ill in 1977 with a heart condition and pneumonia at the same time. It was apparent Carol feared for his health.

"Look, Dave," she said, "he's brought you some books. Here's one on the Big Bands."

Across the room I could see Channel 2's ten o'clock news and I figured Toschi had been watching Maupin's press conference. Nodding toward the set, Toschi said, arms outstretched, "I don't understand what I've done to the man." He put his arm on my shoulder. "I hope you haven't lost respect for me."

"Of course not," I said.

"Now they're saying I forged the last Zodiac letter," he said.

Toschi told me that last Friday at 11:00 A.M. he had been called in by DeAmicis to respond to the complaint and been told to think it over. At 1:00, he was interrogated concerning the allegations.

On Saturday at 3:10, DeAmicis came to the Toschi home and explained that Gain had decided to treat the matter administratively, instead of a formal charge before the commission. Toschi was to be transferred effective Monday; a press release was to be drafted saying Dave had written three letters to Maupin two years ago and signed other names. "Why should there be a press release just because I'm being transferred?" asked Toschi.

Chronicle columnist Warren Hinckle, the colorful eye-patched muckraker, wrote that "a go-getting writer and his side-kick publicist got the cops and the press to jump through a publicity hoop. . . . Maupin made himself famous this week at the expense of Dave Toschi, a decent cop with a weakness for seeing his name in the paper. . . . The whole thing was a set piece of ruining a man's reputation by innuendo. Police Chief Charles Gain couldn't restrain himself from issuing a press release which in effect sentenced Toschi to trial by media before the handwriting experts could have a go at divining the truth."

Toschi told the *Examiner* that "linking those notes with the accusation of forgery made me look guilty to the public of forging the Zodiac letters. The mind naturally leaps from one event to the other. . . . A theory has been suggested to me—namely that Maupin and Maley, the only people to gain anything from destroying me, set the police department up . . . to stage a media event that would call attention to Maupin's article and his book.

"Imagine that—a free-lance writer and his publicist says something about a 'similarity of tone' and twenty-five years of hard work goes down the drain! Can a man be destroyed because of vague accusations about 'tone'? You bet he can!"

I looked at my notes about Toschi's career: How he dove into the surf by the Cliff House and dragged a woman out, how he saved three people from gas fumes in 1953, gave lifesaving first aid to a stabbed bartender in 1956, disarmed a disgruntled employee, and cracked a Reno murder in less than three hours. I saw how Toschi had almost been killed by twin shotgun blasts from a window in the Mission and how he had charged up two flights of stairs, kicked open the door, and arrested two youths.

When Toschi went in to clean out his desk, he learned that they had taken his address book to check his handprinting. Supervisor Dianne Feinstein spoke out after a visit to Toschi's home, where he was put under medical care, "It's appalling. This man is being unjustly crucified by the department without substantiation in a way that I have never seen another case handled."

A week after Toschi's transfer, Gain stated that Toschi had not written the Zodiac letter but he felt neither had the real Zodiac. He still considered the *Exorcist* letter of 1974 genuine.

Morrill and DeGarmo felt that Gain had sabotaged any Zodiac trial in the future.

On August 2, Gain made public for the first time the reports of three handwriting experts. Shimoda, forbidden by his superiors to discuss the Zodiac case, reversed his earlier authentication because he had worked "only from photo copies" before. Terry

Pascoe, a former student of Morrill's, said it was a forgery. Pascoe's boss, Robert Prouty, had been the one to originally cast doubt on the letter. Keith L. Woodward of L.A.P.D. agreed it was a forgery.

"But," said Gain, "the writing is manufactured by someone that knows a great deal about the background or the Zodiac's M.O. They knew every little detail of how he wrote."

If Zodiac did not write the new letter, then who did?

Saturday, August 5, 1978

Over vacation, I took a long look at the April Zodiac letter. The writer had correctly used double postage, inverted the stamps, printed "Please Rush to Editor" with a downward slant, placed the odd punctuation of a colon after "yours truly," used no punctuation after the salutation, and put everyone else's name but his own in lowercase. The letter contained Zodiac's strange spacing between words and letters and used a style of *d* and three-stroke *k* used in 1969.

If the new letter was a fake and was done outside of S.F.P.D., what sort of information would be available to a forger without access to the original letters?

I carefully clipped every letter and envelope reprinted in the newspapers to see just how much information the general public had been given about the writing of the letters. Most letters had never been reprinted; those that were were cropped or reduced in size. The author of the letters was someone who had seen all of the letters, since character formations not used for nine years were in the message.

One thing did bother me: the phrase "that city pig" had not been used before. Zodiac usually called the police "blue meannies" or "blue pigs." The second time I went through the letters, I found that phrase, very small and upside down, in the October 5, 1970, postcard: "city police pig cops." It was hardly the line a forger would reach for in composing a phony letter. But it was a line that would be in the killer's memory.

If it were a forgery, no one outside of the police investigation could produce such a perfect copy, incorporating information never before released. For a jealous insider the motive would be to discredit Toschi. But the forger would have no way of knowing that the letter would ever be found false.

The weather this evening was warm and a shaft of strong sunlight cut through the picture window. I had laid out reproductions of all the Zodiac correspondence on the rug and, taking advantage of the illumination, I held the April letter over copies of earlier Zodiac communications to see if there were any interesting contradictions. There were none.

I took the photocopy of the April letter, tore it neatly in half, and began matching lettering on the top part with lettering on the lower half. They matched perfectly. A little too perfectly. It was as if the writer had used a set of rubber stamps to print the note. No one writes like that.

Was the April letter traced and had Zodiac not returned as I thought? I knew it was common for Zodiac to stop in the middle of a carefully drawn communication and cross out a word, just as he did in the new letter. Why not just redo the letter? It was almost as if he were not writing words but laboriously printing one single character after another.

I tore one of the earlier Zodiac letters in half and held the halves over each other against the intense light. Suddenly, I realized how the Zodiac letters had been done.

The procedure used was probably this:

Zodiac photographed onto a strip of 35-mm film individual letters of the alphabet collected from a variety of sources, such as friends or people that he worked with. The film strip was placed into a photographic enlarger, and each individual character was projected from above by the enlarger one at a time onto the paper and traced with a blue felt-tip pen. A light table, a table with a glass top illuminated from below to make tracings, might be used in tandem with the overhead projector. The size and slant of the individual characters could be changed by a simple touch of the enlarger or turn of the paper.

In using an overhead projector, Zodiac could produce handprinting that was not his own but a conglomeration of other peoples' handprinting.

The process would be agonizingly slow. This would explain why, in writing his first letter in more than three years, the killer had scratched out words in a neatly drawn letter rather than start over. The killer would have had to have access to a private photo darkroom for the considerable periods of time it would take to draft one letter.

In using this ingenious process, the killer totally altered his handprinting. The police could check his natural writing and still find no connection to the Zodiac letters.

Zodiac had left clues to his untraceable technique all through his letters. The fact is inescapable that not even a professional artist could lay out 340 cipher symbols so neatly in block form, each character identical in size and slant, without some sort of projected grid.

Somewhere a master alphabet must exist so that future letters could be penned.

I was sure that the technique used on the new letter provided the one link that all the communications had in common. The April letter *was* from Zodiac. He was back!

Sherwood Morrill confirmed my theory.

Donald Jeff Andrews

Wednesday, August 9, 1978

"I can tell you who Zodiac is," said the anonymous voice on my phone on the evening of August 9, 1978. "He's so full of movies he has a record of his activities on film." Jack Rosenbaum in the *San Francisco Progress* had mentioned I was investigating the Zodiac case. The caller got my name from that.

The caller refused to give me his name, but agreed to my taping our conversation. He went on with his story.

"I have a mutual friend, Greg, who is a ham radio operator who talked to this man at night. He's a guy named Don Andrews.* Back in 1969 he was coming out of a period of deep depression.

"Well, if there's anyone who could be the Zodiac, then it is this fellow, Andrews. My friend Greg told me about him, and I told him he was all wet. But as the years have unfolded, we keep finding out things about Andrews that fit, nothing that doesn't."

The caller then told me that Andrews was the man Narlow in Napa was interested in.

"I don't know why Narlow has held back. I'm convinced that

*Both names have been changed.

he doesn't know what to do. Narlow spent six hours with Andrews one day. Don just talked a mile a minute. Narlow told me, 'He had me so confused I couldn't even write a report when it was over.' This guy takes over when you're around him and talks.

"He's not in bad health. I've seen him since '72. But his eyesight is poor. I wouldn't be afraid of him. I'm six foot three. He would be more terrorizing than physically threatening. His mind would scare you more than his physical strength.

"At an early job he was let go because he couldn't get along with people. He had access to the weather teletype there. I don't know why he got interested in weather.

"Narlow keeps Don's file locked in his desk. All the other suspects out in the open in other places.

"He relates strongly to Lon Chaney. He's got kind of a rounded back like the hunchback.

"One person, Marvin Bernell,* has spent a lot of time with Don. He's storing some old film cans for Andrews and that's where we think the evidence of the Zodiac murders is at."

"Does Bernell know this?" I asked.

"No. He thinks he's just storing a bunch of old film cans, 35-mm. Don told him, 'Don't go close to these. They've got nitrate film in them. They might explode'—which is true. We had seen these canisters at the theater that Bernell runs. The next time Greg and I went down we found they were gone and then discovered that they had been moved to a vault behind red curtains in Bernell's home.

"Do you understand? What we think is that there is evidence from each particular murder and one can has a booby trap with an explosive if you open it up.

"Get to Bernell and be friendly with him to find out. I have some misgivings about him. He's an ex-cop. Probably he suspects nothing. Talk to him. See if he tells you to stay away from part of his film collection. He hauls film back and forth for Don. Andrews lived on Scott Street in San Francisco in the late sixties."

I learned that Paul Avery had been on to Don Andrews and

---

*Not his real name.

at one point had sent his girlfriend around to get handwriting samples. Andrews heard that Avery had been asking around about him and actually had come down to the *Chronicle* to tell him to lay off. The samples Avery had, only "three or four words," did not look like Zodiac printing, but with my new knowledge I realized this did not eliminate Don as a suspect.

"Toschi knows about him," the caller told me.

"Toschi cleared him because when he went to Don's home there was a grisly handprinted sign in the window and it didn't match the Zodiac's printing. Toschi thought it was a big joke."

The caller told me that Don was raised by a stepmother, his father was very religious, and there were family problems.

The caller spoke with me long distance for over an hour. He read to me from notes; I could hear the pages as he turned them. The most promising thing I heard was that he had a thirty-by-forty-inch felt-tip–pen movie poster that Don had done for his friend, Bernell.

After he hung up, I thought for a while. He had known a little too much about the case.

And he had called me at an unlisted number.

Saturday, August 26, 1978

I went to visit Sherwood Morrill in the sweltering heat of Sacramento. A vigorous man, clad in a sports T-shirt, he settled back in an easy chair while I turned on my tape recorder and asked him a few questions. After a while he asked me to turn off the machine. He wanted to tell me something that happened last month, and it was something he didn't want on tape at this time.

"A big guy and his wife in a V.W. drove up," he said, "and asked my wife, Rose, if they could see me. 'I'm real interested in the Zodiac case. I've got some news for Mr. Morrill,' said the man, 'that will make him and me sleep better. I'm only a citizen. I spent a great deal of time coming down from Yountville. It's about that letter. I know it's from Zodiac and not Toschi.'

"Well, I was at lunch with Dave DeGarmo, another handwriting identification expert, he's with the Public Defender's Office now. The couple seemed greatly agitated and Rose told them I wouldn't be back from lunch until 2:30 and they said they would wait.

"When I got back," continued Morrill, "he and his wife both came in. He said his name was Wallace Penny." (The name of this person has been altered at his request.) "His hands were shaking. He's nervous as all hell. He tried to top me every time I mentioned something about Zodiac. He says, 'Wait til you hear this!' He had a great big theory. 'I'll only take five minutes of your time,' he said. He took an hour and a half. He told me, 'Mr. Toschi would sleep better tonight' and then he told me the name of the man he thought was really the Zodiac."

At this point I stopped Morrill and asked him if he would tell me the name of the suspect. He began the name and I finished it for him.

"My God," I said, "that's the name of my suspect! Don Andrews."

It was also the name of Ken Narlow's mystery suspect.

The handwriting samples the couple brought Morrill matched up pretty well with Zodiac printing, with the exception of the letter *K*.

The couple knew many details only the killer should have known. Morrill told his wife after they'd left, "If Don Andrews isn't the Zodiac, then it could be them."

Rose Morrill had shivered, looked at her husband, and whispered, "You might have just shaken hands with the Zodiac!"

"And you know, Robert," said Morrill, "I had the feeling that the man wanted to confess to something."

Tuesday, August 29, 1978

I drove to Vallejo to speak with Lieutenant Jim Husted, head of the Intelligence Section of V.P.D. He was excited about the possible return of Zodiac and promised to show me two of their suspects.

Husted took a file out of a metal cabinet behind his desk. He began to tell me things about this first suspect—his interest in films, his code school training, the unusual items kept in his home. "This man was given a speeding ticket in his white Chevy at Tahoe at the time Donna Lass disappeared," he told me.

I recognized the man as Andy Todd Walker, the first major Zodiac suspect.

Friday, August 25, 1978

By phone I spoke to Wallace Penny, the man from Yountville who had so upset Morrill on July 5. I instantly recognized his voice. He was the same man who had tipped me off anonymously about Ken Narlow's suspect, Don Andrews.

What I learned from Penny was that Andrews was "nervous, frenetic, and temperamental and often exhibited hostility toward sex. However, he seems to have had a female friend.

"He's a Gilbert and Sullivan fan and has quoted lyrics in front of friends," Penny said.

Not only had Andrews had code training, but he had a sewing machine in his home. Was this the answer to where Zodiac was able to get a personalized black hood?

Penny told me that Andrews had showed him blueprints for Zodiac's 1969 school bus bomb based on plans in a book he owned. The Zodiac bomb plans were never printed anywhere.

"Don Andrews collects classic films," said Penny.

The crossed-circle symbol of the Zodiac could be inspired by the projectionist symbol on the film leader.

"Don is ambidextrous. He has told his friends, 'I may look O.K. on the outside but inside. . . .' This parallels Zodiac's statement, 'I'm insane but the game must go on,' " Penny told me.

Zodiac and Andrews both wear glasses that are held on by a band.

According to Penny, Andrews has been known to confide to his friends, "What I have is better than sex."

"Not only that," Penny continued. "Andrews has used so many

names that Social Security asked that he settle on one. Andrews started for Montana in 1961 with a teenager named Jim to apply for a new birth certificate. When he reached Montana, he put his name down on the certificate as Jim Andrews."

Andrews was the only suspect who had any sort of elaborate photo darkroom. He kept a teletype machine in his home. Teletype paper had been used in the first Zodiac letter. I remembered what Ken Narlow, the Napa detective, had told me, "I've got a lulu on Don. Down in his basement he has a teletype machine, a Model 15 AP Teleprinter. I tell you, Robert, there's no question in my mind that whoever drew up the article on the bomb" (Zodiac's November 1969 school bus bomb diagram) "has got to have definite knowledge of that teletype printer." Narlow had shown me the comparison between a photo of the teletype machine's armature rotation system and brush contacts and the killer's schematic drawing of the explosive device.

Zodiac's costume combined naval elements such as bellbottom pants, military shoes, and nylon windbreaker. Andrews was a Navy man.

One month before the first Zodiac letter done in handprinting, Andrews began a friendship with a man named Marvin Bernell. After Andrews and Bernell met, the Zodiac messages were printed in a style of handprinting very similar to that Bernell used in printing black-felt-tip movie posters at his theater. Perhaps Andrews had copied Bernell's style.

Once again, Penny mentioned that he and his friend Greg thought that evidence of the Zodiac killings was in a film canister in Bernell's film vault. "Stine's shirt, sets of car keys, and maybe a film of the Lake Herman Road murders are in that film can. It's marked clearly on the side: 'Do Not Open, Nitrate Film, Danger.'" Penny said he had seen the canister when it was in San Francisco. Perhaps the police had not checked it because Bernell had moved to southern California, where he had a theater.

Saturday, August 26, 1978

I drove to Andrews' place.

No sooner had I gotten over to Don's mailbox than a big man came running over shouting, "What do you want?"

"I was looking for Don," I said, although it was obvious no one was living there now.

"He's not here, he's in San Francisco."

"Damn," I said, reaching for a pen. "What's his new address?"

"If you're a friend find out his address!"

The guy stood there with his hands on his hips until I drove off. I got the feeling I had been expected.

Even though Narlow was unable to establish any sort of proficiency with weapons as far as Don Andrews was concerned, he had told me that "Don is still my best bet."

I had asked him about the prints.

"We had his prints checked. We never brought him in, actually, never asked to roll his prints. We never had enough cause to do it and I'm not sure he would have consented. He might have. The more we started leaning on him, the more naturally defensive he got. The first couple of times we talked to him he was very open. Then it got to the point where he said, 'Either do something or leave me alone.' The first time we went to his house over by the water, we were there several hours. Very intelligent person, very interesting person. He didn't seem to mind talking about his past."

Monday, August 28, 1978

Penny had told me that Don Andrews was "full of movies" and had once worked at a small cinema in Southern California with his friend Marvin Bernell. Bernell had once been a silent movie organist. Their friendship had lasted from early 1967 until the present. Penny had never gotten up enough nerve to approach Bernell and find out if he knew any information about Zodiac or a link to the vintage film theater.

It was night when I arrived in L.A. I took a rental car from the airport to the theater on North Highlands Avenue to see if Bernell was anywhere around. There were no silent films tonight, but Bernell was at the cinema to see part of the 3-D movie being shown.

Even in the blackness of the loge seats I could pick out Bernell from the front row. Because of the black leather jump suit he wore, he seemed to have no body. He reminded me of the giant head of Oz floating in midair.

I went up to him during intermission and started up a conversation. He began to talk a mile a minute, with bold flourishing gestures. An almost Barrymore profile made him one with the old films he had once accompanied on his giant Wurlitzer Pipe Organ.

He was a portly man with a face that, in his sixties, was beginning to grow fat. He had an eye problem, and in order to write his home address he had to put on his dark-rimmed glasses.

"I can't see without glasses," he said. "I'm going to be on vacation and do a little business, but I'll be back in September."

Friday, September 1, 1978

I made the drive to Sacramento to speak with Morrill about the comparisons between Don Andrews and Zodiac.

"Well," said Morrill, "I've talked about Don Andrews with the guy who's the chief special agent of CI&I and I mentioned some of the stuff you told me. Toschi said, 'Armstrong checked these two guys out, Andrews and Wallace Penny. I don't know how he checked them out.' Dave said, 'Do whatever you want with it,' " said Morrill.

"He thinks very highly of you, incidentally. The poor guy, before I got through talking to him, he started crying. And I felt really bad that I even brought the subject up at all.

"Penny laid everything on Andrews. Like I told you, I thought for a while after he left that night that maybe he was Don Andrews. Dave tells me they checked it out and they are two different people. Then Penny kept talking about this third party that's in the middle."

"That would be Bernell, Andrews' friend," I said.

"He never mentioned his name to me, though. I've never seen any of his handprinting and I've never seen any of Penny's handprinting. I wrote to him in hopes that he would answer. I tried to butter him up," said Morrill. "Now Dave DeGarmo, my associate, he's got some contacts over in Marin County and Sonoma County, he's trying to find something out on Don Andrews. So far nothing.

"Penny did leave me some of Andrews' handprinting on a poster, though. I'll get it out in a minute. You know, Robert, if Zodiac is ambidextrous, it would account for the difference in slant, or in the case of transparencies in copying it word for word from somebody else's stuff. When he does the straight up-and-down stuff, I agree they're either tracings or transparencies," said Morrill.

"Penny has had his suspicions about Don Andrews for five, six years," I said, "and hasn't done anything about it, so I'm going to be seeing the organist in Southern California and we'll see what he does. San Francisco doesn't seem to have anything."

"Well, Tedesco [Toschi's replacement] called the other night to see if I would look at all the letters. 'I'm off the case. You can tell Mr. Gain I'm not going to look at anything for San Francisco P.D. anymore,' I told him. Tedesco kind of laughed nervously and he said, 'I think I understand your view.'"

Morrill took out the photo Penny had brought as a sample of Don Andrews' printing. It was a hand-drawn movie poster done in black felt-tip pen.

"That's beautiful," I said.

"Some of the things don't quite match in this exemplar, but enough of them do to make you wonder an awful lot."

I asked Morrill if he had any theories of his own.

"Yeah. Do you suppose, Robert, that there may be more than one guy involved? Now I'm thinking about Wallace Penny and Don Andrews. Penny's sure strong enough, six foot four and 240. Suppose one of them is doing the writing and the other's doing the killing.

"Outside of the letters," he continued, "what evidence do the police have? They're grasping at straws. The day Wallace Penny showed up at my house to tell me about Don Andrews, I sat down with my wife, Rose, and talked with her about the Zodiac case. I didn't realize until Penny left that he knew too much about things that the police have never revealed. I'm not sure I didn't have the Zodiac sitting right here in the room with me and didn't know it, didn't realize it."

"I've started up to go see him at his carpentry shop a couple of times," I said, "but I've canceled out every time. I just get a weird feeling about driving up there."

"Robert, you better be careful," cautioned Morrill. "I'm not worried about him doing anything to me, but I'm real worried about his motives in the Zodiac case. There could be some danger for you. I wouldn't get alone with the guy."

"Penny has the wildest theory in the world," I said. "He thinks that Andrews made a film of one of his murders and has put it in a film canister booby-trapped to explode and destroy the evidence."

"Ha! I hadn't heard that one. The thing you're going to have to find for me, Robert, is some more handprinting. Don Andrews', Penny's and Andrews' friend, Bernell . . ."

"Let's check them all."

"Don Andrews particularly."

"I sure would like to know what Armstrong did to clear Andrews."

"I don't know unless the fingerprint didn't match," said Morrill. "I always thought Armstrong was real intelligent. He and Toschi made a heck of a good pair."

"I was told Ken Narlow went down after the last Zodiac letter and talked to Andrews. Andrews immediately had his phone disconnected. It's a strange reaction," I said. "Narlow talked to him for six hours and he went away with his head spinning."

When I got back to San Francisco, there was a letter in my mail box from Marvin Bernell, agreeing to a meeting at his home on the thirteenth.

When I saw Bernell's handprinting, I realized that it was *he* who had drawn the movie poster that Penny had given to Morrill as a sample of Don's printing.

Wednesday, September 13, 1978

I met with Bernell in the evening at his home near Riverside. He showed me into a large old-fashioned living room. Somehow Bernell knew I had come to talk to him about more than his silent film collection. Perhaps his old friend, the elusive Don Andrews, had seen several newspaper articles that mentioned a book on Zodiac that I was writing. If Don had warned his friend not to say too much to me, did he feel there was some sort of connection between himself and the search for Zodiac?

Bernell sat on a couch to my right. I asked him a few questions about the strange link between Zodiac, himself, and movies.

"To be honest," I said, "when I got your letter from L.A. and saw the handprinting at the bottom, I was really startled. It's amazingly similar to the printing done on the Zodiac letters." I looked at him intently, trying to gauge his reaction, but he remained impassive. I changed the subject.

"Zodiac made several allusions to films in his letters to the papers. For instance, Zodiac mentions *The Most Dangerous Game*. Did that film ever play at your theater?"

"Oh, heavens yes," Bernell trilled. "I don't know how many times."

"Did you show it around 1968–69?"

"I started with the theater about '69," he acknowledged, "and *Dangerous Game* could have come in. But it's been there much more than twice because it's a classic of its kind."

"Marvin, Zodiac mentioned *The Most Dangerous Game* in his three-part cipher and then went on to attack two people at Lake Berryessa wearing a costume with a hood and carrying a knife that was a duplicate to the one that Count Zaroff wore in the movie. I feel that Zodiac may have modeled his knife and his costume, to a certain extent, after that movie. Too, in one of Zodiac's letters, he mentioned the 'Red Phantom.' I've learned recently that there was a silent film called *El Spectre Rojo.*" (An early Pathé Frères Film.)

"I have a copy of it," said Bernell guardedly, leaning forward. "Did Zodiac mention that?"

"He used that as a pen name."

Bernell laughed nervously, covering his teeth with a white hand. "That's pretty funny, because we had a zodiac ceiling in our old theater in L.A.," he said. "A lot of people don't even notice it. Their eyes are more concentrated down front on the screen." He paused. "Now let's see. *El Spectre Rojo* is a silent film, but I don't know how he could have known about it. It was considered a lost film until someone from Thunderbird Films found the original hand-tinted print. It's first announcement of sale was . . ." He thought for a moment. "I could do a little digging."

"Zodiac's letter mentioned the phantom in 1974," I said.

"Well, that would be about right. I first saw that film then and decided to buy a 16-mm copy when it was shown at the annual film collectors' convention in Canada."

I pointed out to him that in one of the killer's letters he mentioned the "piano organist." Bernell had once been a silent film organist. "Then there's his symbol," I continued, "the crossed circle. Isn't the same symbol used on a film leader when they count down?"

"Yeah, you'll find that symbol on the leader beginning a film."

"Of course," I said, "the police have always thought of it as a rifle sight."

"No, when I saw it in the paper I recognized it as an academy [standard] leader. To help sustain the house I've been running commercial films, recent films instead of the classics. Not a very good deal, but we get a modest turnout. I do everything. Do the posters too, but I will not leave my more elaborate posters around the theater; too much chance of damage. On the other hand, these flimsy things . . ." Bernell gestured with an outstretched hand toward the poster blowup that Wallace Penny had offered as a sample of Don Andrews' printing. "Such as you have a copy of there. There is no particular point of preserving those. They're just wadded up and thrown out after the show."

"Then you are the one who printed this poster? We'd been under the impression that a man named Don Andrews . . ." I paused. "He used to work for you, I believe."

"He has," said Bernell stiffly.

"The police, in checking him out as a Zodiac suspect, thought the posters were done by him. They used this copy of a movie poster as his handprinting sample."

I showed Bernell photographic enlargements of the letters, pointing out certain areas where they resembled the poster. "Do you have a sample of Don's real handprinting?"

"I don't have any letters from him," he said softly. "I don't have any occasion to have any correspondence with him anymore."

"My guess is that Zodiac was influenced by the handprinting on one of your movie posters," I told him. "I think he saw the posters you did in black felt-tip pen and discarded and photographed the letters to trace onto his communications to the press."

Bernell had been very nervous. But after he brought back his film records, along with coffee and chocolate cake, we checked the projection dates for *The Most Dangerous Game* and learned it had last played in May 1969.

Bernell was a charming, friendly man and not threatening in any way, but I sensed there was a lot he was not telling me. Alone with him in this old house, I had the feeling that any moment a stocky man in a black hood could step into the room holding a pistol. After all, no one knew where Don Andrews was.

Finally, I went down to the basement with Bernell to see his impressive collection of films. It covered one wall and part of another. I looked at the canisters wondering if what Wallace Penny had told me was true: that Zodiac had hidden evidence from one of the killings and a film of the Lake Herman murders in a 35-mm film canister marked "Do Not Open—Nitrate Film —Danger!" and that he had given this to Bernell to keep for him in case his room was ever searched by the police.

Bernell steered me away from the films after he noticed the intense way I was looking at the canisters. He led me over to where he lettered his movie posters. The felt-tip–pen printing looked like enlargements of the Zodiac handprinting.

If there was a booby-trapped film canister, I tried to imagine what an explosion could do to a ramshackle three-story frame house like this. Decaying nitrate film was, after all, TNT.

Once again Bernell assured me we were completely alone. But I could hear, faintly but unmistakably, the slow, methodical, easy tread of footsteps on the floor above.

I pretended not to notice. I wasn't too worried: my friends knew where I was, and all the information I learned about Andrews I had given to Lieutenant Husted in Vallejo.

I met a second time with Bernell to discuss his friend's possible connection with Zodiac. "I heard that Zodiac may have hidden evidence of his crimes in a silent film canister rigged to explode if opened," I said, "and left this with an unknowing friend."

The organist's broad smile vanished. He flushed, looked embarrassed, and when his smile came back it was in such a way that his lips pulled back over his gums, completely exposing his teeth.

I thought to myself that perhaps in the past Bernell had been asked to keep such a canister by his friend and now suspected he may have been used. I described the label.

"Don has given me such a canister, marked as you say," he said.

Wallace Penny had been right! Such a film canister existed. I tried to look calm, although my pulse rate was accelerating by the second. "Do you know where it is now?" I asked.

"He took it back. Nineteen seventy-two, I think it was."

"Damn!" If Don Andrews was Zodiac, no one would ever see that canister again.

Bernell was staring at the floor. He was terribly worried about the handprinting connection between himself and the Zodiac letters.

"Are you ambidextrous?" I asked.

"No," he said. "I'm right-handed."

"Then you don't have anything to worry about. Zodiac's ambidextrous."

Bernell looked like I had hit him between the eyes with a hammer.

"Don uses his left hand when he cuts films," Bernell said, "writes with his right. I guess he's ambidextrous."

This was a fact about Don that I had known long before I came to Riverside. The look on Bernell's face convinced me that he knew nothing about his friend's possible connection with the murders.

Bernell told me Don Andrews had left San Francisco in 1975 and had been out of state until the beginning of 1978. This might account for the long delay in letters and the phrase "I am back with you . . ."

I asked Bernell if Andrews was back in San Francisco. Bernell thought for a moment, walked across the room, and stood with his back to me, in front of the fireplace. He said he wasn't sure.

Tuesday, September 19, 1978

I had been receiving breathing phone calls at work for some time. They almost always came at 10:30 A.M.

This evening, I called Bernell at his Riverside home to ask him some more questions about his friend.

"Marvin, I've never seen Don," I said. "If I read you this description, would you tell me where it's wrong?" I asked.

"Well . . ."

"I'll try it, O.K.?" I said. "He's a white male adult, stocky, heavyset, about five feet eight inches tall. He has a slightly rounded back, has a paunch, and in '69 he had crew-cut hair that was slightly curled, with sort of a reddish tint. He would be about thirty-five. He wears black thick-rimmed glasses and he holds them in place with a thin band of elastic. He's rather barrel-chested, sort of beefy but firm."

"Well, he is chunky, he is stout," said Bernell. "I guess he has held his glasses in place with a rubber band. There is a fluff to his hair, I suppose."

"They say he has a very full face. Is his face . . . ?"

234

"It goes with the body. It's chunky," said Bernell.

Bernell had plans of getting together with Don and going into business with him. For the time being, Andrews was returning to work in the Bay Area. It was hard to understand how Bernell, as a potential business partner, could not know his friend's new address.

Bernell told me Andrews had been developing arthritis since 1969. Was this the reason Zodiac had stopped killing? Would progression of this condition be noticeable by experts in the later Zodiac letters?

"Don has a prepossessing appearance," said Bernell, "and most people wouldn't cotton to him. He seems smug. He's the kind of man who could do anything under any circumstances. He puts every penny into acquiring photo machinery."

When I asked Bernell about Don's handwriting, he said, "He has a laborious way of working on any sort of writing. He uses felt-tip pens for almost everything."

Don Andrews was an intriguing suspect. But I could go no further until I could find him and until I could speak to Narlow about him.

Andrews had made an enemy of a woman who worked in the personnel section of the radio station he had worked for, and she got me handprinting samples. But these were not enough for Morrill to rule him out or in as a suspect.

I learned the identities of the teenage witnesses to the Stine killing and showed them a picture of Don Andrews. They thought he was "too old and too fat."

I later developed my own doubts that Andrews was the man.

Thursday, May 3, 1979

At 11:05 P.M., Sergeant Ralph Wilson of Vallejo called me unexpectedly.

"It's the weirdest thing," he said. "I've been thinking about the Zodiac killer, and right in the middle of checking out records on a cop who once dated Darlene Ferrin, I got a phone call from an unidentified informant who says he's afraid he's going to be murdered."

I began to get chills up and down my spine. I knew Sergeant Wilson wouldn't be calling me unless something really was up.

"This informant fingered an ex-roommate who he thinks is going to kill him because he knows the roommate is the Zodiac," continued Wilson. "This guy is scared out of his mind. The suspect lived on a ranch. He's moody, an expert with weapons, and he's got photos and exhibits of the Ferrin murder. He's got all the photos of the victims. We now think he was the unidentified man who had the argument with Darlene Ferrin at the restaurant. He's into the occult. He's into cryptography, and he looks like the composite drawing. He was fired from the sheriff's department," said Wilson. "Let me just refer to him as 'Jack' to avoid any problems."

As far as I was concerned, Don Andrews was the best suspect in the case, but I wanted to hear every possibility.

According to Wilson, access to the roads where the crimes were committed had been a problem during the short time in 1969 when Jack was a prime suspect in Darlene Ferrin's murder. There seemed to be no way he could get to the murder scenes and back home in the time allowed. Now, thanks to the unknown informant, Sergeant Wilson learned of a small road that opened out on Lake Herman Road. The road was closed by a gate with three combination locks. Jack supposedly knew the combinations and used this ranch road to commit his murders and return home. This could explain why Mrs. Borges did not see Zodiac's car when she drove straight into Benicia on narrow Lake Herman Road and flagged down a patrol car.

Sergeant Wilson promised to get back to me the minute something broke. He had to wait until the informant called again and let him know who he was. "I knew this Jack," said Wilson. "He's capable of anything."

Sunday, June 24, 1979

Toschi dragged after a ten-hour work detail, nursing a throbbing ankle. But he had to give a pleased smile when he saw a Sunday *Progress* article about him. It told how, after not quite a year, he had been reinstated to his former rank. Reminded, he gave a relieved laugh. Now he had worked all the four units of crimes against persons: Sex, Homicide, Aggravated Assault, and now Robbery. He was back on top again.

I felt good. At our morning editorial conferences I had had an opportunity to speak to two mayors, Moscone and Feinstein, about promoting him. I would like to think that might have helped.

Tuesday, June 26, 1979

I learned that "Jack" had sold his ranch and used the money to buy a bar in Nevada. To see if he compared physically to Zodiac, I made the trip by car.

When I arrived in the evening, he was playing at the second of two plush pool tables. He was tall, thin, and bald as an egg.

His fingerprints had been checked against the bloody print on Stine's cab and come up negative. The photos he had of Darlene's body at the scene he admitted he had taken as a "souvenir" when he left the police department. They were official autopsy and crime scene photos.

I was convinced that he was not Zodiac.

⊕17
Zodiac

Friday, July 27, 1979

Since March I had been working on breaking the large 340-symbol cipher that had defied the most sophisticated codebreakers and computers at the CIA, NSA, and FBI (Zodiac's sixth letter, November 8, 1969; see facing page).

Most people thought that this cipher was a joke on the part of the killer and that it had no meaning. But in the sixth line of the cipher, Zodiac had made a correction. Since he had worked so painstakingly to create an almost flawless block of symbols, it was unlikely that he would mar it by crossing out one and writing a different one if the symbol meant nothing.

If Zodiac had mentioned Herb Caen, the *Chronicle*'s famous columnist, in 1978, then it was possible that he had mentioned Caen in 1969 as well. The first three letters of the large cipher were "H E R." I asked myself if any of the symbols in the 340-character cipher bore the same meaning as those solved by the Hardens in Zodiac's first letter. I found they did. The remaining five symbols spelled out " C E A N B ." Combined with the "H E R," this was an only slightly transposed version of "HERB CAEN."

It was only fair to figure that Zodiac had transposed some of the remaining cipher as well. There were many spelling and coding mistakes in the Harden solution, and I also took this into account.

Caen's name was the key word in the cipher. Using these eight symbols as a Rosetta Stone, some of the cryptogram began to make sense.

On the third line from the bottom of the cipher were the letters "POSHT/." I knew that "H" stood for *H* and that the word could be an anagram for "TOSCHI."

Once again I tried to imagine what Zodiac might have been like in 1969, what thoughts he might have had, and whom he might have considered his enemy. Herb Caen, for one. And I found what could be Sergeant Les Lundblad's name on the ninth line.

I think one reason the 340-symbol cipher remained unsolved for so many years is that Zodiac mentioned many of the proper names of his antagonists and places where his murders occurred. To cryptographers in the East, these names would be just so much gibberish.

Slowly, the cipher began to produce words and parts of words. The word "SEE" and the incomplete word "RN___AOD" were revealed. The last was the transposed word "PARDON"; this gave me a symbol for *P*. In the fifteenth line "ECBU_____" was likely "BECAUSE"; this gave me more meanings.

The letter that Zodiac enclosed with the cipher was a great help. It reminded me of the formal way of speaking he adopted, his manner of being polite and vicious at the same time, and his anger at "the lies" the police were telling about him. He wrote of having killed seven victims, so I looked for letter patterns that might spell "eighth," referring to his next victim. He mentioned the police telling lies about him in a letter written the next day (November 9, 1969), so I looked for the recurring word "lies." He often ended his sentences with "etc," so I looked for that.

Zodiac had started by creating a substitution cipher, symbols substituted for alphabet characters, and then transposed these symbols, creating a substitution-transposition cipher. Each alphabet character could be represented by multiple symbols. Transposition ciphers are more difficult to solve than substitution ciphers.

The killer had used sixty-five different symbols in the cipher with forty-three of these occurring five times or less. Only two ("+" and "B") occurred more than ten times. Zodiac was using something very different from the cipher broken by the Hardens.

If only the cipher had been a few lines longer! Experts stated that more symbols would have given a computer enough material to check all possible combinations and hand back the answer.

Sunday, July 29, 1979

I felt that I was nearing an answer. I worked every night on the code. Sometimes when I stopped to look up at the white walls of my office, I would see the lines of the symbols in front of me.

By 11:00 P.M. I finally thought I had the answer to one of the great "unbreakable" ciphers of the last decade.

The Hardens had solved the three-part cipher by looking for double-L combinations, the most common. I found triple-L combinations, deliberate misspellings to throw off cryptoanalysts: "PILLL," "ALLL," "ALLLSO," and "WILLL."

In my solution, I found Zodiac had used ten different characters for the letter E, nine for S, and seven for A. The recurring symbol, the backward C, turned out to stand for nothing.

In the morning, I sent my solution to the cryptographers' convention then meeting at Kent State. If my answer was valid, they would know. And they might improve on any mistakes I had made.

Monday, August 6, 1979

While I was working on my editorial cartoon ideas for Tuesday, my phone rang. It was Greg Mellen, from the American Cryptogram Association. "Congratulations," he said, "you've broken the Zodiac code."

At that moment, San Francisco was hit by the biggest earthquake it had experienced in sixty-eight years. High-rise buildings in the downtown area began to sway, and people in my office stood up and some left the room.

"What's going on?" said the code expert.

"We're having an earthquake here. People are leaving."

"Do you want to call me back?" said Mellen.

"No," I said, "this is more important. Go on."

Just then, the city was hit by the aftershock.

Mellen decided to write me the details rather than talk any longer.

Wednesday, August 8, 1979

"Dear Mr. Graysmith," Greg Mellen wrote, "As I was saying just before the earthquake . . . Congratulations on having broken the second Zodiac cipher. Both Zodiac messages are homophonic ciphers [ciphers using multiple substitutes for a single letter], with the second complicated by an added, apparently random, transposition of the letters of each word. Homophonic ciphers date from at least the fifteenth century [1412] and are not uncommon. . . .

"The errors in spelling and in encipherment are to be expected and are within an acceptable range. I regret I can't supply you with additional 'clues' in breaking the second message; you have abstracted all the information that is there."

Eugene Waltz of the American Cryptogram Association wrote to me also. "I had an opportunity to speak with Greg Mellen at the ACA convention and we are both agreed that your solution is good and valid. We also hope that it leads to an early arrest of Zodiac. The successful solution of a cipher such as this requires intuition, good luck, and most of all *dogged perseverance* to spend hour upon hour of ofttimes fruitless effort to add a value or to determine the validity of values already assumed. You are to be congratulated, not only for breaking the cipher, but for your willingness to spend the hours and the effort to do so."

Earlier, I had turned the cipher key and solution over to the Vallejo P.D. Here is what the cipher said.

Zodiac had used a series of nulls including a backward c and multiple l's and the word "it" placed at random. The letter k stood for both k and s. I have left these out as well as adding punctuation and spacing so that it reads as a letter to Herb Caen, which I believe was the cipher's original purpose.

> HERB CAEN:
>   I GIVE THEM HELL TOO.
> BLAST THESE LIES. SLUETH
> SHOELD [SHOULD] SEE A NAME
> BELOW KILLEERS FILM. A PILLS
> GAME. PARDON ME AGCEPT TO
> BLAST NE [ME]. BULLSHIT.
> THESE FOOLS SHALL MEET
> KILLER. PLEAS ASK LUNBLAD.

Here Zodiac mentions Detective Sergeant Les Lundblad, the man who had hunted him in Vallejo. The mention of drugs confirms police theories that Zodiac wrote the letters while he was high.

> SOEL [SOUL] AT H LSD UL
> CLEAR LAKE. SO STARE I
> EAT A PILL, ASSHOLE. I
> PLANT MR. A. H. PHONE LAKE B.

("Lake B." is probably a reference to Lake Berryessa, which is near Clear Lake. "Mr. A. H." might refer to *Chronicle* columnist Art Hoppe.)

> ALL SSLAVES BECAUSE LSD
> WILL STOLEN EITHER SLAVE
> SHALL I   HELL SLASH TOSCHI?
> THE PIG STALLS DEALS OC [OF]
> EIGHTH SOEL [SOUL] SLAIN.

The cipher did stir things up. After my appearance on the evening news, and with the second mention of Toschi in a Zodiac letter, the San Francisco Police Department applied for a federal law enforcement assistance grant of $92,000 to go on with the case. By August 29, the sum desired had been reduced to $70,000.

Why was Zodiac killing when he did?

There had been instances when a serial killer had murdered only on holidays (the Fourth of July murders in Michigan, 1967–69). Is this what Zodiac was doing?

Cheri Jo Bates was killed close to midnight on October 30, 1966. Did the killer stand talking to her for hours waiting for midnight, and the beginning of Halloween—the age-old celebrations of the dead?

Zodiac attacked at Blue Rock Springs five minutes after midnight on the Fourth of July. Kathleen Johns was taken on her terror ride in 1970 on Palm Sunday.

Paul Stine was killed while San Francisco was already celebrating Columbus Day.

September 27, 1969, the killing of Cecelia Shepard, was the first day of the Jewish holiday Tabernacles.

But the December 20 slaying of David Faraday and Betty Lou Jensen fell short of Christmas. This bothered me.

Zodiac's first letter was mailed November 29, 1966, only two days before Thanksgiving. His letters of April 1970 were postmarked the first and last days of Passover.

It was an unacceptable, tenuous theory, but there was a consistency, a rhythm about the Zodiac attacks and communications that transcended holiday celebrations.

Zodiac and astrology. What if the stars did control his actions? Could the unknown maniac who had been terrorizing California be following the phases of the moon?

I checked October 1969 first to see if any of the phases of the moon coincided with an attack or letter. The first day of the new moon fell on October 11, the day Paul Stine was murdered. I went on to the phases of the moon for November 1969. The first day of the new moon fell on November 9, the day the 340-symbol cipher was mailed to the *Chronicle*.

The September 27, 1969, murder occurred the night of an eclipse of the moon and only two days after the beginning of the full moon.

The July 5, 1969, killing followed by five days the June 29 full moon. On the day of the killing, the earth reached aphelion, when the sun, earth, and moon are in a direct line and exert their strongest gravitational pull. Near summer Solstice, this is one of the most important astrological events of the year.

December 20, 1968, the murder of Jensen and Faraday, was a new moon plus one day and only minutes before Winter Solstice. Cheri Jo Bates was slain on a full moon plus one day, a moon known as the Harvest Moon. Kathleen Johns was abducted one day past the Vernal Equinox during a full moon.

Zodiac's three letters containing the cipher puzzle broken by the Hardens were mailed on July 28, 1969, the first night of the full moon.

In all of the killings, Saturn was visible as an evening star. In the Shepard slaying, the moon passed above Saturn, which rose early and was in the sky most of the night in Aries. Saturn was in Aries in the July 5 murder, as well as the October 11 murder. Even in the 1966 Bates murder on Halloween (which begins the age-old celebrations of the dead), Saturn was the evening star.

Faraday and Jensen were killed at the time of the ancient Roman festival of Saturnalia (December 17–23), when children were sacrificed to the gods. The name of Saturday is derived from "Saturn's day." Each of the victims was slain on Saturday (except for Faraday and Jensen, who were shot minutes before Saturday). When Saturn was in ascendancy, perhaps Zodiac felt he was caught in the power of the ancient god.

Zodiac was writing his letters and killing at the times of consecutive lunar phases. Nowhere was this more apparent than in the choice of times he wrote to the *Chronicle* in 1970: the April 28, June 26, and July 25 letters were mailed on the first day of the last quarter phase of the moon.

In 1974, when six occultations of Saturn occurred and Saturn was the evening star, Zodiac broke a long silence. He wrote when Saturn was in retrograde motion and less than one-degree south of the moon (January 29), two days into the full moon (May 8), and once again when the earth was in aphelion (July 8) four days into the full moon.

In 1978, one day after the full moon, between the time the sun entered Aries and Saturn became stationary, Zodiac wrote he was "in control of all things" (April 24).

Many believed that in all liklihood Zodiac was an Aries who is active in his clandestine pursuits around the full moon or new moon when Saturn is in ascendancy.

However, Alex Hoyer, the astrologer, revealed in the *Chronicle* "the chances are the killer was born under the sign of Taurus, whose people are generally loving, kind, and gentle. . . . Such a person, . . . while very loving by nature, has periods of violence and rashness when thwarted and can go berserk."

As an artist I have knowledge of visual symbols. This led me to realize what the strange symbol on the Halloween card death threat really meant. It was formed of the Hebrew symbol and the Greek symbol for Taurus.

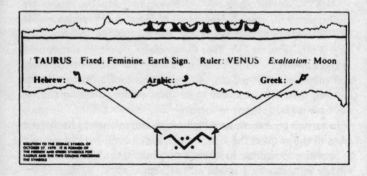

And now I realized what had bothered me about the three circled figure eights in the "my name is" cipher of April 20, 1970. The tops of the eights were not closed. They were actually three circled Taurus symbols.

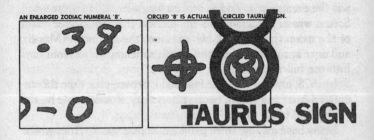

AN ENLARGED ZODIAC NUMERAL '8'.

CIRCLED '8' IS ACTUALLY CIRCLED TAURUS SIGN.

TAURUS SIGN

Zodiac had cleverly hidden five Taurus symbols in his letters. Was this his birth sign, or did he only think he was a Taurus?

Whether Zodiac was a follower of astrology or only sensitive to the waxing and waning of the moon, perhaps his future actions could be predicted. He had, after all, broken a three-year silence in a month when a major coincidence of cosmic cycles occurred in January 1974. This biological tide could have triggered an emotional explosion.

Was Zodiac unconsciously being dominated by the moon? Or did he plot his crimes by some sort of astrological horoscope? If he was working from a horoscope, did he draw it up himself or have it done for him? Perhaps there was an astrologer somewhere in the Bay Area who had drawn up a Taurus chart for the killer and might remember him. If Zodiac did cast a horoscope for himself, then his name was more than window dressing and he did have a real interest in astrology.

In various books on ancient languages and sciences, I had found a few of the symbols the killer used in his ciphers, but not enough to convince me Zodiac had used a particular text to form his signs. Finally in one book I found *all* of them.

This book was *As Above, So Below* by Alan Oken, who had created several of the symbols specifically for his horoscope book. All of the symbols Zodiac used in his 340-character cipher were the same ones used in casting a horoscope. (See last illustration in second photo section.)

And finally the answer to the meaning of the Zodiac's own symbol, the crossed-circle. He had killed the day before Winter Solstice, at aphelion and the nearest full moon to Autumnal Equinox, and attacked the day after Spring Equinox. Winter Solstice, Summer Solstice, Autumnal Equinox, and Vernal Equinox create a cross upon a circle. It was at these four points on the circle that Zodiac murdered (see facing page).

Zodiac had used two of the five major symbols of astrology, the Circle (spirit) overlapped by the Cross (matter), to signify not only himself but the days on which he was to kill.

"Your information on the Oken book is startling," Toschi wrote to me. "To think that Zodiac probably used the same text that you have read is fascinating. Your thoughts that Zodiac is a 'follower' fits into what I have been thinking for many years. . . . I believe that you are truly on the right track, especially with the cross and circle, which when shown visually by you pretty much explains that you are onto something big."

The common elements in the Zodiac murders had not been added to in a decade, but now that I knew what timetable the killer used, perhaps I could find links to other unsolved killings in Northern California.

"So I shall change the way the collecting of slaves," wrote Zodiac in 1969. "I shall no longer announce to anyone when I comitt my murders, they shall look like routine robberies, killings of anger, & a few fake accidents, etc." Who were the unknown victims?

As I've noted, all of Zodiac's victims were young students killed in or around their cars, near bodies of water, and on weekends when the moon was new or full. Sexual molestation or robbery was not a motive. The killer used a different weapon each time. In some of the attacks, the killer carried a large flashlight.

My thoughts kept going to the right side of the car, the passenger side. The only window down at Lake Herman Road was on the right where Betty Lou was sitting; Mageau's window at Blue Rock Springs was down, and Stine's fly window was open on the

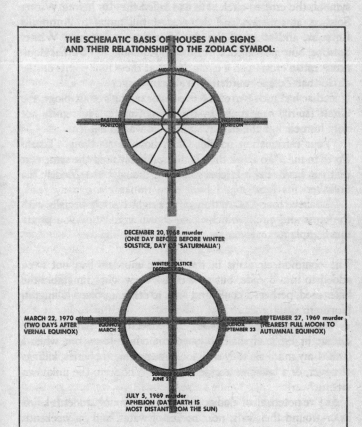

THE SCHEMATIC BASIS OF HOUSES AND SIGNS
AND THEIR RELATIONSHIP TO THE ZODIAC SYMBOL:

MIDHEAVEN

EASTERN
HORIZON

WESTERN
HORIZON

NADIR

DECEMBER 20, 1968 murder
(ONE DAY BEFORE BEFORE WINTER
SOLSTICE, DAY OF 'SATURNALIA')

WINTER SOLSTICE
DECEMBER 21

MARCH 22, 1970 attack
(TWO DAYS AFTER
VERNAL EQUINOX)

EQUINOX
MARCH 21

AUTUMNAL
EQUINOX
SEPTEMBER 23

SEPTEMBER 27, 1969 murder
(NEAREST FULL MOON TO
AUTUMNAL EQUINOX)

SUMMER SOLSTICE
JUNE 21

JULY 5, 1969 murder
APHELION (DAY EARTH IS
MOST DISTANT FROM THE SUN)

THE CIRCLE (SPIRIT) overlapped by THE CROSS (MATTER) two of the five major symbols of astrology.

passenger side. Zodiac went to some difficulty to pull Stine to the passenger side of the cab. At Lake Herman Road the killer fired a shot in the rear window and, moving around the station wagon, fired another bullet into the left rear wheel housing to successfully force the couple to leap from the passenger side. Did Zodiac associate the passenger side with hitchhikers? Were these his other victims?

If Zodiac was positioning bodies in a ritual way, the most common posture was one of the victim hanging part or all the way out of the right passenger side of the car, on his back, palms up, with his head pointing away from the car. Even Mageau, after he fell from Darlene's car, accidentally adopted this posture. David Faraday and Paul Stine, both victims of bullets near the ear, were on their backs. David's head pointed to the east and Paul's to the north.

The one thing that had never ceased to puzzle me was how Zodiac knew, on pitch-black Lake Herman Road, that "the girl was on her right side feet to the west"; that in the dark Blue Rock Springs lot Darlene "was wearing paterned slacks"; and that he had shot Mageau in the knee while the boy was thrashing about with his legs. If Zodiac knew such details, could they have been observed during a rushed killing after which he had only moments to get away? He must have followed the victims earlier in the evening. It was a good possibility, because he attacked his victims almost immediately after they parked. If he knew the areas so well, was he a Vallejo resident? Or, someone who had access to the coroner's and police reports?

The missing Lake Tahoe nurse, Donna Lass, last seen alive just before the Autumnal Equinox, has never been found and is considered a possible Zodiac victim. Judith Ann Hikari, also a nurse, was found April 26, 1970, in a shallow grave in remote Placer County. But this was thirteen days before the Vernal Equinox. Nancy Bennallack, a court reporter, was found dead in her apartment October 26, 1970. The next day the *Chronicle* received a letter from Zodiac claiming fourteen victims. Police felt that if Zodiac did, in fact, kill Donna Lass at Lake Tahoe, he might be responsible for the deaths of the other two women.

Marie Antoinette Anstey was abducted from the Coronado Inn in Vallejo, where Darlene Ferrin used to go dancing. This was seven days before the Vernal Equinox on Friday, March 13, 1970. One year to the day she disappeared, Zodiac mailed the *Chronicle* a letter. One year to the day that her body was discovered, March 21, 1971, Zodiac mailed the *Chronicle* a postcard.

The next Friday the thirteenth in 1970 came in November. It was on this night that a car pulled off Ascot Avenue and drove thirty feet into a field on the northern edge of Sacramento dragging a body through the weeds and throwing it face up next to a wire fence. The victim's throat was then cut. So badly beaten was the woman that dental charts were necessary to establish her identity. She was another nurse, Santa Rosa resident Carol Beth Hilburn, who had once studied to be an X-ray technician at Sutter General Hospital in Sacramento. The strawberry blonde had been estranged from her husband for three months and was staying with her sister in Santa Rosa. A mysterious girl known only as "Dee" accompanied Carol to Sacramento on Thursday, November 12, to see some friends who were members of local motorcycle gangs—"motorcycle types" and "the wrong people," as her husband called them. Dee dropped Carol off at an after-hours club on West Capital Avenue frequented by motorcycle gangs. Carol was wearing a hip-length black jacket with "Santa Rosa" printed on the front in yellow letters. She had gone to the bar to keep a date with a boyfriend and was still at the bar at 4:00 A.M. After that, she was not seen again. When her body was found the next day, she was wearing only one of her suede boots and on the other foot a single "ped." Her panties had been pulled down around one knee. Was her killer keeping her clothes and purse?

The name of the after-hours club was the Zodiac.

The third Friday the thirteenth victim (July 1973) was Nancy Patricia Gidley, who was abducted from her motel in San Francisco and dumped in the parking lot of Washington High School. All of her clothes had been taken. Stine the cabdriver had been killed on Washington Street.

Cosette Ellison was killed seventeen days before the Vernal Equinox, and Patricia King fifteen days before. Eva Blau was killed on the Vernal Equinox. All died in 1970; all were found tossed in ravines. In 1969, Leona Roberts had been killed ten days before the Winter Solstice. Police believed that one man killed all of these women.

On July 6, 1979, a corpse with hands and ankles bound to its neck with clothesline was found in a shallow grave near Calistoga Road in Santa Rosa. This discovery rekindled speculation about seven unsolved murders dating back to 1972.

The seven were:

Maureen L. Sterling, twelve, and Yvonne L. Weber, twelve, who vanished on their way home from the Redwood Ice Skating Rink in Santa Rosa at 4:00 P.M. Friday, February 4, 1972. Their skeletons were discovered down a sixty-foot embankment off a rural road in the Franz Valley area of east Sonoma County. They had been murdered elsewhere and dumped where they were found, on December 28, 1972. The killer had kept their clothes and had also taken one gold earring from each girl.

Kim Wendy Allen, nineteen, a Santa Rosa Junior College student, vanished while hitchhiking to her residence in Santa Rosa on March 4, 1972. She had come from her job at the Larkspur health food store and was seen hitchhiking north on 101 around 5:00 P.M. It was a Saturday, and sixteen days before the Vernal Equinox. Her nude body was found in a creekbed twenty feet from Enterprise Road. She had been strangled with white clothesline; her wrists and ankles showed marks of having been bound as if she had been spread-eagled. She had superficial cuts on her chest. One of her gold earrings had been taken as well as her clothes and possessions.

I obtained a list of what Kim Allen had been seen carrying when she left work. One was a straw carrying bag, twenty-four inches high, with straw handles, filled with health food. The second object was a wooden barrel, two and a half feet tall, empty, with the word "soy" printed on the side in black ink. The soy sauce barrel also had some Chinese writing printed on it. The killer kept the barrel.

And now I thought I knew where the killer had gotten the

symbol at the bottom of the *Exorcist* letter from. I got one of the barrels and found this particular Zodiac symbol matched some of the Chinese characters closely.

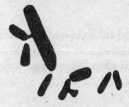

Zodiac symbol   Barrel symbol

Lori Lee Kursa, thirteen, was last seen alive in the U-Save Market in Santa Rosa on November 21, 1972. Her nude body was found on December 12, 1972, with a broken neck. Her first and second cervical vertebrae had been dislocated. She had two wire loops in her pierced ears, no earrings attached.

Carolyn Nadine Davis, fifteen, a runaway from Anderson in Shasta County, was last seen leaving her grandmother's house in Garberville on July 15, hitchhiking south on 101. Her nude body was discovered 2.2 miles north of Porter Creek Road on Franz Valley Road in the *exact* spot as Sterling and Weber. She was found July 31, 1973. The police discovered that Carolyn had bought a one-way ticket to fly from Redding to San Francisco. She had been poisoned by strychnine.

Therese Diane Walsh, twenty-three, disappeared exactly on the Winter Solstice 1973, hitchhiking on 101 from Malibu Beach to her home in Garberville. Her body was discovered near the spot where Kim Wendy Allen's was found. She had been hog-tied with a one-quarter-inch nylon rope, strangled, and thrown into a creek. She had been sexually assaulted.

Jeannette Kamahele, twenty, was the victim found on July 6, 1979. A Santa Rosa Junior College student, she was last seen hitchhiking near the Cotati on-ramp of Highway 101 and was traveling north to Santa Rosa on April 25, 1972. Her body was discovered in a Sonoma County ravine in a shallow grave near

Calistoga Road. The coed had been tied with her hands and ankles bound to her neck; white clothesline was wrapped around her neck four times. She was found 100 yards from the spot where Lori Lee Kursa's body was discovered.

There were other possible Zodiac victims that my research uncovered. Betty Cloer, twenty-one, was killed two days before the Summer Solstice in 1971. In the year 1972, Linda Ohlig, nineteen, was murdered six days after the Vernal Equinox and Alexandra Clery, twenty-four, was killed eighteen days before the Autumnal Equinox. Susan McLaughlin, nineteen, was murdered eighteen days before the Vernal Equinox and Yvonne Quilantang, fifteen, eleven days before the Summer Solstice in 1973. Nineteen days prior to the Winter Solstice, both Cathy Fechtel, twenty-seven, and Michael Shane, thirty, were killed and dumped off a Livermore highway. Six days after Autumnal Equinox in 1974, Donna Marie Braun, fourteen, was murdered. On Thursday, October 16, 1975, Susan Dye was strangled while she was hitchhiking home; she was discovered under a freeway overpass near Santa Rosa.

Almost all were hitchhikers, some with minor involvement in drugs. Any hitchhiker would occupy the passenger seat, Zodiac's usual focus of attack. The killer had a knowledge of knot tying consistent with a seaman. The victims were found near areas of water, as most Zodiac victims had been: Walsh in a creek, Roberts at Bolinas Lagoon, Anstey was drowned, Dudley on the bank of Lake Merced, and Braun floating in the Salinas River.

Few had been sexually molested; none of the clothing of the nude victims has ever been found. The killer struck over weekends at dusk or night and bound his victims in Santa Rosa with white clothesline of the type used on the victims at Lake Berryessa. Three of the girls had it wrapped around their necks.

All of the victims were killed away from where they were found. When the murderer dumped the bodies, he parked his car in the road and not on the shoulder, so that he would not leave tracks. The victims had been lifted and tossed over drainage ditches and fences and down hillsides, indicating he was an extremely strong man. The killer knew the area.

The students were tortured, stabbed, poisoned, strangled, drowned, smothered, or broken. Since the bodies were being dumped in the same spots, layered, with months separating each dumping, the police were convinced that the same person was committing all or most of these killings. The truly horrifying part to me was that it seemed that someone was experimenting in different ways of killing people.

CI&I, as of July 1974, had 103 murder cases that had the above characteristics, including cases in Washington and Oregon. They were certain at the least fourteen of them involved the same man.*

From the office of the attorney general a secret report was issued stating that "over the past five years (1969–74), there have been fourteen young women murdered in Northern California, and all of these murders appear to have been committed by the same person. Eight other women have mysteriously disappeared in the states of Oregon and Washington over the past year." The report, developed by the California Department of Justice with the aid of many local law enforcement agencies, stated that they thought the killer was "familiar with witchcraft or the occult, because of a witchcraft symbol found during the Caroline Davis case and the possible occult involvement in the missing female cases in the states of Oregon and Washington." The report concluded: "The murders will probably continue until such time as the perpetrator is identified and apprehended."

Were these the missing Zodiac victims?

Santa Rosa came up over and over. They were either students at Santa Rosa Junior College or Santa Rosa residents killed elsewhere. Was there a Zodiac suspect who had links to Santa Rosa?

When I asked Toschi if there was a major Zodiac suspect who had ties to Santa Rosa, he said, "Yes, there was. But that's all I can say until the case is closed."

*My source is a special report: "Unsolved Female Homicides, An Analysis of a Series of Related Murders in California and Western America." Marked Confidential and printed February 1975 by the Department of Justice, California.

Then there was a suspect I had yet to find. Other investigators were also evasive. What were they keeping back?

Meanwhile, I continued looking for Don Andrews.

Friday, February 29, 1980

I felt that to the people around him the Zodiac killer might well appear to be a well-controlled man, calm, reasonable, a loner with few contacts with others. He was, however, wrapped up in a dream world of movies, fantasy, and melodrama; this was the part of his personality that carried over into his dark side.

In a secret evaluation of the murderer of Cheri Jo Bates written in July 1967 for the Riverside District Attorney's office by the Chief Psychologist of Patton State Hospital, the girl's killer is described as: "so hypersensitive . . . that virtually any little misperceived act could be blown up out of all proportion to the facts. He is obsessed and pathologically preoccupied with intense hatred against female figures—all the more so if he sees the young woman as attractive. Because of his own unconscious feelings of inadequacy, he is not likely to act out his feelings sexually, but in fantasy, as a rule. The fantasy can take on aggressive aspects, as in the case of the Bates girl's murder."

At the end of the report is this warning: "I would like to emphasize that there is a real possibility that he can become homicidal again."

Friday, February 29, 1980

I was sitting across from one of the nation's leading experts on mass murder, Dr. Donald T. Lunde, clinical professor of psychiatry and lecturer in law at Stanford University. The young-looking, light-haired doctor was currently examining Kenneth Bianchi in connection with the Hillside Strangler trial. I had seen him several times on TV. We met in Lunde's fashionable, book-lined office on the second floor of the Stanford Law School.

"Dr. Lunde, you say there are two distinct types of mass killers, sexual sadists, and the more common, the paranoid schizophrenic.* Having seen copies of all the Zodiac letters, are you inclined to believe that Zodiac is a sexual sadist?" I asked.

"Most likely if I had to make a choice it would be that," said Lunde. "Unlike the paranoid schizophrenic, the sadistic sociopathic killer does not suffer from hallucinations but selects his victims for the purpose of venting certain deeply rooted sexual and sadistic urges, such as the need to mutilate parts of the victim's body to achieve sexual satisfaction.

"I had the impression that there are more of these people around than ten, twenty years ago. When I saw [Edmund Emil] Kemper," [who killed eight women in Santa Cruz, killing his mother last] "I went back through the literature and found very few cases, one every decade. So I thought it was just a rare event and I probably would never see another person like that again.

"In the last year I alone have seen several and it's amazing the characteristics that they have in common. It seems there were very few sexual sadists reported in the twentieth century. But the seventies! Just full of them.

"Now that I've been able to personally study several of these people, there are an awful lot of similarities. Bianchi's† responses on psychological tests are almost verbatim like Kemper's. The whole sort of thing of seeing animals torn apart and blood and animal hearts."

A psychological profile of a sexual sadist—and most likely of Zodiac—would read like this:

He is always male, usually under thirty-five, clever, stealthy, strong, and intelligent. He has a passive, cruel, or estranged father and a seductive, dominant mother who gives affection and rejection erratically. The sexual sadist seeks revenge toward his

---

*A paranoid schizophrenic is controlled by external forces such as voices telling him what to do and often kills women because of confused sexual identity. He suffers from disordered thinking, hallucinations, persecution, and delusions of grandiosity. Contributing factors are environment and heredity or the taking of drugs such as LSD or PCP. If the paranoid schizophrenic reaches his mid-thirties the rage may burn itself out or go into remission.

†Kenneth A. Bianchi, confessed to five killings in the L.A. Hillside Strangler killings.

mother, fantasizes her death, but is perversely in love with her. Sex with other women is impossible. In most cases, he has few social or sexual affiliations and has never had an experience of normal sexual intercourse. Murder is the only successful relationship he can have with a woman. All of his victims are only substitutes for his true target, his mother, who is often the last victim.

He has a past history of animal torture in his early teens. Richard Trenton Chase [the Sacramento Vampire Killer], for example, drank human blood and kept animal kidneys and livers in his freezer. He strangles and poisons his pets as substitutes for human victims.

For reasons unknown, sexual and aggressive impulses intertwine early in childhood in these sadistic types and eventually find expression in vicious sexual assaults and sadistic murders.

He kills to achieve sexual pleasure. Murder produces a powerful sexual arousal and pleasure and is a replacement for sex. He may masturbate while reliving the crimes.

The sexual sadist often taunts the police in letters, uses deliberate misspellings, and under stress may use handwriting that is unrecognizable from his true writing. The pleasure of baiting the police may actually become the motive for the slayings, and though he takes great pains to appear normal and avoid capture, he often throws suspicion upon himself.

The sexual sadist has a strong self-mutilation drive. As a child he may play at his own execution and eventually become suicidal.

He will be fascinated with the tools of policework and with policemen, and may pretend to be one. He collects weapons and instruments of torture and has great skill in their use.

The sadist seeks the dehumanization of his victims into objects that cannot reject him and that he has power over. He is incurable, feels no remorse for the cruelty he inflicts on others, and will most likely repeat his crimes.

He chooses victims with specific characteristics, such as students or hitchhikers. The sexual sadist can describe his assaults in great detail. If caught for one murder, he takes delight in confessing to all the others in an effort to dismay the police.

The sexual sadist may be clever enough not to have a history of identifiable mental illness.

"Why are there so many around now?" I asked.

"A possible explanation is that these people were perceived by parents as weird because they did things like cutting up animals and putting the parts in the refrigerator or whatever," said Lunde, "and under the old laws, that was enough to get someone committed, but now it isn't.

"I suspect there were a bunch of people put away for life who were potential Zodiac-type killers. But now that you can't keep people longer than ninety days* people like that are getting out. Until 1969, for instance, people could be committed for life to a mental hospital on pretty flimsy grounds. There was this drastic change where it became very difficult to commit someone. You had to have concrete evidence of either suicidal acts or an act of violence toward others."

"How often," I asked, "have you personally seen a sexual sadist? How many have you talked with?"

"A dozen," Lunde replied, "which is a lot more than one. But it doesn't, on the other hand, compare to the thousands of paranoid schizophrenics. There's something spooky about the incredible similarities among sexual sadists."

"Is it inconsistent," I asked, "for a sexual sadist to be a child molester as well?"

"No. The thing about all these people and the one thing they have in common is an abnormal relationship with women. They are limited or incapable of forming normal adult sexual relationships. And so what are the alternatives? One is sex with dead bodies or killing for sexual satisfaction. Another is sex with children.

"There are the common threads of inadequate normal adult sexual relationships and also the need to have power over the sexual object, which you can achieve either through violence,

---

*The Lanterman-Petris-Short Act was passed in 1967 and determined that a person can be detained only if he is a danger to himself or others. The reduction of 50,000 psychiatric beds in California in 1960 to 5,000 today deposited patients in local communities ill prepared to handle them.

strangulation, tying up, or whatever—or with children. The common thing is the power relationship and the need to be all powerful vis-à-vis the sexual object."

I remember what Kemper, the archetypal sexual sadist, said of his murders at his trial: "It was kind of a triumphant-type thing, like taking the head of a deer or an elk or something would be to a hunter. I was the hunter and they were my victims."

Sunday, March 2, 1980

Because of Zodiac's gigantic ego, I had always felt that somewhere along the line he would have to write Toschi using his real name. I asked the inspector if he had ever received a letter from any of the Zodiac suspects.

"Well, there is only one," he said, "a Vallejo student named Starr." (Not his real name.) "As I recall the phrasing was:

" 'If I can ever be of any help to you just let me know. I'm sorry I wasn't your man.'

"After the April 1978 Zodiac letter surfaced, a guy named Jim Silver with the California Department of Justice told me, 'You know, Starr is out of prison and he's been out for about six months. And you got this new letter and it's been authenticated.'

"I told him, 'Yeah I know. I got a letter from Starr about six months ago. He wrote me to let me know he was out and I thought at the time it was unusual."

" 'Jesus Christ,' said Silver, 'he's weird. He's a weird son of a bitch. He's such a good suspect we've got to watch him all the time.' "

I asked Toschi how the letter was addressed.

"Well, it was addressed only to me, not to Armstrong. It was addressed to me by my full name, Inspector David Toschi."

"I bet he typed it."

"That's right, Robert. It was typed," said Toschi.

Monday, March 3, 1980

I had the day off from work to speak with Lieutenant Husted of the Vallejo P.D. I had a hunch that Starr was the Santa Rosa link, and I was going to see if Husted could verify it.

Husted came in late, dressed in rough western clothes with an outside holster. As usual, he was tanned and fit. Husted, in an off-hours job, ran the Stress Management Hypnosis Institute on Marin Street. He was an expert in hypnosis. He worked for the state in some trials. After putting witnesses in a trance in a soundproof room, he would record their testimony on his built-in closed-circuit TV system. It was Husted's idea that we fly in Kathleen Johns, the woman who had escaped from Zodiac with her daughter, and have her put under deep hypnosis to enable her to describe the man she believed to be Zodiac. But the police had been unable to find her.

Husted was glad I had brought him information about Don Andrews, Narlow's favorite suspect. "Otherwise, Robert, we could not morally search for the Napa suspect, without stepping on Narlow's toes. I'm glad you came up with the information on your own. I'm interested in his whereabouts. Do you know where Andrews is now?"

"He's somewhere in San Francisco now," I said, "but to be honest, I've begun to have my doubts about him. The witnesses at the Stine killing say that he's too old and too fat."

Then I asked Husted about Starr, the suspect who had written Toschi.

"This Starr really has my interest," I told him. "I get strong feelings from the letter he wrote Toschi."

"I know what you mean," said Husted. "He's always been my favorite."

The rest of the day we talked about Starr, who was no longer a student but had moved in 1971 to Santa Rosa, where he was a salesman. His mother bought a house there in August 1975.

And that night, I began to put together a report on the best Zodiac suspect I had found yet.

Robert "Bob" Hall Starr

At the time of the known Zodiac killings (1968–70), Robert "Bob" Hall Starr (this name has been changed) was a "professional student" and lived with his mother in her house in Vallejo. He was highly intelligent, with an IQ of around 135. In 1971, he kept a trailer in Santa Rosa. In 1969 he had looked like the Zodiac composite description. He always kept to himself, collected rifles (he owned two .22s), and hunted game. To his sister-in-law and brother he spoke of "man as true game." Starr often spoke of man as the "most dangerous game."

In November 1969 Sheila*, his twenty-six-year-old sister-in-law, noticed a paper in Starr's hand and asked him what it was. He had been keeping it in a metal box in his brother's room in the North Bay. Hiding the lines of strange symbols, Starr said, "This is the work of an insane person. I'll show it to you later." He never did. The family became increasingly concerned. When he was asked by his sister-in-law about a bloody knife on the front seat of his car the day of the Berryessa attack he said, "That's chicken blood. I use it to kill chickens."

Sergeant Mulanax already suspected Starr of another terrible

*Not her real name.

crime, that of molesting a child at a school where he had once worked. This would fit in with Zodiac's knowledge of school bus routes and vacation times for the "kiddies."

Men of Starr's type, although they have a great underlying hatred of women, are capable of great personal charm. Starr tended to have a taunting way of speaking and often suffered from painful headaches.

Husted had a theory about the car Zodiac used in the Blue Rock Springs murder. Starr had been fired from a job at a gas station the week before Darlene's death. A friend of Starr's parked his Ford sedan there overnight to be repaired, and Starr could have used the car to commit the murder, returned it, and made the call to VPD. Starr and the owner of the '58 Ford often talked of death and murder. In August, Starr's friend also died from natural causes.

It was early in 1971 that Starr's family, his mother, brother and sister-in-law, began to suspect, on the basis of his erratic behavior, that he just might be the Zodiac killer. After consultation with Starr's uncle and much agonizing, the family dialed Toschi and told them of their fears. Armed with information turned over to them by Starr's relatives, Armstrong and Toschi began laying the groundwork for a search warrant.

Fred Wisman of the D.A.'s office in San Francisco called the Sonoma County D.A.'s office, who in turn put Toschi and Armstrong in charge, along with two Sonoma detectives.

"Jesus," thought Toschi, "Starr lives part of the time with his mom in Vallejo, camps out with his brother and sister-in-law in San Rafael, and has his own trailer near the campus. Which do we search?" The investigators decided on the trailer, since Starr had been there on Tuesday.

Starr had a job at a chemical company in Petaluma and a locker there. Toschi hoped that any evidence they wanted wasn't being hidden there.

Friday, June 4, 1971

San Francisco P.D. was very excited over the suspect. Even Toschi's secretary, Kate, looked up from typing the warrant request and information to say, "Good luck! I think you have him."

"Kate," said Toschi, "we're going to give it a try."

The request was taken to a Sonoma superior court judge. He read the affirmation and signed it. "I believe you have enough information to execute the search warrant," he said. "Gentlemen, I wish you luck."

The warrant specified "pieces of bloody shirt, rope, pens, glasses, trousers with pleats, blue or dark parka navy-type jacket, a knife in a sheath and a black hood." Even the dark clip-on glasses seen by Bryan Hartnell were mentioned.

Starr's family had told the two San Francisco detectives where his trailer and car were. The suspect's family had never visited him there but they did know the trailer was off wheels. Toschi had the manager of the trailer court show them specifically which stall the student used. The lot manager said that he had driven off just before they'd arrived at the trailer lot. The detectives found the door to the trailer standing open and decided to make a cursory search while they waited for Starr to return. Bob Dagitz, the print expert who had covered the Stine killing, was with Armstrong and Toschi, along with the two deputy sheriffs.

The men moved into the yellow trailer. Papers and debris were everywhere. There was a sour smell that filled the room. Toschi moved Starr's bed away from the wall and found the largest jar of Vaseline he had ever seen and several large, uncleaned dildos that rolled out onto the floor at his feet. They carefully replaced rubber dildos and moved the bed back. Then they went into the small, unkept kitchen.

"My God," said Toschi. "Bill, get a load of this!" The detective had opened the freezer and seen little animal hearts, livers, and mutilated rodent bodies. "It's not everybody who keeps dead squirrels in their freezers," thought Dagitz.*

*I later learned that Starr was working toward a degree in Biology, and had received permission from the state government to collect and experiment on small animals.

They waited forty-five minutes for Starr to come back. When they heard Starr's auto drive up, they rushed to the door of the trailer. The car was dirty; there were clothes in the back seat, and papers, books, and exams that went back years.

The student got out and lumbered up to the door.

"What's this all about?" he said coolly, without a trace of panic. He already knew who these detectives were from a visit they had paid him at one of his jobs last May. After a two-hour interrogation, they'd brought him back. Later Starr was fired from this job; he felt it was caused by the detectives' inquiries.

"We want to talk to you. We have a search warrant for your vehicle, for your trailer, and for your person. We have information that you are a very good suspect in the Zodiac murders," said Armstrong.

"I thought that guy was arrested," said Starr. "I live in Vallejo."

"We know."

"Well, help yourself," said the stocky man.

Toschi looked over as the student pointed at the trailer. Starr was wearing a Zodiac watch (a Clebar skindiver, underwater Chronograph made by the Zodiac watch company). He was also wearing a "Z" ring. When Toschi gestured toward it, Starr told him that his sister had sent it to him in 1967.

The detectives began a more complete search, rolling back furniture and moving the bed. Toschi pulled back the sheets and then once again pushed the bed all the way from the wall. The dildos rolled out at his feet.

"Are these yours? asked Toschi.

"I just sort of fool around," said the stocky student.

He did not seem embarrassed at all to the detectives. But as they continued the hour-long search, which "tore apart his place pretty good," Starr began to become uneasy and anxious. The two detectives were aware of how physically powerful Starr was in the close quarters.

"We have to take your prints," Toschi told the student. "We have to take your tips. These things have to be done."

Starr was obviously annoyed and fought against having his prints taken.

The print man, Dagitz, finally got good examples, and started making comparisons quietly by the lamp in a corner of the trailer. Dagitz had been pretty excited about Starr, especially when he heard the suspect was familiar with the area, was ambidextrous, and was good with weapons.

Meanwhile, Toschi and Armstrong were getting samples of Starr's handprinting. Toschi had two sheets of paper with typed sentences supplied by CI&I's Morrill. He told the suspect he had to reprint the sentences on the page. "We want you to print right-and left-handed and in uppercase and lowercase," said Toschi. "We want you to print this list of sentences."

Toschi handed him a black felt-tipped pen. He showed him the phrase, "up until now I have killed five" and said, "We want you to just print the way you normally print."

"I don't do it left-handed," said Starr.

"I understand you have some ability with your left hand."

"Who told you that?"

"We've done a very good background," said Toschi. "We know what you can do and what you can't." Starr was naturally left-handed, was forced to be right-handed in elementary school, and eventually reverted to left. His family and friends all said he could write and shoot with either hand. Morrill felt that the Zodiac letters were written right-handed.

The stocky man wrote with his left hand and appeared to have some difficulty. "I can't," he said.

"Do the best you can. Print capital letters, small letters. Print what we tell you," said Toschi.

The student didn't like that, but Toschi had decided that they were going to "do everything they could with Starr but stand him on his head."

The detectives had him go from A to Z and from 1 to 100. It was obvious to Toschi that the student was altering his printing, but it had the spacy quality that was found in the Zodiac letters.

"Why can't I print what I want?" said Starr.

"Because this is what we want you to print," said Toschi, impatience beginning to show in his voice. The detectives had him print "yours truely": and then asked Starr to print "This is the Zodiac speaking."

"What are you making me say? That I'm Zodiac?"

"No, but we have to compare. If you're not the man, we'll leave you alone. We'll just walk away from you, rule you out completely. But we have to be sure," said Toschi.

The student still balked, but he wrote out the phrase.

Toschi produced a second page of quotes. They had Starr write "In answer to your asking for more details about the good times I had in Vallejo, I shall be very happy to supply even more material." Starr copied it faithfully but repeated the word "more." Then Starr was made to write "All people who are shaking hands shake hands like that." Toschi noted that the last lines tilted toward the bottom right side of the page, as was common in the Zodiac letters.

At last, the detectives made their way out of the stifling trailer into the cool evening air. They adjourned to a coffee shop some six blocks away to have a snack and discuss the search.

Dagitz was depressed. "If the prints on Paul Stine's cab," he said, "were those of Zodiac, then they don't match Starr's. It's a positive no."

Back in San Francisco, Armstrong and Toschi sent the Starr printing samples off to Morrill in Sacramento and went home to wait for an answer. Within a day, Morrill got back to them on the phone.

"Sorry, Dave, there's just no match."

At this time, no one had any idea that Zodiac was using some sort of tracing technique in his letters. Toschi was also unaware that, as I learned from later research, stress produces dramatic changes in the handwriting of a sexual sadist. I also obtained samples of Starr's real handwriting on job applications; it was tiny and very different from the samples he made for Armstrong and Toschi.

"Everything sounded just perfect," Toschi told me later,

"but we couldn't find a way to prove that he was the Zodiac killer."

My feelings were that a mistake was made in not searching Starr's mother's Vallejo residence, where Starr often stayed, but it was in another county. Zodiac had used the two-county technique right from the beginning. He killed in areas that bordered on unincorporated sections of cities or that were areas of disputed jurisdiction between police and sheriff's departments. If Starr was Zodiac, then after the Santa Rosa search he had only to go back to Vallejo and destroy any physical evidence that might exist in his mother's basement.

I learned through the Department of Motor Vehicles that Starr owned two trailers in 1979. What if in 1971 Starr had had other unregistered trailers? He might have had a trailer in every county where the killings took place and the detectives had had the misfortune to search the wrong one.

Starr's father died just before the Riverside murder (1966). He passed on to his son a love of sailing. The Zodiac killing costume consisted of old-fashioned Navy clothes, pants with pleats. Was Starr, out of hatred or even love of his father, dressing up in his father's clothes to do the killing? Had these clothes hung in his father's cedar closet in Vallejo until 1975, when the house was sold?

Zodiac spoke of his "death machine" in his basement. Starr's room in his mother's house in Vallejo was a basement. It was a basement that swarmed with the little animals Starr liked to experiment with.

Starr had studied chemistry; the Zodiac bus bomb was a chemical bomb.

Starr spent some three years at an institution for the criminally insane as the result of a child molesting charge in 1975. When he was released, he returned to living under his mother's house, this time in Santa Rosa. She spoiled him, buying him a plane and two boats.

But the really interesting thing about Starr was this timetable:

1971, March 22: Zodiac postcard to *Chronicle*.

1971, June 4: Starr's trailer searched.

From June 1971 until January 28, 1974: Zodiac letters unexplainedly ceased. The murders directly connected with Santa Rosa began at this time, February 1972.

1974, January 29: First Zodiac letter in three years.

1974, May 8: Letter to *Chronicle* from Zodiac.

1974, July 8: Letter to *Chronicle* from Zodiac.

1975, December: Starr committed to institution for child molesting. The linked murders of young hitchhikers around Santa Rosa cease.

1977, December 30: Starr is released. He immediately writes Toschi a typewritten note.

1978, April 24: Zodiac writes again for the first time in four years.

1979, February 24: The first linked murder occurs since October 16, 1975, when Susan Dye was strangled in Santa Rosa, Teresa Matthews was strangled on a Saturday and left by a body of water (Russian River).

If Starr were Zodiac, then the search of his Santa Rosa trailer had caused him to stop writing until the heat was off. When Starr was released from prison, Zodiac wrote again.

I had asked Starr's parole officer if he had received a letter from him and he told me that he had. It was typed and had double the needed postage on it. The address slanted downward, stamps inverted.

I told Toschi, "Not only that, Inspector, until recently the parole officer had no idea that his guy was a Zodiac suspect. In fact, the day he found out, the P.O. was home looking at copies of the Zodiac letters. All evening he kept getting these calls where someone would just breathe. The P.O. told his girlfriend, 'I think that he knows that I know and that he knows that I know that he knows.'

"The P.O. did this impersonation of Starr for me where he tried to probe the suspect to see what sets him off. It was at their monthly meeting.

" 'You say you don't like to come to these meetings, Bob. But if you don't then you're going to have to go back to jail,' said the P.O.

"At this Starr gripped the sides of his chair, lowered his head, looked up at the P.O., and said, 'I wouldn't like that at all.'

"He kept saying this over and over again. He became very menacing. It was a total change in personality."

"That sounds exactly like Starr," said Toschi. "He cooperated with us, but only under much duress."

"I found out something I bet you didn't know, Dave. Starr has an enlarger. Isn't that interesting. Now you have two people with enlargers, Andrews and Starr.

"They talked Starr into seeing a psychiatrist, and Vallejo P.D. discovered that he had been boning up at the library on what the proper responses to psychiatric tests should be," I said. "Starr would take a test in this manner: he would study the board for a minute and then react swiftly, finishing the test immediately. These would be physical tests involving shapes and pegs. Dave, I saw a report from the psychiatrist that read, 'He [Starr] was a study of economy in motion and laughed when others tried to duplicate the ease in which he solved problems.' "

It was obvious that Starr took all of his tests the same way. He would not smile or show emotion, and would speak in a slow monotone.

"The test analyst gave Starr an ink blot test in 1978," I told Toschi, "and was warned to look for answers that contained the letter Z.

" 'The odds of more than one answer beginning with Z are very remote,' the analyst told VPD. 'I don't expect any.'

"Well, the first ink blot that Starr was shown reminded him of 'a zygomatic arch.' The analyst was shaken by this and at the end of the tests found that Starr had given five Z answers. As you may remember, Stine was shot in the zygomatic arch."

When Toschi was demoted to Pawn Shop Detail, Starr expressed his feelings to his P.O. He felt that Armstrong and Toschi's visit to his office in 1971 had cost him his job. "Now Mr. Toschi will know what it feels like!" Starr said through his teeth.

"Starr works at a store as a salesman but hates working for a living," his P.O. told me. "He still lives in the basement, but now it's the basement of his mother's new home here in Santa Rosa. And he still has live chipmunks running around the house.

"But I'll tell you one thing," said the P.O., "he's got his act down great."

Wednesday, March 5, 1980

I turned out the lights on my car and coasted to a stop under an elm about twenty-five feet from Starr's front window. It was 8:30 P.M.; there was a chill to the night air. To the left of Starr's house was a driveway and garage. There was only one V.W. in sight. I wondered where he kept his campers and boats and other cars. I stayed for hours, watching the window overlooking Starr's porch and front door. I could make out the silhouette of a large hulking shape, which I took to be some cabinet or appliance. At 11:00 P.M., it moved.

I had been watching the shadow of Starr.

Saturday, March 8, 1980

Starr worked in a store. The store was so large that I decided it would be safe to get a closer look at him.

It was a bright shining morning. I parked blocks away so that he couldn't see what kind of car I drove or get a glimpse of my license number. I brought my two little boys and a friend with me. Starr had never seen me; I, of course, knew exactly what he looked like from photographs.

I found him in the back of the store ringing up sales. I had intended to buy something from him in order to get a sample of his handprinting, but there was such a feeling of menace and of animal strength radiating from him that I left quickly. I had expected a mild, overweight man who would be, like Son of Sam, the last person you would suspect of being a mass murderer, but this man was powerful and dangerous looking. His eyes were cast into darkness beneath a heavy brow; he still wore a close, blond crew cut. He was heavy all right, but the girth came from solid muscle, especially in his neck, shoulders, and arms.

I gathered up my boys from the front of the store where they were waiting and took them for a soft drink at a nearby 7-Eleven store. My youngest got a prize on the bottom of his Slurpee drink.

It was a ring with one of the signs of the Zodiac on it.

Sunday, March 9, 1980

Once again I spoke with Starr's parole officer in Santa Rosa. He had knowledge of the man's movements since his release from prison.

"Is he still living with his mother?" I asked.

"Oh, yeah, his mother is still there and she, ah . . . it's a strange situation. I talked with him about his mother. It's one of the major things in his therapy and the way he relates to life.

"Do you think Starr hates his mother?" I asked.

"Oh, yeah. He absolutely hates her. . . . She would say about the father, 'That miserable son of a bitch, he's gone all the time. He never takes care of his family and satisfies my needs. He never takes care of his familial responsibilities. Men are all assholes. They all do the same thing. They're all miserable sons of bitches.' Then she would tell her son, 'You're just like all other men. You're this, you're that.'

"Years and years of that completely demolished his ability to have regular heterosexual relations with an adult female. One of the things he does frequently is when his mother says, why are you the way you are, he says, 'I'm all fucked up. The reason I'm all fucked up is because of you. You made me the way I am.' And she feels really guilty and all the guilt comes out and she refuses to do anything to stop whatever behavior he's involved in.

"I told him one day, 'Bob, you're suspected of being the Zodiac killer.'

" 'I know,' he said to me.

" 'What do you think about that?' I asked him.

" 'I think that was real wrong to do that to me. I think it was unfair.'

" 'It was?'

" 'Yeah.'

" 'Have you read the reports?'

" 'Yeah, I know what they are talking about. That's all a pack of lies,' Starr said.

" 'That's fine. Who in hell is going to admit to being the Zodiac.'

"Robert, the greatest phrase I ever heard in dealing with child molesters and mentally disordered sex offenders was 'Whatever gets you off gets you off.' And it doesn't make any difference whether you go to Atascadero [institution for criminally insane] for four years and they bring you back and they say you're sane and you're cured and you're no longer a MDSO. What basically happens is, whatever gets you off, gets you off. You may be able to repress what gets you off, but that is still what gets you off."

Tuesday, March 11, 1980

In Vallejo again, I learned even more about Starr.

In 1965, before there were any murders, before there were any letters, before there was such a creature as the Zodiac, Starr and two friends, Kenn and Bill, (not their real names), from Torrance went hunting. The following conversation took place, as reported in a police deposition filed July 1971.

"I would rather hunt people than wild game," Starr told his friends. "I think of man as true game. Man, after all, is the most dangerous game.

"This is what I would do," said Starr, warming to the subject. "I would hunt them at night with an electric gun sight, a flashlight taped to the barrel of my gun."

"Christ! But why?" asked Kenn.

"Because," said Starr, turning and locking his unblinking gaze on his fellow hunter, "I want to. And not only that, I would write taunting letters to the police and the papers. And I would call myself the Zodiac."

My sources told me several more stories about Starr and his life in Vallejo. In 1973, a doctor's report on him said that he was "potentially violent, he is dangerous" and "he is capable of killing." The doctor suspected that Starr had "five separate personalities." When Starr's parole officers first visited Starr's Santa Rosa home, he had neighborhood children riding bicycles and waving red flags to direct them up the driveway. "Another example of Starr's dark sense of humor," said the senior parole officer.

Starr's physical strength could be verified by a boyhood friend, who was now a retired highway patrolman. When Starr was a teenager, the friend passed him walking down a San Francisco street and in the rearview mirror of his car saw five Marines closing in on him. "There's going to be real trouble now," the friend thought. But before he could back up, bodies were flying everywhere. Starr was the only one left standing. "I backed up my car and asked if he was all right and if he needed a lift home," the friend told me. "He said that he was going for a walk, and no thanks."

At a store where he once worked, he was hassled by the men there. He dared one to come at him. He picked the man up and hurled him across the room into a stack of cardboard boxes.

Was he strong enough to lift dead coeds in Santa Rosa and hurl them over railings far into the bushes?

In the Navy, Starr had had code training, was a wire operator and a sail maker. In spite of weight and blood pressure problems, Starr still did scuba diving.

When Starr was arrested as a child molester and when he was released on bail, he told all of his friends that he was being arrested because "he was the Zodiac."

During the trial, he took to harassing the deputy who was testifying against him by standing outside the man's house at night. Finally, one evening the cop came out and chased him off.

When Starr was convicted, the police came to his home and

were let in by his mother. They found him in the center of his basement room howling and shrieking, live chipmunks crawling all over him and "squirrel shit dripping from his shoulders."

During his time in prison, Starr wrote his friends that he "hoped Zodiac would kill or write a new letter to the papers. That will clear me."

After his release in 1978, Starr was talked into a series of psychiatric tests by a Santa Rosa psychologist, Dr. Thomas Rykoff (this name has been changed by request). My source told me, "The Santa Rosa shrink came to the conclusion that Starr is 'extremely dangerous and is a sociopath [feels no guilt]' and that he is 'highly intelligent and incapable of functioning with women in a normal way.' " The sociopath label was certain by the next to the last session. When Starr talked of Zodiac he cried. Dr. Rykoff felt that Starr was "repressing very deep hatred."

The psychologist was midway in his study of Starr when, as part of a training program for a social rehabilitation group he was organizing in Santa Rosa, he hypnotized a young woman. As the woman told Rykoff more and more of her feelings and suspicions about her brother-in-law and his dark side, the doctor began to realize that the character being sketched was frighteningly familiar. "What's this?" thought Rykoff. "That sounds just like Starr. The potential for danger is just the same."

Rykoff said nothing to the woman, whom he had correctly deduced was Starr's sister-in-law. The doctor wondered if he was being set up. First he had seen Starr as a favor to Lieutenant Husted and Starr's P.O., and now the patient's sister-in-law showed up with more suspicions about Starr. The coincidence was just too much. Rykoff had to know just who this man was and why were so many people interested in him. The psychologist was becoming more and more terrified of his patient.

On November 1, 1978, the doctor asked his brother, a San Francisco policeman, to look into Starr's background and find out what he was really suspected of. Late the next day, his brother got back in touch with the psychologist.

"I've found out he was a major suspect in the Zodiac case," said Rykoff.

"Oh, shit," said the doctor. "Find out anything you can about him, and how I should deal with him."

The forthcoming answer was anything but reassuring.

"We felt strongly then and now that Starr was our best suspect," Toschi told the doctor's brother. "We cut him loose because we weren't able to find any physical evidence. Believe me, we did everything we could with the guy. Personally, my gut feeling is that he is the man. Tell Dr. Rykoff that when he talks to him to do it in a place that he can get out of in a hurry. Keep at an oblique angle to him. Don't get too close. And above all, don't make him angry."

Rykoff had Starr's sister-in-law Sheila back in and, with Husted, put her under deep hypnosis on November 15. When she remembered a paper with strange lines of symbols she had seen in Starr's hand in 1969, Husted decided to see if she could redraw these figures. In automatic writing, she slowly drew four lines of symbols. Automatic writing is usually sprawling but hers was straight and even, gridlike, just like the Zodiac's. The symbols closely resembled the third line of the Zodiac 340-character cipher. As the hypnotic session progressed and the woman spoke more and more about Starr, she began to tremble and shake; her knuckles turned white. Finally, Rykoff had to stop the hypnotic session.

Rykoff and the sister-in-law weren't the only ones afraid of Starr. His own mother possibly feared him. Though she lived in the same house, she kept traveling constantly around the U.S. and Europe. Was it to get away from him? Both the P.O. and sister-in-law thought so. Pension money from Starr's deceased father was probably the capital used to finance the trip.

Starr's Parole Officer was observant enough to notice that Starr wore pleated, old-fashioned pants. At the time the P.O. first discovered that Starr was a major Zodiac suspect, he looked out of the window of the apartment he was sharing in Bodega and saw the student standing two stories below by the complex's swimming pool. He was smiling, staring straight up at the P.O., looking like some white, beached whale and holding the hand of a little nine-year-old girl. There was no reason for Starr to be there; he looked totally out of place among all the young people. He had obviously taken the hand of the young girl so that he would fit in with the crowds of families.

Once, officers on the way to the Santa Rosa area that a killer had used as a dumping ground for the bodies of Santa Rosa coeds stopped in their tracks on Sully Road. Walking down the road toward them and from the murder area was Starr. He traveled the road to go skin-diving, he told the open-mouthed policemen.

Wednesday, March 12, 1980

This evening, again I watched Starr at work in the store. At one point I stood closer than two feet away, listening to his soft, quiet voice as he spoke with customers. His brow was even more massive than I remembered, his body sturdy and strong. But the paunch around the middle was there, as Zodiac had been described.

Starr wore a bright red overcoat with the name "Bob" on a patch sewn over his left breast pocket. He had previously worked in the rear of the store doing stock work, but now he worked practically all the time near the front window. On the wall was a sign; the lettering, done with a felt-tip pen, looked similar to the Zodiac printing. I would have to get a copy of the sign.

Later, I shot a few photos of Starr from across the street, when he had his head turned partially away from the window. I was afraid he would see me. At 5:15 I left and made some time-exposure shots of Starr's house. Then I drove back to the store.

I planned to get a photo of Starr in silhouette as he left work and passed under the bright vapor lights of a drugstore. At 6:30 P.M., I saw him leave the store and start across the street toward me. I positioned myself in the shadows and waited for him to pass between me and the lights. But he didn't.

I realized that he wasn't walking home tonight. He must have brought his car to work. I raced for my V.W. In a few seconds I was behind the wheel. I didn't see Starr anywhere. I started the engine, turned on my lights, and was about to pull out onto the darkened street when the V.W. coupe parked behind me came to life and slid onto the road, lights off. The car had been hidden under the shadows of a large tree; I hadn't realized it was occupied. The driver peered into my car as he drove slowly alongside. It was Starr.

He turned the corner and started east. I waited a moment, turned out my headlights, and then followed him. He was heading away from his house.

Three blocks away, he stopped, and I parked about a block away from him and began walking toward him. When I was close enough to make him out in the dusk, I could see that he was looking around to see if anyone was watching.

Suddenly, he walked over and opened the door of another car parked on the street. He got in and raced off into the blackness. By the time I sprinted back to my car, he was gone.

My aim had been to see if I could find out where he was keeping his trailers, or at least to know where he hung out. Why had he switched cars? Was he actually afraid people were following him? Next time I followed Starr, I would have to use a different car.

Even if Starr was not the Zodiac, he was up to something very strange.

Friday, March 14, 1980

Lieutenant Husted was buying a pony for his daughter. I watched him from the wire gate a hundred feet away. It was a stormy day, and the sky was filled with black clouds; the grass in the field waved in the wind. Husted's truck leaked a steady drip of rusty water on the edge of the road. On the other side of the barbed fence, a watchdog barked at me.

Husted believed that Zodiac was responsible for the string of Santa Rosa coed killings. That afternoon, he had shown me a two-page list of victims.

"There's a lot I haven't told you and can't," he said as he unlocked the truck. "I was thinking that if you could be brought into the case officially then I could tell you much more. We need some new stuff . . . something we can get a warrant with. I want to hypnotize some of the witnesses again, and if you were there as a police artist we could put together some good composite drawings and also learn some things that might help your book."

"That would be fine with me," I said.

"Starr has a friend I haven't told you about before," said Husted, "and Starr seems to have confided in him that he is the Zodiac killer and told him details of some of the murders.* I'd like to put the friend under, and the sister-in-law as well. And of course Kathleen Johns, if we can ever find her. Have you had any luck on that?"

"She was living in Riverside until December. I have the address, but she moved and my letter came back 'unable to forward.' "

I had mentioned searching for Starr's trailers earlier to Husted.

"I think we know where one is now, but I don't think there's anything there," said Husted. "I think any evidence is in his basement, not out in the open where we could see it. The guy's a carpenter . . . good with his hands. I would go in with sonar equipment and look for a hidden room. I think, Robert, that's where you'll find the bloody clothes, keys, and maybe even photos.

"I think Starr has built himself a place to relive his crimes."

Sunday, April 20, 1980

Driving on 101, almost to Santa Rosa, I tried to imagine how the killer of the coeds had managed to pick them up on the freeway. Most of the Santa Rosa Junior College students got rides on Mendocino Avenue in front of the school or at a gas station at the College Avenue onramp. For the killer to pick up a hitchhiking student, I felt that he had to be in Santa Rosa initially.

The victims were found dumped on Franz Valley Road a distance of seven to eight miles from Santa Rosa. I wondered how

---

*Of course, such a "confession" would not mean Starr had committed the crimes. False confessions are common in notorious murder cases.

in that scant distance the killer was able to strangle them and in some cases elaborately tie them up and then dump them on a road so narrow and so winding that a parked car could be happened upon any second. In three cases, the girls were poisoned with strychnine. Fast-acting as that alkloid is, how did the murderer get the women to ingest it before he got to Franz Valley Road? The killer must have had a home to take the women to for at least a short period; I was certain that the murderer must be some sort of resident of Santa Rosa or at least have lodging there.

Starr, I remembered, had a trailer in Santa Rosa.

In the driving rain I made my way on Mark West Springs Road until I came to a fork. To my left was Franz Valley Road; to my right was Porter Creek Road. Bodies had been found on both roads; I was reminded of Zodiac's killings on Lake Herman Road and Blue Rock Springs. In both cases the killer came to a fork in the road. One time he went right and next he went to the left, in search of victims.

On Franz Valley Road, I drove until I came to the area where seven bodies had been found, and parked my small car on the shoulder of the road. I made my way down the embankment through heavy trees and underbrush to the floor of the ravine, some sixty feet below. The killer must have been incredibly strong to hurl bodies over a fence and past the heavy shrubs and foliage to the bottom of the ravine.

Drenched, I drove my car to the end of Franz Valley Road, where I realized that even if the killer had taken the Porter Creek fork he would have met up with Franz Valley Road again at Calistoga. And for the first time I became aware of how very close to Pacific Union College at Angwin I was. Shepard and Hartnell had been students there.

Friday, April 25, 1980

As I drove to Santa Rosa, I thought of Dean Ferrin. He had begun to receive crank calls about his wife's death at the hands of Zodiac.

Starr was not at the store when I stopped to look for him, so

I got back in my car and drove past his home. All of his cars were there. One was a gray Skylark, one was a blue-white Corvair, and the other car was a 1967 V.W. Karmann Ghia, an almost exact duplicate of Bryan Hartnell's car from the Lake Berryessa attack. He also had two sailboats and somewhere else three "special construction" trailer-campers.

I figured he had taken a long late lunch. At 3:00 I went back to the store; there was still no sign of him. I decided to take another look at the poster in back with its printing that resembled Zodiac's. As I had feared, it was gone. But as I turned away, I saw something that brought me up short

Hanging slightly above my eye level were six clipboards with notes and writing on them. One of them had block handprinting on it in felt-tip pen that was the closest to the Zodiac printing that I had ever seen. The block of printing was signed. It was signed by Starr.

V.P.D. had told me that they had no samples of Starr's printing (though I had seen script letters that the police had in their files that Starr had mailed from the mental institution) and that he now typed everything.

The store was crowded and dark and I knew that taking a photograph without arousing the attention of the staff would be next to impossible. Too, Starr could return any moment for his clipboard; I didn't want to tangle with him. I came back a short time later with a friend and we bought a few items, then moved to the back of the store. I pretended to take a picture of my friend clowning around with a wooden spoon. What I was really photographing, with the lens wide open, was the lettering almost four feet away. We did this in an open, loud, obvious way, and it came off perfectly.

Now I had to get the photo of the clipboard developed and enlarged. I couldn't believe that anything could possibly come out under the circumstances, but I decided to get the best photographer I knew to try and bring the printing up enough for Morrill to examine.

My absurd backup plan, if the photo was a dud, was to make a copy of the note in felt-tip and tape it down to a brown clipboard exactly like the one in Starr's store. I would then go back to the store and make a switch with my copy. I knew I was a good enough artist that if I put the two side by side and moved them around Starr himself couldn't tell which was his and which was the one I brought into the store.

Monday, April 28, 1980

Gary Fong developed the film for me.

"It's going to be a bit grainy," he said.

"That's fine," I said. "I'll be happy just to get anything to send to Sacramento."

It wasn't until midafternoon that Gary had enlarged it enough to please himself. I got a sharp, clear black-and-white eight-by-ten from him. At 4:30, I mailed it to Morrill in Sacramento by special delivery. The people at the post office assured me that he would get it early the next morning.

Tuesday, April 29, 1980

At 10:17 A.M., Morrill called and told me that he had gotten my exemplar and, with the other handwriting expert there, Dave DeGarmo, from Pleasant Hill, had looked at the sample.

"On the basis of the exemplar you sent me, Robert, I cannot rule this man out as the Zodiac killer," Morrill said. "They look good. I've got DeGarmo here with me. Could you get us more samples of his writing?"

I promised I would.

I decided to use the direct approach.

Thursday, May 1, 1980

I called Starr's employer at home at 8:30 P.M. I explained that I needed help in regard to an urgent, serious, and confidential matter and needed specimens of printing from someone who worked at his store. I emphasized that I wasn't interested in the content of the handprinting but only in the shape and spacing of the individual characters. I held back Starr's name because I didn't want to jeopardize the job of an innocent man. And at no time did I mention that it involved a murder case.

"Wait a minute! Are you insinuating that there is the possibility that there is someone in my employ who might be a criminal?" the boss said. "Sir, I don't employ criminals!"

"No, it has to do with threatening letters received over a ten-year period," I said.

"I've got to think about it," the boss said. "I don't think I'd like anyone doing that to me."

Over the next few weeks he changed his mind several times, but in the end, I was denied access to the freight files and Starr's requisition slips.

Because of the search warrant served on Starr in 1971, the Vallejo P.D. was hesitant to request another, especially now that Starr had moved to another county. Husted, saddled with other cases, would, I imagined, have preferred that a civilian gather handprinting samples. As a favor to me, Morrill was checking them out.

Thursday, August 7, 1980

And so for some time, in an effort to get samples of Starr's handprinting, I asked my friends to buy things from him.

"Did you know that I used to be a teacher?" Starr told one female friend of mine. "I taught one class of eighth graders, but I really enjoyed teaching elementary school kids. My kids did well —one little girl in the third grade knew tenth-grade math by the time she graduated. My entire class could read at seventh-grade level. I loved working with elementary school kids."

"That's a great age," my friend agreed.

"I thought that would be the up and coming field. And now I can't get a teaching job, so I end up working here, six days a week for $5.32 an hour. The only day I get off is Friday."

"Do you always work six days a week? That must be hard."

"Yes, except for one time when I took a few days off without pay, but it was like pulling teeth to get them," said Starr.

"Well, you know how hard teaching jobs are to get in California."

"True, but I'm going down tomorrow night to apply for a job teaching adult education—twenty hours a week at $10.00 an hour. It sure beats what I make here.

"But this job is all right. I like dealing with people," he said, looking straight through her.

Zodiac

Tuesday, August 12, 1980

I drove to Napa to ask Ken Narlow if he thought that Zodiac was involved in the Santa Rosa murders.

The broad-faced, heavyset lawman didn't pause a second but answered, "Not really. We considered some of them, but the characteristics were not compatible."

"We've all got our favorites," he said. "Toschi and Armstrong were always high on Starr. I've been high on Andrews. We're all just guessing."

Narlow and I began looking through Don Andrews' file, comparing it to the information we had on Starr.

"Don Andrews Engine Repair," said Narlow, "might be a cover or he might have actually repaired them. Father was Oscar Andrews [this name changed], mother was Betty Moran [this name has been altered]. Here he was booked as a transient by L.A.P.D. Identification was recorded as Walt Hansen [this name has been changed], January 11, 1945. Occupation given as stage singer.

"Well," said Narlow, pounding his desk for emphasis, "I'll tell you, if Andrews isn't the Zodiac, I'll take one just like him."

A 1969 photo of him was very close to the Zodiac composite drawing when Narlow laid them alongside each other.

"See, here he gives his occupation as engine builder," said the detective, still looking through the file. "Walt Hansen is the same as Don Andrews. Here's an affidavit of registration in 1967. He lists his occupation as engine builder. Here's his rap sheet. You definitely have a Don Andrews alias Oliver Walter Hansen.

"Kathleen Johns said the Zodiac wore a band on his eyeglasses. So does Howard.

"In 1969 Napa had three homicides within ten days, which just tore a small department like ours apart, manpower-wise. We were kind of fragmented in the investigation division so I requested that an investigator from the Department of Justice be assigned to help us with this case the moment we found out it was tied in with the slayings in Vallejo and Solano County. We were assigned Mel Nicolai, a very close personal friend of mine.

"Informational time charts (PERT Charts) were done on all the Zodiac crimes with the assistance of the Department of Justice so that the officers involved could keep in contact with all the evidence and time sequences. We do it on major homicides and surely on something as complex as this, involving so many different police agencies. All the palm prints Napa has have been checked against the suspects. Now San Francisco's got fingertips. One in blood."

I asked Narlow about the story of Bob Hall Starr and the two hunters, when he predicted in 1966 that he would kill couples and call himself Zodiac.

"That story is so bizarre you don't know whether to believe it or not. Sometimes people concoct things like this, for whatever reason. Maybe they firmly believe it. I don't know, but that story about him talking about those things is so pat that if he in fact did say it, then he almost has to be the Zodiac.*

"It would be difficult at this point if a man were to come in here and confess to the Zodiac killings. It would take a considerable length of time for us to unravel some of the things he said to

---

*I later learned that there was some antagonism between Starr and one of the hunters that could cause the report to be suspect.

determine whether it came out of newspaper clippings or interviews with people. Of course, there are certain little things that we've held back," said Narlow.

Saturday, October 25, 1980

It had become apparent to me over the years that the police departments were not exchanging their best Zodiac information with each other. I remember Toschi telling me, "Narlow could never put Don [Andrews] down in the area of Riverside but we could. Still we don't know how long he was down there in Riverside."

After a visit to see Husted in Vallejo, I called Toschi.

"This guy, Andy Todd Walker, they were so hot on, he supposedly was the one sitting in the restaurant all the time bugging Darlene. But Bobbie Ramos told me, 'No! That wasn't the one. I told them it wasn't him!'

"There *was* a guy doing these things, poking around in Darlene Ferrin's life. I just don't think Walker was the one. They all say they saw a man in a white sedan with old California plates. Bobbie saw this guy, stocky, light curly hair. You know, the whole bit. A lot of people have seen this man," I told him.

"Obviously," said Toschi, "you've got so much information I'd like to see it all come together. I think it's terrific. I really think it was someone from Vallejo or close to Darlene. Right now it looks that way. The more information you keep getting, the more it leads to the area there."

Saturday, November 8, 1980

In answer to a letter I wrote, Darlene Ferrin's sister Linda called me. Since Darlene's death her life had been chaos and she was calling me from near Stockton.

I had only one question at this time, "Linda: did Darlene go to Lake Berryessa?"

"Yes," she said, "she liked it up there. And that's why . . . I believe Darlene knew Cecilia Shepard."

Saturday, December 20, 1980

My attempts at following Starr were as worthless as before. I was certain he was on guard. However, I got hold of some job applications he had recently filled out and some business receipts from 1980. I drove to Sacramento and arrived at Sherwood Morrill's just before 8:00 at night. Morrill was anxious to see more of Starr's printing.

He studied the samples for five minutes and then looked up at me. "Well, right off, Starr has none of the three-stroke *k*'s we associate with Zodiac. And take a look at Zodiac's *n*. It's either like a checkmark or a hump. Now Starr's *n*'s are rounded. Starr's *y*, too, is all wrong. But outside of that the samples are close enough that I still want to see more."

Sherwood thought that the printing that Starr was doing since he'd gotten out of prison was contrived and not natural to him.

Monday, January 12, 1981

I called to set up an appointment with Jack Mulanax, the policeman who had replaced Lynch and Rust on the Ferrin-Mageau investigation. He was a private detective now, but wouldn't touch a case if he thought the client was guilty.

"I understand that you had a suspect you liked a lot," I said. "Was this suspect named Starr?"

"Yes. Starr was the only suspect I ever developed that I had any strong feelings about," said Mulanax.

"I have a file on Starr that you might like to see," I told him. "I got his scholastic record."

"Starr was down in Southern California on the first Zodiac murder," said Mulanax. "Down at Riverside. He was a student at the college."

"Bob Starr? That's astounding. Starr seems convinced that he is the Zodiac now. He evidently told some people that he is," I said. "He's working at a store right in Santa Rosa now."

"I don't feel there's any proof now. But at the time I was real high on him. I think Bill and Dave Toschi were too."

"Did you ever have anyone besides Starr?"

"The only one that ever turned me on was Starr. I didn't realize that he was still around here [in the Bay Area]."

"I go in all the time and buy things from him. But I can't get him to print anything. I know Morrill saw some of Starr's printing. His writing has changed a lot over the years."

"I wasn't aware that this Starr was still around. We'll have to use a little discretion," said Mulanax. He sounded worried.

"Assuming it isn't Starr, do you think the Zodiac is still alive?"

"It's the consensus that the guy is either dead or in a mental institution or penal institution."

"But that's where Starr has been, in 1975 to 1978."

"I wasn't aware of that."

"And what I thought was interesting is that after Toschi and Armstrong talked to Starr in his trailer we stopped getting letters from the Zodiac," I continued. "By the way, how did you get on to Starr?"

"Some people who knew him."

"Oh, the hunters, the two guys in the woods with him."

"Yes."

Wednesday, January 14, 1981

Over coffee Toschi and I discussed Starr. "Dave, I've got something I'm not sure you know," I said. "Starr was at Riverside College in 1966."

There was a long pause as Toschi absorbed this.

"His family had told us something about Starr being around the Riverside area in the middle or late sixties," Toschi said. "It's never been confirmed."

"I was surprised, to say the least. I was able to place him there only in the early seventies before.

"If Starr were actually at Riverside College maybe someone saw him with scratches on his face the day after the Bates killing. He's the first suspect that I've run across who was also at RCC.

"We knew he was in the area but not at RCC."

"That's what I thought."

"When the family came to us," said Toschi, "we told V.P.D. about Starr. They had already scanned him very, very briefly. Mulanax's eyes really popped. He actually thought we had him."

"You might have. Starr has a friend that Husted knows about. He's afraid of Starr, and his wife asked him not to speak to the police. Seems one night while they were out drinking, Starr hinted to this friend that he was Zodiac. This is the man that Starr wrote to while he was in the institution. There is a remote possibility that he was also a patient at Atascadero when Starr was there."

"I wish I could give you a better suspect than Starr," Toschi said, "We exhausted every avenue. We just didn't know which way to go after we searched his trailer."

"Since you're off the case, if I was able to come up with some proof on Starr, whom would I give it to?" I asked. "Would you have trouble presenting it to your department?"

"You might be better off staying with someone in V.P.D. Starr is outside of our jurisdiction."

"Right. I've been passing everything along to Husted anyway. I was just concerned."

"I know you are," said Toschi, leaning back in his chair.

"A guy who's only under the delusion that he's the Zodiac," I said, "couldn't really plan to be in Riverside in 1966, because the Riverside murder was only uncovered long after Starr became a suspect. Zodiac even attempted to conceal his connection to the crime, only belatedly taking credit, as if he had made some sort of slip. There's an awful impressive case against the guy."

"We sure tried to get him," sighed Toschi, "and everything we had we passed on to Vallejo. But I'm aware after talking to you that so much of what V.P.D. had was not relayed over here to us, and I'm sorry. It was like a one-way street."

"Starr does have a .22."

"We knew that. Well, he was an outdoorsman, and all that. Rifle, handgun. But not enough for us to book him on a warrant."

"And why does he change cars all the time if he's not up to something?"

After I arrived at Jack Mulanax's home in Vallejo, he decided to take me out to the crime scenes again. The heavy rain had stopped and was now mist. Mulanax carried two handguns in holsters with him to his truck. As the big man slid behind the wheel, he stashed the weapons under the front seat. There was a rifle rack on the truck. Besides being a P.I., Mulanax was an avid deer hunter.

After we had looked at the Lake Herman site, he took me out to Blue Rock Springs and told me about a trap the police had set up, a decoy, a couple of dummies in a car to the west of the parking lot. The car was parked partially in the woods and a stakeout set up. Nothing came of it.

Mulanax said, "I was real surprised when you told me Starr was working in the Bay Area. Is his mother still alive?"

"She spends her time traveling."

"Evidently there is some money in that family."

"He's got a new Karmann Ghia and quite a few other cars."

Mulanax rummaged among the notes he had taken. "I don't know if this was indicated in our reports. I just read this part this morning," he said.

At this point I learned a stunning piece of information.

"There is a voiceprint of Zodiac speaking to Nancy Slover [the police operator at V.P.D.] on the night of the murder."

I ran to a booth in Vallejo and dialed Toschi in San Francisco.

"Dave, did you know that there is a tape of Zodiac calling Nancy Solver? Mulanax told me that Linda, Darlene's sister, has heard it as well."

"Oh, really. I was never aware of it," Toschi said gravely. "That's interesting. She says she heard a tape. I'd like to know about that. Try and verify that."

"It does seem terribly important."

"Well, sure it does."

"I wanted you to know. I'm looking into it," I promised. I told Toschi about the composite drawing that Linda had produced for V.P.D. of the man she saw at Darlene's painting party and how closely it matched the Zodiac composite on the wanted poster.

"Ours? For Chrissake."

"Also, according to Linda and some of her friends, there was a man bringing Darlene presents from Mexico. All they knew was that he was called Bob. She described him with close-cropped hair, paunch, muscular. It sounds a lot like Starr. Evidently she got the connection across because the police were looking into people named Bob."

I told Toschi that Bobbie Ramos, when asked by the police who Darlene's closest friends were, answered, "Sue Gilmore, Robbie, and this guy named Bob who used to bring her presents from Mexico." The presents were a silver dollar purse and a belt.

Thursday, March 5, 1981

I drove the thirty-six miles to Vallejo in a downpour to check out a hunch I had about the Blue Rock Springs murder. I passed the oil refineries to my left on the way, thousands of twinkling lights amid blue-white steam billowing from the towers.

Re-creating the crime, I left Darlene's house at 11:40 P.M. (although the sitters told me it was closer to midnight when she actually left), and drove on Georgia Street straight to Mike's house on Beechwood. I arrived there at 11:45. I waited only one minute, and then drove to Blue Rock Springs and stopped in the lot at 11:51. I allowed enough time for the shooting at midnight, and then drove down Springs Road to the phone booth used by Zodiac to phone the Vallejo Police Department. Even with the rain, the poor visibility, and obeying the speed limit and all stop signs and lights, I got to the booth at 12:09. Zodiac's call to the police was made at 12:40.

That left thirty minutes unaccounted for.

The booth was less than a block from Darlene's house and in front of the Sheriff's Department parking lot. The lot is large and open, and Darlene's home was easily visible across it. I had to ask myself, would Zodiac park almost directly in front of the Sheriff's Office, in a car that may have been seen leaving the scene of the crime? And for over a half an hour? Isn't it more likely that he lived near the police and sheriff's departments and went home to hear the sirens of squad cars rushing to Blue Rock Springs. When this didn't happen, might not he have walked to the phone booth and reported the shooting, so that he could get his kicks in exactly the same way he was to do later in Napa? By 12:47 the police knew exactly where the call was placed and anyone in the Sheriff's department could look across the lot and see a person in the lighted booth.

After Zodiac finished his call, a call he knew was in the process of being traced, he was seen by an unidentified black man. Would he dare use another booth in the area to place his one o'clock crank calls to Darlene's house and Dean's relatives? Particularly if the area was mostly black? My thought was that he made at least the second calls from his own home. He finished at the booth at 12:45 and made his crank call at 1:00, fifteen minutes later.

If Zodiac arrived home at 12:09, he would have hidden his car in the garage, hidden his gun, and waited for the sound of sirens. Lynch did "not roll immediately" on the report of shooting, and so, tired of waiting, Zodiac leaves at 12:25. He walks to the booth, about a fifteen-minute walk, and makes his call to the police. Then the roughly fifteen-minute stroll home, slowly so as to not attract attention, and perhaps irresistibly past Darlene's so that he could look into the darkened window. Was Zodiac's home in the direction of Darlene's from the booth?

With the phone booth in the center, was Zodiac's home within a fifteen-minute walking distance?

Few homes in Darlene's neighborhood had garages, and I felt that the killer needed a garage to hide his Chevrolet. Starr had one. Going by the Zodiac letters, he would also have a basement, another rarity in this neighborhood. Starr had one. His house at the time was exactly a fourteen- or fifteen-minute walk away from the phone booth.

Beyond everything else, I still firmly believed that Zodiac knew Darlene and that she had known who he really was. Zodiac knew Darlene's nickname. With no word of the attack on radio or television, he knew her home phone number, not yet listed in the phonebook since she lived in a new house purchased two months earlier. He knew her, because with all the booths available in Vallejo, he called from within sight of her home.

Darlene was hounded by a man in a white Chevrolet sedan, a man who sat in front of her house, who frightened her at the painting party and asked about her at Terry's.

Fifteen minutes before the killings on Lake Herman Road, and throughout the evening, a white Chevrolet sedan was seen parked exactly where the murderer's car was parked. If the killer of Faraday and Jensen drove a white Chevrolet and the man asking about Darlene drove a white Chevrolet, then chances were that they all belonged to the same man, Zodiac.

Zodiac was able to describe Darlene's outfit in detail even though he saw it only briefly; knew her well enough to follow her from her boyfriend's home and then call V.P.D. across from her own home on Virginia. If he knew her, then he may have been the man calling all day for her that July Fourth. Darlene knew "something big was going to happen." Too, she was a friend of other victims. More than one person had told me that she knew Cecelia Ann Shepard.

Saturday, March 7, 1981

I arrived at the home of Detective Sergeant John Lynch in Vallejo. He was a small, solid, older man, with penetrating eyes. We sat in his dining room.

"What about Mike Mageau?" I asked.

"That guy was a tough guy to fathom. . . . I never did figure out what was wrong with him. To tell you the truth, I never talked to anybody that I even remotely suspected."

"You wrote Dean off as a suspect?"

"That night. You know when it happened that's what we at first thought."

"Darlene dated a lot of guys?"

"Oh, all kinds of guys. She was a goer."

"What about Bob?" I asked.

"Bob? Oh, Bob Starr. I talked to him at great length several times. He was up the coast at Bodega Bay. He's a skin diver. On that Fourth of July, 1969, he said he was with three or four other guys."

"When did you speak with him? In 1971?"

"Long before that. Within one or two months of the killing. I don't know how I got his name in the first place. He's a great big guy. Have you seen him?"

"He's bigger now," I replied. "Husted likes Starr the best."

"I like him the least. I was positive it wasn't Starr. The minute I looked at him, I said mentally that isn't Zodiac. I only typed in five or six lines on the report on Starr. Only in order to get Starr's name in. I talked with him for about an hour. Checked on his car, and he had his scuba gear in the back of the car. Real old, dirty car, that didn't even remotely resemble—"

"He's had a lot of cars though," I interjected. "He's got four now."

"Oh, I didn't know that," said Lynch.

I thought to myself that Lynch had cleared Starr because he did not match Lynch's visual impression of the killer.

Lynch's replacements over the years did not go back and check the early suspects cleared by Lynch.

Sunday, March 29, 1981

Sheriff Al Howenstein had been in a whirl. In two years he had collected over two thousand suspects in his search for the notorious "Trailside Killer." This murderer had stalked Marin County's steep hiking trails, shooting and stabbing seven young people, always preceding the attacks with threats of rape accompanied by an arcane presexual ritual and followed by actual sexual attack in a few instances. Oddly, many of the deaths occurred around holidays.

The Trailside Killer's victims were:

Edda Kane, forty-four, shot by two .44-caliber slugs in the back of the head.

Barbara Schwartz, twenty-three, stabbed by butcher knife, which was found nearby along with the killer's bloodstained hornrimmed bifocal glasses.

Anne Evelyn Alderson, twenty-six, shot by a large-bore weapon in the head.

Diane O'Connell, twenty-two, and Shauna May, twenty-three, shot in the head execution-style.

In the search for O'Connell and May the badly decomposed and fully clothed corpses of Cynthia Moreland, eighteen, and Richard Stowers, nineteen, were found, also shot in the head but a month earlier. Police realized that May and O'Connell had been killed to call attention to the earlier murders.

Today there were two more victims, one hundred miles from the last trailside murder: Ellen Marie Hansen, twenty, who was killed instantly and Steven Russell Haertle, twenty, who was only wounded. They were in the mountains above Santa Cruz.

After surgery, Haertle described the man in great detail and a set of composite drawings was made. The killer was between forty-five and fifty-five years old, about five foot nine inches tall, and weighed 175 pounds. He had gray, close-croppped hair, hazel eyes, and wore dark horn-rimmed glasses with faded stems. He spoke in a "slow and deliberate manner" and had very clean hands. The slayer wore blue bell-bottom Levis and white running shoes, a green baseball cap, a gold nylon windbreaker with "Olympic Drinking Team, Montana" on the back. He had crooked yellow teeth. Witnesses saw the killer flee on foot, take off his glasses, and speed out of the campground in a red "foreign car."

Stowers, Moreland, O'Connell, May, Alderson, and Hansen were all killed with the same .38 with round-nosed bullets. Both Marin and Santa Cruz investigators announced that they "strongly believed" that the Santa Cruz slaying was the work of Marin's Trailside Killer.

Obviously, this Trailside Killer reminded me of Zodiac.

Starr's file computer number had been sent to Santa Cruz police on April 2 by Husted. The next day, KTVU-TV announced that, based on similarities to the composite drawing, the Trailside Killer might also be Zodiac.

Police eventually arrested and convicted David J. Carpenter as the Trailside Killer. He had been cleared as a Zodiac suspect by Toschi in 1970 and Husted in 1979, on the basis of handwriting and fingerprints. Additionally, I learned that he was in jail during the time three of the Zodiac murders took place.

Friday, May 15, 1981

A furious and crestfallen Toschi spoke to me. "We've sent all our Zodiac files to Sacramento. Seems the agencies involved have decided to let the State Department of Justice coordinate the 'dead Zodiac investigation.' I was hoping that Lieutenant Jack Jordan of Homicide would hold onto some parts of the case. They never wanted to be bothered by the Zodiac, mostly because it meant a hell of a lot of work. Deasy himself drove everything to Sacramento. He never bothered to learn the case," said Toschi bitterly, "and now they've even sent copies of our latents from the cab to the Department of Justice.

"A state employee will be coordinator. What the hell he'll be doing is anybody's guess," Toschi snapped. "I'm very saddened by this. What a shame. We haven't kept any of the files." He shook his head. "All the handprinting reports by Morrill, the fingerprint reports, all gone to Sacramento. I think S.F.P.D. made a mistake not keeping something."

An expression of annoyance crossed Toschi's face. "When I think of the man-hours and months and years compiling the unreplaceable alphabetical files on suspects: Whenever someone asked me, 'Toschi, what the hell have you been doing on the goddamn Zodiac case?' I could always point at my cabinets and sit back and see the look of amazement on his face. Now if someone asks me, all we have is one manilla folder in a 1969 unsolved drawer," he said with emotion. "Sure doesn't show much. Now some poor guy who has no idea what the Zodiac is really like has to investigate."

Toschi got to his feet and walked to the window. "How can we expect this poor guy to know what he's doing. Sad. Very sad," he concluded. "They'll never catch him now."

After the Zodiac case had moved to the State Department of Justice, I began working with a source there.

Thursday, June 18, 1981

"A few good leads," my Department of Justice source told me, "brand-new people and a few old names. However, everybody kind of thinks it's this one guy that used to live in Vallejo."

"Yeah, Starr. He's a fascinating guy," I agreed.

"I figured you were writing about him. Everybody seems to be leaning toward him. . . . I don't know if we're barking up the wrong tree, because there's no evidence to indicate that Starr's anything but a nut. I've got all the files from S.F.P.D. on three-by-five cards. All they seem to be looking at, concentrating on, is the fingerprint on Stine's cab," he confessed.

"Do you believe that is Zodiac's print?" I asked.

"I don't know. You know the witnesses indicated that he wiped the cab down to remove any prints. Right now I've been looking at the handwriting. There was one tip that came from a Bay Area town. I'm checking that guy out."

"That wouldn't be Santa Rosa, would it?"

"How did you know?"

"That's where Starr's living now."

"Like I say, Robert, I have gotten so many damn calls on this Starr, I spend my time trying to do a background. I don't want to be left holding the bag. The last person on the case."

He told me about a new suspect from Montana, who had lived in Marin County. He had no criminal record in California. "One of the handwriting experts, Prouty, has indicated that there are some characteristics noted between the handwriting of this man and those of the Zodiac letters," my source told me. "But these are not enough to warrant identification to a degree of probability of authorship. They do indicate to the examiner that more handwriting samples and comparisons are called for."

I suddenly realized that this "new" suspect was Don Andrews. My source was going to be repeating a lot of work that had already been done. It was good to hear that Prouty agreed with Morrill that Andrews' movie poster writing was as close to Zodiac writing as anyone had yet found.

"Look, Starr might be the guy," he continued, "I'm not saying he's not. Starr goes to libraries and does a lot of research on crimes against women. He uses this to scare his friends into believing that he might be the Zodiac killer. Every investigator I've talked to thinks it's him."

"I'll give you something to read," I said. "I'll send you my chapter on Starr in the morning."

"That's great. You treat me right, I'll treat you right. If there's something there that'll get you started on something, I'll let you know."

While I was in Sacramento, I dropped in on Sherwood Morrill, who was busier than ever in his retirement. I had some letters from Penny in the trunk of my car, and Morrill and I compared them to the Zodiac printing. They did not match in any way.

"I get them all, Robert. A group of San Francisco people have been calling me for years telling me that a wealthy banker in the area where Stine was killed is the Zodiac. They got into his yard, swiped all his garbage cans, and drove them up here and dumped them all over my lawn and started rooting through them to show me his handprinting on letters and bills." Morrill sighed. "I just threw up my hands and went in the house."

Wednesday, January 6, 1982

The years of frustration finally caught up with Toschi. This evening, in his floral-patterned yellow kitchen, Toschi rose to get a glass of milk from the refrigerator. As he leaned forward, he suddenly doubled over in pain and slumped to the floor. Carol called an ambulance and Toschi was rushed to Children's Hospital with massive internal bleeding.

Yet when he finally returned home, he could not stop working on the case in his mind.

Wednesday, August 3, 1983

After months of working on finding Don Andrews, I found him effortlessly, and in a matter of seconds. Suddenly I knew exactly where he was. As I crossed the room, I didn't rush; my hunch was that strong. My mind had gone back to my conversation with Narlow when we were trying to determine if Don had used the alias of Hansen. "See," said Narlow; "here he gives his occupation as engine builder. Walt Hansen is the same as Don Andrews."

In the yellow pages for San Francisco, under "Engine Building," I found this listing: "Andrew Donaldson." (This name has been changed.)

I had my friend call the number listed, then she called me back.

"I had a *long* conversation with him under the pretext of having some work done. He told me that he hasn't been in Southern California except for San Diego. He said he'd never been to Riverside. I told him I'd been a student there. He told me that he doesn't do engine repair full time.

"Donaldson told me he's listed in both the yellow and white pages. He said he wanted to be different, but didn't say how. You'll love this. He said, regarding his listing with a number and no address, 'Anyone who knows me will know it's me.'

"I'm supposed to call back tomorrow to get the address and make an appointment. Is he the right one?"

"The dates match up. When you get the address, let's pay him a visit."

The man who answered was Don Andrews, all right. The dark horn-rim glasses were held on by an elastic band in the back just as I had been told.

As Narlow had said, Andrews was interesting and intelligent and talked on and on. I was impressed by the multiple layers of his personalities that I knew lay beneath the identity he had assumed for his latest role in life. Earlier in the evening I had paid a visit to Don's old house in the Haight. Don had lived there in 1969, the same time as Darlene and her first husband, and Darlene had lived only one block away.

My friend described her car, a white Renault Caravelle with stripped gears. This was the kind of car that Don had owned at the time of the Lake Berryessa killing. This got a big response out of him—a quick uplifting of his head. I could tell the man was instantly suspicious. As I watched my friend and Don talking about how she would be bringing her car by in the morning (a visit I knew she had no intention of ever following through on), I looked around the spacious apartment with its movie posters and film stills. He seemed to identify strongly with Oliver Hardy. Everywhere, there were photos of Hardy without Stan Laurel.

I could tell as we left that my friend was very impressed and considered him more of a suspect than ever. "My god, he seems shrewd," she murmured as we went carefully down the steps in the dark. "He seems so really intelligent. I think he really could be the Zodiac."

I said nothing, but deep inside, my suspicions about Don had faded. He was a fascinating suspect, but I no longer believed it was he. It was Starr who seemed to dominate the case, from as far back as the murder of Cheri Jo Bates in Riverside.

Zodiac

Tuesday, December 20, 1983

Evening. The wind rolled the mounded trees of Lake Herman Road, trees lost and found in the curves of the road and the unusual white fog. Exactly fifteen years after Zodiac killed Betty Lou and David, I drove out to where it all began, by the old pump house near the gravel entry road. The few cars that passed me appeared suddenly and swiftly vanished.

I pulled up to the metal gate to the pump house and cut the engine. There were no lights anywhere. As I looked at the spot next to my car, where the killer's white Chevrolet had been parked so long ago, I wondered: With the wealth of information we had had about Zodiac, where were we going wrong? What was the mistake in perception that prevented us from seeing who he truly was? Narlow had said, "There's enough here we ought to be able to break this case. Either that, or he's just sending us around in circles."

I thought of all the theories that had come to me over the years. Was Zodiac a mental patient who was released or escaped periodically and during these intervals of freedom became active as a killer? Was he so sick that his double identity was unknown even to himself? No. I knew this could be true of a paranoid schizophrenic, but not a sexual sadist (which Zodiac is). He would know what he was doing and would remember.

Were there two Zodiacs, one doing the killing and one doing the writing of the letters? Were there multiple Zodiacs such as Sergeant Lundblad had once suggested? I doubted such a great secret could be kept by more than one person.

Was there no Zodiac? Could the entire case have been one monstrous hoax, the work of someone who took credit for unrelated crimes? If so he would at least be the killer of Paul Stine or a confederate of the killer because of the bloody shirt scrap mailed with some of the letters. The printing on the car door at Lake Berryessa also linked Zodiac to that crime.

Zodiac might be a traveling salesman who sold death county by county, state to state. Could he have been, as he hinted, a hunter (the expert marksmanship and the killer's knowledge of the area pointed to this), who had grown bored with animal game.

Perhaps a military man, a sailor stationed for a while in the Bay Area and then transferred? The gaps in the murder activities were about right for this. The Wing Walker shoes, the cipher training, crew-cut hair style, navy garb, and the highly polished shine on his shoes would fit. However, for Zodiac to keep arranging to return to a Bay Area post was improbable.

Most chilling of all, was he a man on the inside, a cop turned killer? The Highway Patrol driving techniques, shooting skill, knowledge of police I.D. techniques, the outstretched flashlight led this way. Had he actually helped in the search for himself? Was he a reporter for one of the papers that Zodiac contacted? His command of punctuation and grammar was above normal. Both of these jobs would have given Zodiac access to progress in the investigation. Or was he merely a police groupie giving the detectives ideas on how to catch the killer?

As to the fate of the Zodiac, he may have been arrested for another crime, become a suicide, died in an accident, or have been killed by one of his intended victims. But in all of these cases evidence to his other identity as a mass murderer would certainly have been found out.

He may have burned out and stopped killing, or people who were sure of his guilt may have "taken care of him," especially if the killer were a policeman. Or the most horrible possibility of all —was he still killing after all these years?

Of the 2500 Zodiac suspects, only one remains that excites the investigators' interest and my own.

Bob Hall Starr, the "gut-feeling choice" of most detectives. Nobody knows who Zodiac is but based on the evidence I have seen Starr is the best suspect found so far.

Starr still carries a mysterious gray metal box he allows no one to look into. Dr. Rykoff, the police-appointed psychologist, says that Starr has five distinct personalities and doctors at Langley Porter and UC at Berkeley have seen his case file.

He, of all suspects, can be placed at the scene of all Zodiac murders.

Bryan Hartnell was driven by Sergeant "Butch" Carlstadt to hear Starr's voice at his job. Later he told me, "There was nothing about what I heard or saw that would rule him out."

Starr has confided to his friends that he is Zodiac. Perhaps he just thinks he is.

I climbed out of the car, zipped up my jacket, and looked down dark Lake Herman Road. People around the Vallejo area have seen a man in a white auto who tailgates women on moonlit nights. They even have a name for him: "The Phantom of Cordelia." I could imagine that phantom Chevy, ghastly white, roaring down dusty California backroads, the stocky man hunched behind the wheel, his moon-round face leaning into the lunar light. The whisper of tires and the obsession.

There is a white fog tonight out on Lake Herman Road and the killing is fifteen years into the past.

But not for Pam, Darlene's sister. She's being followed again, all the way to Lakeport. And someone is leaving notes. And there are the calls—one at her boyfriend's home in Antioch and one at her new home in the East Bay.

It's always the same man, saying the same line: "This is the Zodiac speaking. . . ."

Sunday, July 22, 1984

Starr is now working in Santa Rosa.

I was curious to see if Starr was still refusing to print anything and my friend agreed to help me find out.

We parked behind the rusty old anchor in the parking lot and walked around to the front of the store.

I asked my friend for her thoughts on our visit to Starr. Here's what she later wrote down:

> Starr guided me in my purchases, helping me to select just the right item. When my arms were too full of purchases, he offered me a basket, finally throwing my list back on top of the supplies.
>
> "I need just one more thing," I said. "I need an itemized receipt for these things."
>
> "One of these people up here at the front cash registers will help you," he replied. "I'm not authorized to do that anymore."
>
> "Oh, you've been so helpful. Well, thanks so much for all your help and for your time."

From across the room, I observed Starr turning to face her, putting a massive hand on each of her arms and grinning. In a second, he released her. I could see his lips moving but I was too far away to hear what he was saying.

She turned away, and Starr reached out and patted her shoulder.

Across the blindingly bright illuminated showroom, Starr was reflected in the brass compass, duplicated in the shiny varnished sides of the Chris Craft, reflected in the deep and highly polished floor, mirrored in the brass work around him, and copied in a hundred polished shaft bearings. He was reproduced full length in the floor to ceiling show window.

Starr was everywhere I looked.

Epilogue

Many of the people involved in the Zodiac case are gone now. Sergeant Les Lundblad and coroner Dan Horan are deceased as well as the mother of Stella Borges, who discovered the Lake Herman Road victims, and Darlene Ferrin's mother.

Former San Francisco Police Chief Charles Gain now runs a profitable mobile home court in Lemoore in Kings County and says he is "deliriously happy".

Clement D. DeAmicis, Gain's former deputy for administration, was sacked when the new chief, Cornelius P. Murphy II, replaced all of Gain's deputies in January of 1980. DeAmicis filed for retirement and is now working for a Fidelity Savings and Loan in a security capacity.

In July of 1979 John Shimoda ended his five-year relationship with S.F.P.D. and refused to do any more documents work for them. I suspected this was because of the pressure put on him during the April 1978 Zodiac letter investigation. One policeman told me, "There are many angry cops around here because now we have to go to CI&I in Sacramento and on an emergency case that's a long ride. The department will now be forced to train one of its own men."

Maupin's informant retired in late 1978 to the East Bay. Eric Zelms, the junior patrolman in the radio car that stopped Zodiac in Presidio Heights after Stine was shot, was killed in the line of duty on a New

Year's Eve shortly afterward. His senior partner has been promoted and is still with S.F.P.D.

Inspector Bill Armstrong learned of an opening in the Bunco Division in late winter of 1976. "I've looked at my last homicide," he told Toschi. He retired at age fifty, October 1978.

It was a bad back that forced Edward Rust to quit VPD. He and Sergeant Lynch have both retired, in Vallejo.

Lieutenant Jim Husted, the obsessed and driven Vallejo investigator, lost his intelligence division and has been hurt in a string of work-related accidents. He has been divorced, and spends much of his time at his ranch and developing his private business.

Paul Avery, the *Chronicle* reporter who broke the Riverside Connection, is now a prize-winning reporter for the Sacramento *Bee*.

As far as the surviving Zodiac victims are concerned: Mike Mageau is living in Southern California under a new name.

Bryan Hartnell, completely recovered, is a successful lawyer in Southern California. He sees Cecelia Shepard's family often.

Terry's Restaurant has been closed. Blue Rock Springs is no longer isolated; new roads and housing developments have sprung up there as well as Marine World/Africa U.S.A.

Janet, Darlene's babysitter on July 4, 1969, recalls, "Only about a week ago it was on the news about the Zodiac again and I started thinking, 'Don't have him turn up again. I baby-sat for the woman who got killed by the Zodiac and it is part of you and every time you hear his name you just kinda think, Oh, no!' "

As for Dean Ferrin, Carmela Leigh comments, "He was a good husband. He's remarried, and he and his wife have a couple of children. But it will always be with him."

After five successful years in Robbery Detail, Dave Toschi transferred in May of 1984 to the Sex Crimes Detail. Then, on July 3, 1985, after thirty-two years on the force, he retired to become head of security at the Watergate apartment complex in Emeryville. "Zodiac was the most frustrating of all my cases. I really believe it gave me bleeding ulcers," he said.

Although several people claim to have heard it, the tape of Zodiac speaking to the Vallejo Police Department has never been found.

Appendices

1. **BATES, CHERI JO***
   Oct. 30, 1966   Sun.   Stabbed   Riverside   Clothed

2. **JENSEN, BETTY LOU***
   Dec. 20, 1968   Fri.   Shot   Vallejo   Clothed

3. **FARADAY, DAVID***
   Dec. 20, 1968   Fri.   Shot   Vallejo   Clothed

4. **MAGEAU, MICHAEL****
   Jul. 5, 1969   Sat.   Shot   Vallejo   Clothed

5. **FERRIN, DARLENE***
   Jul. 5, 1969   Sat.   Shot   Vallejo   Clothed

6. **HARTNELL, BRYAN****
   Sept. 27, 1969   Sat.   Stabbed   Lake Berryessa   Clothed

7. **SHEPHERD, CECILIA***
   Sept. 27, 1969   Sat.   Stabbed   Lake Berryessa   Clothed

*Definite Zodiac victim.
**Survived attack.

8. STINE, PAUL*
   Oct. 11, 1969   Sat.   Shot   San Fran-
                                    cisco   Clothed

9. DAVIS, ELAINE
   Dec. 1, 1969   Mon.

10. ROBERTS, LEONA
    Dec. 10, 1969   Wed.   Exposure

11. ELLISON, COSETTE
    Mar. 3, 1970   Tues.   Unknown   Nude

12. KING, PATRICIA
    Mar. 5, 1970   Thurs. Strangled   College   Nude

13. HAKARI, JUDITH
    Mar. 7, 1970   Sat.   Beaten   Nude

14. ANSTEY, ANTOINETTE
    Mar. 13, 1970   Fri.   Blow   Vallejo   Nude

15. BLAU, EVA
    Mar. 1970   Blow/Drugs   Clothed

16. JOHNS, KATHLEEN**
    Mar. 22, 1970   Sun.   Attempted Murder   Escaped

17. LASS, DONNA
    Sept. 26, 1970 Sat.   Nevada

18. BENNALLACK, MARY
    Oct. 25, 1970   Sun.   Throat cut Sacramento

19. HILBURN, CAROL
    Nov. 13, 1970   Fri.   Beating   Sacramento   Almost
                                                     nude

20. KANES, LYNDA
    Feb. 26, 1971   Fri.   Strangled   Angwin   Almost
                                                     nude

21. CLOER, BETTY
    Jun. 19, 1971   Sat.   Shot/Beaten   Almost
                                                     nude

22. LYNCH, SUSAN
    Jun. 19, 1971   Sat.   San Fran-
                                        cisco

23. DUDLEY, LINDA				
Aug. 20, 1971	Fri.	Stabbed	San Francisco	Nude

24. WEBER, YVONNE				
Feb. 4, 1972	Fri.		Santa Rosa	Nude

25. STERLING, MAUREEN				
Feb. 4, 1972	Fri.		Santa Rosa	Nude

26. ALLEN, KIM				
Mar. 4, 1972	Sat.	Strangled	Santa Rosa	Nude

27. OHLIG, LINDA				
Mar. 28, 1972	Tues.	Beaten	Half Moon Bay	

28. KAMAHELE, JEANETTE				
Apr. 25, 1972	Tues.			

29. DERRICK, LYNN				
Jul. 26, 1972	Wed.	Strangled	San Francisco	Almost nude

30. CLERY, ALEXANDRA				
Sept. 4, 1972	Mon.	Beaten	Oakland	Nude

31. KURSA, LORI				
Nov. 11, 1972	Sat.	Broken Neck	S. Rosa	Nude

32. McLAUGHLIN, SUSAN				
Mar. 2, 1973	Fri.	Stabbed		Almost nude

33. VASQUEZ, ROSA				
May 29, 1973	Tues.	Strangled	San Francisco	Nude

34. QUILANTANG, YVONE				
Jun. 9, 1973	Sat.	Strangled	San Francisco	Nude

35. THOMAS, ANGELA				
Jul. 2, 1973	Sat.	Smothered	San Francisco	Nude

36. GIDLEY, NANCY
   Jul. 13, 1973   Fri.   Strangled   San Fran-
                                          cisco   Nude

37. DAVIS, CAROLINE
   Jul. 15, 1973   Sun.   Poisoned   Santa Rosa   Nude

38. FEUSI, NANCY
   Jul. 22, 1973   Sun.   Almost
                                                      nude

39. O'DELL, LAURA
   Nov. 4, 1973   Sun.   Strangled   San Fran-
                                          cisco   Nude

40. LANE, VALARIE
   Nov. 11, 1973   Sun.   Shot   Yuba   Clothed

41. DERRYBERRY, DORIS
   Nov. 11, 1973   Sun.   Shot   Yuba   Clothed

42. FECHTEL, CATHY
   Dec. 2, 1973   Sun.   Shot   Livermore   Clothed

43. SHANE, MICHAEL
   Dec. 2, 1973   Sun.   Shot   Livermore   Clothed

44. WALSH, THERESA
   Dec. 22, 1973   Sat.   Strangled   Santa Rosa   Nude

45. MERCHANT, BRENDA
   Feb. 1, 1974   Fri.   Stabbed   Marysville   Semi-
                                                      clothed

46. BRAUN, DONNA
   Sept. 29, 1974   Sun.   Strangled   Monterey   Nude

47. DYE, SUSAN
   Oct. 16, 1975   Thur.   Strangled   Santa Rosa   Clothed

48. MATTHEWS, TERESA
   Feb. 24, 1979   Sat.   Strangled   Sacramento   Nude

49. RIVERA, CARMEN
   May 20, 1981   Hayward

1. July 31, 1969 (Thursday), 1A to *San Francisco Chronicle*, contains one-third of a cipher. "This is the murderer . . . brand name is Western."

2. July 31, 1969 (Thursday), 1A to *San Francisco Examiner*, contains one-third of a cipher.

3. July 31, 1969 (Thursday), 1A to *Vallejo Times-Herald*, contains one-third of a cipher. "I am the killer . . . print this."

4. August 7, 1969 (Tuesday), to *Vallejo Times-Herald*, three pages. First use of the name Zodiac. "In answer to your asking for more details."

5. October 13, 1969 (Monday), P.M. 1B to *San Francisco Chronicle* on Stine killing. Bloody scrap of shirt.

6. November 8, 1969 (Saturday), 4A P.M. 340-symbol cipher and greeting card with dripping pen.

7. November 9, 1969 (Sunday), P.M. no postmark. Seven-page letter "change my way of collecting . . ."

8. December 20, 1969 (Saturday), no postmark, P.M., ca. at bottom center. "Dear Melvin . . . Happy Christmas . . ."

9. April 20, 1970 (Monday), 4A A.M. "My name is . . ." and bomb diagram.

10. April 28, 1970 (Tuesday), H. P.M. Man on a dragon greeting card. "Enjoy the blast . . ."

11. June 26, 1970 (Friday), 1A A.M. Mt. Diablo and Phillips 66 road map.

12. July 24, 1970 (Friday), 6B P.M. Mention of Johns and baby.

13. July 26, 1970 (Sunday), no postmark, P.M. "Got a little list . . ."

14. October 5, 1970 (Monday), 1A P.M. 3×5 card to *Chronicle*. "Pace isn't any slower . . ."

15. October 27, 1970 (Tuesday), 6B P.M. "Your secret pal . . ."

16. March 13, 1971 (Saturday), Pleasanton 94566. Los Angeles *Times* "Blue Meanies . . ."

17. March 22, 1971 (Monday). Four-cent postcard. "Peek through the pines. . . ."

18. January 29, 1974 (Tuesday), 940 A.M. *Exorcist* Letter.

19. May 8, 1974 (Wednesday), Alameda County. *Badlands* Letter.

20. July 8, 1974 (Monday), San Rafael 1B P.M. "Red Phantom . . ."

21. April 24, 1978 (Monday), 8B P.M. "I am back with you. . . ."

1. Riverside, November 1966. No stamp, no postmark.
2. Riverside, April 30, 1967 (Sunday). No postmark. To Riverside *Press-Enterprise;* "Bates had to die. . . ." In pencil. Double postage.
3. Riverside, April 30, 1967 (Sunday). No postmark. To Riverside Police Department; "Bates had to die. . . ." In pencil. Double postage.
4. Riverside, April 30, 1967 (Sunday). No postmark. To Joseph Bates, "Bates had to die. . . ." In pencil. Double postage.
5. Desk-top poem, found around the same time as Letters 1, 2, and 3. Ballpoint pen, "Sick of Living . . ."

Bryan Hartnell's car door at Lake Berryessa, September 27, 1969 (Saturday).

ZODIAC'S HANDPRINTING

Small, cramped style; blue felt-tip pen, double postage; writing trails downward toward right. Stamps are pasted in odd angles; writer has exhortations to rush and hurry on outside of envelope. He always abbreviates California.

He uses few contractions and has good knowledge of punctuation.

He uses military way of numbering pages.

Abbreviates "San Fran Chron" or "Chronicle."

Writes "Editor" on back.

His spelling is good because he spells words correctly after having spelled them incorrectly earlier in the same letter.

Left margin and printed lines were ruler straight. Size of letters showed patience, concentration, and an interest in details and in follow-through.

Variability in spacing and letter size means he is a manic depressive.

Slant downward at end of letter means depression.

Letters on Eaton bond, 7½ × 10", with matching envelope.

In signing "yours truly:" odd punctuation.

Always begins with phrase "This is the Zodiac speaking"; no punctuation after this opening phrase, it runs directly into the first sentence with a period at the end of "that." (This varied only twice, in the first letter to Vallejo *Times-Herald* and *Chronicle*.)

Everyone else's name is lowercase but "Zodiac" and "I" are always uppercase.

Cursive *d*, sometimes three-stroke *k*.

Letter *i* with dot circle over it. Letter *n* very small, not too round. Most important: checkmark *r*.

W changes the most—rounded and then pointed.

Even in the middle of a carefully drawn letter, Zodiac would cross out a word rather than begin again.

ZODIAC'S SPEECH PATTERNS

October 22, 1969: Voice to Oakland Police Department was sure, not young.

July 4, 1969: Call at 12:40 to Vallejo Police Department (Nancy Slover), no trace of accent. Man was reading or had rehearsed speech. Voice was even and consistent, soft but forceful. When Slover attempted to interrupt, the man just talked louder. At the end of the short statement, the man's voice deepened and had become taunting. The caller sounded mature.

September 27, 1969: Remarkably calm voice, twenty to thirty years old, not high- or low-pitched. The most monotone voice that Bryan Hartnell had ever heard (spoken through hood). "That voice . . . it was like . . . a . . . a student. But kind of a drawl, not a Southern drawl, though." Even words; soft-spoken. "He had a pronounced way of saying things. He volunteered nothing." Hartnell had to "suck it out of him."

Call to Napa Police Department: Calm voice in twenties; did not use contractions.

March 22, 1970; Kathleen Johns: Monotone voice with no trace of accent, no emotion. "No anger, no kind of emotion. Nothing. The words just come out." He spoke very precisely.

ZODIAC'S PHRASING

Spelled clues as "clews" (British); "boughten" for past tense of "bought"; awkward construction, as "my collecting of slaves" instead of "collecting slaves." Formal asides: "as one might say" instead of "so to speak." Understatement: "I took them for a rather interesting ride."

Military: "waiting for me to come out of cover." Uses military numbering on pages. "Will pick off all stray people." "I shall wipe out a school bus." "Just shoot out the front tire and pick off the kiddies as they come bouncing out." "Kill rampage." "All I had to do was spray them." "Move in on someone else's territory." "Unflappable," adjective meaning calm and clear-thinking, Air Force phrase.

"Happy Christmas" and "boughten" British terms. "Boughten" was past tense of bought in 1850s U.S.

"The good times," "very happy," "Happy Christmas," "having a good time," and "cheer up," phrases that point out the killer's depression. "Have some fun," "it would cheer me up considerably," "I am rather unhappy."

Strange phrasing: "some bussy work," "mask the sound," "doesn't it rile you?" "noze rubbed in your booboos," "will positively ventalate anything."

British type: "It could be rather messy if you try to bluff me"; "clews."

Imperious tone: "They have not complied with my wishes"; "I have grown rather angry"; "I shall no longer announce to anyone when I committ my murders." Correct usage of "shall" and "will."

Formal asides: "as one might say" instead of "so to speak."

Uses phrases common to the young in 1969: police are "pigs" or "Blue Meannies" (from the Beatles' movie, *Yellow Submarine*), "do my own thing," "set the shit off."

Cops: "As one might say, I gave the cops some buzy work"; "Two cops pulled a goof"; "By the way it could be rather messy if you try to bluff me"; "I was leaving fake clews."

Blacks are referred to as Negroes.

Uses "kiddies" for children (Australian or British usage).

"Fiddle & fart around" is a phrase used by older people around Texas, most common in Lubbock County.

Quotes Gilbert and Sullivan lyrics from memory.

Threat: "I will do something nasty, which you know I am capable of." "Peek-a-boo—you are doomed." "I will loose all control of myself." "I am finding it extremely difficult to hold it in check. "They did not openly state this." "This kind of murder-glorification can only be deplorable at best."

The Taurus sign occurs five times hidden in the October 27, 1970, sign and the "my name is . . ." cipher. Either Zodiac was born between April 20 and May 19 or he thinks he is a Taurus.

315

October 30, 1966: Riverside, heavyset young man; 5'11"; with a beard.

November 22, 1966: man thirty-five, 5'9" tall; with chunky protruding stomach.

December 18, 1970: Contra Costa, burglar with a dark nylon ski jacket, dark pants, navy blue knit cap, wearing welding goggles. Thirty; 5'9". The man had wrapped adhesive tape around the ends of his fingers, handkerchief over lower part of face.

February–July 3, 1969: man following Darlene Ferrin—heavyset with a very round face and with curly, wavy dark brown hair; middle-aged? Man (same as above) at Darlene's May 1969 painting party: dark-rimmed glasses; curly, wavy hair; an older man. Man at Terry's: thirty-five to thirty-eight. 175; 5'11".

July 4, 1969: the man appeared to have a very large face, was not wearing glasses. He looked to be between twenty-six and thirty years old; had short, curly, light brown hair. To Mike Mageau "the man's build was beefy, heavyset without being blubbery fat. He had slight potbelly, combed hair up in kind of a pompadour.

July 8, 1969: second Mageau description: twenty-six to thirty; short, curly, light brown hair worn in military crew cut; pants had pleats; he wore a Navy-type windbreaker jacket. 5'8"; 195–200 pounds.

July 10, 1969: third Mageau description: blue shirt or sweater; 160 pounds. Man seen arguing with Darlene Ferrin: thirty, 6'; 180–185 pounds; hair the color of champagne, combed straight back.

September 27, 1969: lone man seen by three girls: twenty-five to thirty-five, over 6'; 200–230 pounds; no glasses; hair straight and parted. Black-sleeved sweat shirt, dark blue pants, sports or suit pants, T-shirt hanging out at rear; nice-looking and clean cut. Chain smoker.

Man, most likely Zodiac, seen quarter mile from Hartnell-Shepard attack site: white adult male; 5'10"; heavy build; dark trousers and a long-sleeved dark shirt with red coloring. Blue windbreaker jacket.

Shepard and Hartnell description: black ceremonial hood with four corners (like a paper sack) came down over man's shoulders almost to waist. Stitching around edges, sleeveless with the front and back panels. Emblazoned in white on front with 3" × 3" cross over circle. Slits for eyes and mouth cut into the cloth; a pair of clip-on sunglasses over eye slits. Dark sleeves were clamped tight about his wrists, trousers tucked tightly above half boots (probably with blousing rubbers used by the military). On left side was a bayonetlike knife. Holster on right with blue-steel .45 semiautomatic. Weight is solid, not flabby; the man's stomach hung over his trousers or he had puffy air-filled jacket. Several lengths of common variety white, hollow core plastic clothesline hung at the man's left side (or in back pocket). Another pair of glasses possibly under hood. Dark brown, sweaty hair seen through slits. "Could have been a wig," according to Hartnell. Man wore a light-weight blue-black windbreaker over a reddish-black wool shirt. The crossed-circle symbol was sewn on very professionally. Hooded man was 5'10" to 6'2"; 225–250 pounds. Footprint size 10½, compaction test showed 220-weight, boot was chucker type called the "Wing Walker." Uppers manufactured by Weinbrenner Shoe Co., Merill, Wisconsin. Soles are manufactured by Avon, Avon, Massachusetts. One million shoes manufactured in '66, under government contract; 103,700 pairs shipped to Ogden, Utah, district to Air Force and Navy installations on West Coast. Hartnell: "He had to be fairly lightweight (without puffed-up jacket). All the guys the police had me look at were really fairly husky guys. This guy I think was in his thirties and fairly unremarkable."

October 11, 1969: heavy build; 5'8"; dark navy-blue or black parka-type jacket, dark trousers, reddish or blond crew cut, thirty-five to forty years old; wearing glasses.

Weight is now 200 pounds or more, he is barrel-chested and wearing a navy blue or black waist-length and zippered jacket. Description of officers changes composite: Older and heavier, 5'11", thirty-five to forty-five, short brown hair with red tint, glasses.

March 22, 1970: Kathleen Johns Description: a clean-shaven and very neatly dressed man; "I remember thinking he may have been a service-man . . . he was that kind of clean cut." Shoes spit-shined, dressed in a dark blue-black nylon windbreaker type of jacket over black woolen bell-bottom pants. Black thick-rimmed glasses (held in place by elastic band like a machinist might wear); chin had acne scars; nose not especially small; his jaw wasn't weak, not a weak person; average brow, crew-cut brown hair. Ten years later: "The man in my car weighed about 160." White shirt, dead-pan eyes, navy shoes, general appearance military.

April 19, 1970: (Christopher Edwards/steward P&O liner *Oronsay*) man dressed in blue slacks and sweater who claimed to be a British engineer, looked like composite. Late-model hard-top car at Bay St. and the Embarcadero.

April 7, 1972: light-colored car swerved at Isobel Watson in Tamalpais Valley; 5'9"; wore heavy black-rimmed glasses; neat brown hair.

The clothes of the Zodiac killer point to a military man, most likely from the Navy or Air Force. The well-made Zodiac black hood had a crossed-circle design sewn on the front. (In the Navy a proficient skill in sewing is required.) The pleated pants may point to an older man (as do slang words he uses that have been out of vogue for a quarter century).

ZODIAC'S CARS

October 30, 1966: car seen; 1947–1952 tan-gray Studebaker with oxidized paint.

July 4–5, 1969: white Chevrolet impala sedan, 1961–63.

Car similar to 1963 Corvair, "older and bigger, old plates." "May have been a 1960 Falcon, California plates." Lighter in color than the bronze Corvair driven by the victim (1963 Bronze Chevrolet Corvair two-door coupe).

Description of man following Darlene Ferrin: American-made sedan, white with a large windshield.

September 27, 1969: lone man seen in silver or ice-blue '66 Chevrolet two-door sedan, with California plates.

Moulages made of two different-size tires (front), very worn; width between the wheels was fifty-seven inches.

March 22, 1970: (Johns) late model car, American make, light-colored, two-door, with old California license plates (black and yellow). Interior of car was very messy, with papers and clothes strewn about the front and back seats and even on the dashboard. Mostly men's clothing but mixed in with small T-shirts with patterns such as a child eight to twelve years old might wear. Black four-celled flashlight with a rubber grip on dash, along with two colored plastic scouring pads. "A sporty console-style auto; transmission gear shift box was between two black bucket seats, a special built-in cigarette lighter on its right side and an ashtray at the front end."

November 11, 1970; man following woman in Santa Rosa. White Chevrolet, young twenty-three to twenty-four-year-old man from Vallejo; cited but ticket purged from records.

Guns

Used at Lake Herman Road:
.22 caliber semi-automatic, J.C. Higgins Model 80 or High Standard Model 101 (ammunition: .22 caliber Super X copper-coated long rifle).

Used at Blue Rock Springs:
Browning 1935 High Power (FN GP35) 9-mm. Manufactured in Canada. Thirteen rounds (ammunition: 9-mm Winchester Western).

Used at Lake Berryessa:
may have shown Colt (1911A1) to (surviving victim). Blue steel semiautomatic.

Used at Washington and Cherry, San Francisco:
second Browning High Power used in San Francisco (ammunition: 9-mm Winchester Western).

Knives

Used at Riverside City College:
Small knife with blade three and one-half inches long and one inch wide. Broken tip, piece left in Riverside victim.

Used at Lake Berryessa:
foot-long knife, one inch wide, wooden handle with two brass rivets and one-inch-wide adhesive tape around handle. Wooden sheath. Sharpened on both sides, rivets replaced guard.

ZODIAC'S MATERIALS

An enlarger, light table, or overhead projector.

A cipher encoding wheel.

Portable Royal typewriter, elite type, Canterbury shaded.

Handle-type boat flashlight.

Blue felt-tip pens.

Eaton watermark Monarch-cut bond paper; this paper is cut imperfectly and may be a bulk remainder such as is sold to the military.

Complete news files on the Zodiac case.

A gray metal box (from psychic).

A basement workshop.

Teletype paper. UP model 15 teletype. Bomb plans based on the circuitry of this teleprinter.

Owned boat-type lantern flashlight with handle; may have boat.

Possibly a four-celled black flashlight with rubber grip.

Gloves, worn while writing the letters.

Zodiac brand wristwatch.

Timex watch, ripped off at Riverside, 7 inches circumference, black band.

Wing Walker shoes sold only at military outlets.

Portions of Paul Stine's bloody dark-gray-and-white striped shirt, and Stine's car keys.

Books on cipher and horoscopes.

Polaroid camera.

Hole puncher.

ZODIAC'S TRAINING

Explosive devices.

Cryptography.

Meteorology.

Charts and terminology used in conjunction with the compass.

Knowledge of Gilbert and Sullivan *Mikado*, light opera.

Extremely good knowledge of punctuation; fakes poor spelling. Touch-types.

Knows car engines (distributor cap wire sabotage).

Chemistry (bomb plans).

May have access to computer.

Knows how to cast own horoscope and knows astrology.

Knowledge of ancient cults.

Movie fanatic. *Badlands, The Exorcist, The Most Dangerous Game.*

Knowledge of disguise. This may relate back to light opera training.

Knew about using glue on fingertips to prevent leaving prints; may have been in jail where he learned this.

Knows drafting.

Training with guns. Five shots in a tight formation in victim's back from ten feet away while running.

Police training? Used highway Patrol cut-off technique at Blue Rock Springs, shone light in eyes of victims. They reached for their I.D.'s because they thought it was a policeman.

Sews well.

Ambidextrous.
Probably Navy background.

ZODIAC'S METHOD OF OPERATION

Kills on weekends, in areas near water, on the full or new moon.

Attacks couples. Uses different weapon each time. Cars usually involved.

Always young students, all at dusk or night; robbery was not a motive.

No sexual molestation. Killer has compulsion to brag after murders by phone or letter. Kills in lovers' lanes.

Different weapon each time. A flashlight is often used. Killings on a gravel surface twice, on asphalt twice, on ground once. Three victims killed near parking lots.

PSYCHOLOGICAL PROFILE OF ZODIAC

Paranoid delusions of grandeur.

Psychotic.

Sexual sadist: You will find that the Zodiac probably tortured small animals as a child, had a domineering mother, weak or absent father, strong fantasy life, confusion between violence and love. Is the type of person who would be a police groupie, carry police equipment in his car, collect weapons and implements of torture.

Calm in a crisis.

Plans carefully. May rehearse crimes. Look for similar attacks in areas weeks prior.

Enjoys taunting the police.

Secretive and guarded in his dealings with the world.

Very angry that the police tell lies about him. Zodiac is reasonably truthful in what he writes. The police did stop and talk to him, but denied it.

Crank calls; "Rush to Editor." Zodiac can hardly wait to contact the police and tell what he has done. The note to Joseph Bates demonstrated that he likes to torment relatives of his victims. The crank calls to the Ferrin family fit in here as well; he may even know them.

Zodiac is an imitative person, not inventive. Everything he has done he has seen or found written down somewhere.

Makes sure the woman always dies.

Makes phone calls close to police department to be sure and hear sirens rushing to crime scene.

Plans ahead; cut up clothesline (at Berryessa) beforehand.

Zodiac feels he is persecuted.

Masturbates after each attack and during the writing of the letters.

Zodiac kills at close range because he wants his victims to see him.

Suicide (or an institution) lies at the end for a person like this.

Affected by the moon and tides.

Usually this type is a voyeur and a prowler.

Taunting way of speaking and painful headaches.

An inkblot test on this man would elicit Z shapes and answers.

Will repeat his crimes. The pleasure from taunting the police may in the end become the real motive for the crimes.

Most often highly intelligent, strong. He is incurable. He feels no remorse.

He will often choose victims with specific occupations (all victims, even Stine, were students).

He will keep souvenirs. Polaroid photos were taken by Santa Cruz serial killer Edmund Emil Kemper.

He will stab victim until he achieves orgasm.

Will remember in great detail the particulars of the murders.

Will have a fascination with police work. May have applied for this job.

If like Bundy, Bianchi, etc., may be abnormally strong.

These types are limited or incapable of forming normal adult relationships. The alternatives are: sex with dead bodies, or killing for sexual satisfaction. Another alternative is sex with children. Have a need to be powerful.

Homosexuality is not inconsistent.

Often play at execution of themselves as children. Mutilate dolls.

Skillful and charming liars. May even move to a state that has the death penalty, which they unconsciously desire.

Fantasy of killing mother.

This type of killer will scout out a certain type, even to the point of a prepared questionnaire to select them (Edmund Emil Kemper did this).

They think of the victim as an object.

When writing letters Zodiac was either smoking marijuana, drinking, or taking some kind of narcotics.

The sexual sadist kills to achieve sexual pleasure. May never have had sexual intercourse. He seeks dehumanization of his victims into objects that he can have control over, power over. He takes great pains in appearing normal and in evading capture.

Sources

Police Investigators' personal case notes and reports, including rough drafts.

San Francisco Police Department, Vallejo Police Department, Napa Sheriff's Department, Benicia Police Department, Vallejo Sheriff's Department, Santa Rosa Police Department, and Riverside Police Department incident reports and files. Included in these reports are ballistics and crime lab results, autopsy reports, fingerprint comparisons, and suspect files.

Information was also obtained from two confidential reports from CI&I and the California State Attorney General's Office ("Zodiac," "Linked Murders").

In addition to FBI and NSA reports on the Zodiac codes (contained on computer cryptoanalysis printouts) I made use of a secret psycholinguistics study made of Zodiac's personality as manifested in his letters and prepared by the Syracuse Research Institute. I also had access to a confidential report on the psychological makeup of the Riverside murderer.

A hundred hours of taped interviews were made with surviving victims of the Zodiac killer, relatives and friends of the victims, and major suspects in the investigation. I also spoke with the investigators of each Zodiac homicide. I was allowed to read and copy letters, notes, journals, and address books of some victims. I studied employment records and phone logs of some suspects as well as fingerprint files from Washington State and Mare Island Naval Shipyard.

Academic files from Riverside City College and Hogan High School yearbooks.

Hypnotic interviews conducted with witnesses.

Suspect letters from Atascadero State Hospital for the criminally insane.

California Department of Motor Vehicles and some insurance records.

Newspaper and television accounts of the Zodiac case, including reporters' notes, rough drafts, computer files, and unpublished stories.

Composite sketches and police diagrams of murder sites.

Visits to all scenes of the crimes.

CI&I Handwriting reports.

Files on the case that had been discarded. Files on Zodiac taken home as collector's items.

Anonymous tips from citizens.

The letters from Zodiac.

Selected
References

Dickensheet, Dean W., ed. *Great Crimes of San Francisco*. New York: Ballantine, 1974.

Jane's Small Arms of the World. Great Britain.

Kahn, David. *The Codebreakers*. New York: Macmillan, 1967.

Laffin, John. *Codes and Ciphers*. New York: Abelard-Schuman, 1964.

Lunde, Donald T., M.D. *Murder and Madness*. New York: W. W. Norton & Co., 1979.

Oken, Alan. *As Above, So Below*. New York.

Pratt, Fletcher. *Secret and Urgent*. New York.

Sest, Mann, Flangan, Cowen. *The Phenomenon Book of Calendars*. New York: Simon & Schuster, 1978.

Snyder, LeMoyne. *Homicide Investigation*. Springfield, Illinois: Charles C. Thomas Co., 1977.

Index

A Supplemental Report to the Reader
on David Fincher's *Zodiac*

"I am interested in an impression," David Fincher tells me. "I am interested in your hair standing up on the back of your neck. I'm interested in the things that can't be articulated." This crisp January morning in 2004 David Fincher, the celebrated film director of *Se7en* and *Fight Club* is dressed in Levi's and a gray cardigan over a white V-neck T-shirt. His beard is short, slightly graying. Sandy-colored hair peeks from beneath a black baseball cap. The forty-one-year-old Denver native is tall, six foot one, and weighs about 180 pounds. He is intense, a devouring listener and watcher. "I do this for a living. My whole gig, the only thing I do, is I watch TV and I watch people, how they behave. Take 7, you go, 'That was it!' [Fincher claps his hands together explosively]. You shoot Take 8. It's not right. Take 9 and now you're just fucking gilding the lily and it's no good. Take 7, that's the one. You put it in the movie and people cry. I don't know why. It's this thing that you get. So I trust that implicitly and that's the difference, that's the thing we need to do now. We need to construct *Zodiac* from its emotional truth as opposed to its factual truth."

The broad, wood-paneled suite is a room of contrasts—white furniture against dark carpet. Across the room, shadows envelop two young men, Brad Fischer the producer and Jamie Vanderbilt the screenwriter. The illumination from Geary Street makes Brad paler than usual. His short black hair and dark brows stand out boldly in an earnest, inquiring face. "David is beyond *Zodiac* being a reconstruction," says Brad. "He is interested in the progression of events that he can accurately capture on film and that dispel any myths in the case."

The Bay Area is familiar territory for Fincher, childhood grounds. "I was about seven years old when all this Zodiac stuff was going on," Fincher says. "I was going to Isabel Cook in San Anselmo when I first started to realize we were being followed by a couple of highway patrol cars on the way to school. I remember riding the bus and coming home from school and asking my dad about it. 'Why is the highway patrol following us?' but got only a vague answer. I remember that people were killed and then later on when I was at Berryessa having lunch at a picnic table somebody said this is where the Zodiac stabbing took place. I was probably eleven at the time." He believes *Zodiac* is a movie about "a time and a place and a process and a series of events that shaped California in an interesting way."

"For Brad and me this is a labor of love," adds Jamie, who adapted *Zodiac* and *Zodiac Unmasked*. "It's important to us to get this right with the right guy, which David is. I like the fact that Fincher even rebels against being a rebel. 'Don't label me,' he says about that. 'It's not like some cool thing. I just want to make movies.'" Jamie's sideburns and blondish hair are as long and unruly as a movie Tarzan's, but within a few months he will resemble a swashbuckling pirate with a goatee (which he will vow not to shave off until the $80 million Warner Brothers/Paramount motion picture is green-lighted). I first met Brad and Jamie in 2002 at the premiere of Paul Schrader's *Auto-Focus*, a motion picture of my 1993 book about *Hogan's Heroes'* star Bob Crane (Greg Kinnear). "David began on such a technical side of the movie industry working with visual effects," says Jamie. "I think that contributes a lot to how clinical he is about stuff. Usually those guys who make music videos (as David did) never make very good movies because they're lacking in emotion and are more interested in the technical stuff. The old version of *Zodiac* was much more like *JFK*, where there is a final summation. Oliver Stone wanted to convince the audience."

"I don't want this to be about convicting Arthur Leigh Allen [aka Bob Starr]," David tells Jamie. "If the characters in the movie believe Arthur Leigh Allen is the Zodiac (though I think it's him), I'm completely fine with that, but I don't want to make a movie about convincing the audience. Certainly Robert came to his conclusion and it was good enough for him. He felt like he knew who the guy was and he knew the hardware store he worked at. When Leigh died, he felt like it was put away. That's what we want to present. We also know there has to be a scene in it where the Department of Justice says, 'This is all really interesting stuff. I wish we could follow through on it, but the reality of the situation is that we can't put this guy on trial so if there's not going to be that kind of public satisfaction there's no real upside. And we want to talk about the politics of that. The case against Leigh is a good one. I buy it. But it's circumstantial and we have to kinda present that and go, "We think everyone can rest easy." I look at it and it's incredibly compelling."

"I love revenge pictures," says Jamie, "but I understand why David wants to take it to task. He wants to make the film that ends the serial-killer genre. He has made a type of serial-killer movie before. The danger for us would have been to get a director who wanted to focus on all the purulent details. If anything he's got that part of it out of his system and is so much more interested in the people."

Brad Fischer will accomplish many great advances in the Zodiac case. In the long fact-checking phase for a *Zodiac* motion picture he will track down Blue Rock Springs victim Mike Mageau in Las Vegas and discover an important parking ticket. Jamie will find a hand-drawn map of Lake Berryessa signed by the prime suspect. All three Hollywood detectives will gather together the original detectives and go over the murder sites with them. Theirs is a fascinating adventure that I documented over years, but that's another story. *This* is the story of how David Fincher filmed *Zodiac*.

Nearly two years pass. On a bright September morning, as vintage buses and cars crawl past the *San Francisco Chronicle*, Jake Gyllenhaal bounds up the wide sidewalk and extends a hand. It's an odd feeling to have the finest actor of his generation play yourself in a major motion picture. Gyllenhaal is dressed in the same kind of sweater vest and cords I wore in 1968 when I was a young political cartoonist at the *Chronicle*. He is twenty-four (born six days before Christmas 1980), over six feet, blue-eyed, muscular, and roguishly good-looking. Jake does a number of jumping jacks, takes a few puffs on a cigarette, and sprints into the adjacent alley where he raps on the window of a car parked across from Hanno's. Reporter Paul Avery, hungover, awakens with a jolt. For the role of Avery, a driven, substance-abusing former war correspondent, before Fincher considered such an unusual choice, he had to mull it over before telling Brad, Jamie, and Laray Mayfield, the casting director. The brilliance and rightness of Robert Downey Jr. as Avery is confirmed.

Around the corner Fincher studies a monitor—seeing only what the cameras in the car and behind Jake see. GRAYSMITH: "I've been thinking—" AVERY: "God save us all . . . All fascinating pieces of minutiae, Roberto, but it's a little early in the day—" GRAYSMITH: "It's eleven." As Avery staggers into the *Chronicle* we see a gun tucked inside his waistband. Downey has just married film producer Susan Levin at a private home in the Hamptons and is in fine fettle. My friend San Francisco stage actor Penny Wallace is anxious to see the magnetic actor up close. When I mention I knew Avery, Downey dashes over to us. "Tell me more," he says, inches away. First I tell him that Avery was much taller, lankier, and blonder than he is.

On September 5, 2005, I spent the day with Jake Gyllenhaal inside Fincher's sprawling two story office (plus tower) on Hollywood Boulevard. At the rear, in front of an electronic gate, hopeful actors have left their resumes in little cardboard boxes. "David, your office is a building," says Jamie. "Who else is in here?" asks Brad. "No one, just me," says Fincher. He's been there a couple of months. He gets up, checks a fact on the Internet behind his desk, then reaches for one of the dozen black Sharpies in a cup on his desk and makes a note. The office is modern, stylish, and crowded with Sony high-tech equipment. Fincher is reading—*Force Majeure, The World Is Flat,* and *Freakonomics.* Today the Viper has arrived, wrapped in brown paper and waiting in the lobby. Fincher is as excited as a kid with a new toy. "For *Zodiac* I'm to make it sit up and do tricks. Let's go check the Chronology." They get up from a grouping of couches and chairs to study the low-tech big board pasted up with notecards and Scotch tape. The conference area with its high-tech A/V resembles the war room out of *Dr. Strangelove.* All the ceilings are twenty feet tall, and a giant oval-shaped light twenty feet in diameter covers half of the ceiling.

Jake has spent the morning changing diapers and drawing political cartoons. He asks what kind of pen I use (Gillott #170 and #658). The 19th Century dip pens are too difficult to master, so I give him my Radiograph #2 and he sketches a passable Nixon. Raised in Hancock Park, Jake springs from a show-biz environment; father, Stephen, is a director (*Losing Isaiah*); mother, Naomi Foner, is a screenwriter (*Running on Empty*); older sister Maggie even played his on-screen sister in *Donnie Darko.* Jake is hot—his action film, *The Day After Tomorrow,* took in a $187 million domestic box office and he has two big movies headed into theaters. One is Ang Lee's *Brokeback Mountain* with Heath Ledger, a tragic story about two cowpokes who fall in love in 1960s Wyoming. It will earn Jake his first Oscar nomination. The other is Sam Mendes's *Jarhead,* the story of a young Marine sniper during Operations Desert Storm and Desert

Shield. "Can I take your picture?" Jake asks me, but his camera/phone has been dented and sandblasted by fierce winds near the Mexican border where he underwent basic training. "I've got a tape recorder in my car," Jake tells me. "I'll be right back." He runs out and comes back with a space satellite—microphones, video camera, long arms sticking out, blinking red lights, and props it precariously on the edge of the couch. A light stubble covers his cheeks, and his dark brown hair has grown back, but the Friday he met with David Fincher to discuss *Zodiac* his scalp was still shaved for *Jarhead*. From the very beginning David thought Jake Gyllenhaal would be "really interesting" for the Graysmith part. "I'll do it if you'll do it," David tells Jake, sliding the enormous script across the table to him. "Read it over the weekend." It is a first draft because he and Jamie are still refining a version that could easily make a three-hour movie with a marathon shooting schedule of over a hundred days. The exhausting length doesn't intimidate the athletic actor. He's got stamina. He's got game. "Hey, it WAS two hundred pages," he later deadpans to *Premiere*. After Jake looked the script over he saw that for the first three-quarters of the movie my character is deferential and polite, a product of my Southern upbringing and military family. "But I am the hero of this movie," Jake says, then comes back and tells Brad and Jamie. "Oh, I get it. It's a comedy."

Brad and Jamie worked with casting director Laray Mayfield on their film *Basic*, but she and Fincher go way back. When Laray first came to LA with her boy, she didn't realize the incredible odds against a single woman surviving and succeeding in this tough town. It was Fincher who made her realize what a woman on her own could accomplish. "I had a friend who was a music video director," she drawls, "and in 1987 I went to work as his assistant at this small production company, a little satellite company of a big commercial house that doesn't exist anymore." A few months later, when Fincher cofounded Propaganda Films, a production company, David asked her to work for him. "I did, and nineteen years later here we are. My relationship with David is very close because he forgives me for all my shortcomings." She is also beautiful enough to be a star herself. They cast Brian Cox, the original Dr. Lector, as attorney Mel Belli. "He will eat that role alive," says Jamie. "The biggest struggle in this draft was to get it to the point where Fincher not only felt it was true to life (he's obviously very invested in that), but to get the feeling of ebb and flow

342

of the information." In the script, the fingerprint on Stine's cab is a great source of debate. Jamie doesn't necessarily want to show one way or the other if Zodiac is wearing gloves. "We do see the Stine killing, but we're not going to see the face of the person."

"When Zodiac stops writing for three years," says Fincher, "we've got to feel he stops writing. We can't just cut to the next scene." A way of showing the passage of time is the skyline of San Francisco; we see the TransAmerica building in time lapse as its construction is finished.

"We balance what Toschi was doing and what you were doing," Jamie tells me. "We follow both of you before you meet, which I think is a really cool structural thing, where we know the two main characters, we know they are going to be on screen together at some point, but we don't know when. So when you finally intersect, it's a really cool moment."

Over the last two or three weeks Fincher's office has become a full-service production center. "It's a bit of a maze," says Brad. "It's a gigantic facility. People get lost in here." On the ground floor, production designer Don Burt's office sits at the southwest corner. There's *Zodiac* stuff everywhere, on the walls, laid out on all the tables but especially in the back area where Burt has camped. The first assistant director, Mary Ellen Woods, a dark intense woman, has an office in the northeast corner; then there's art director Keith Cunningham's office. David is in the southeast corner next to his longtime partner, producer Cean's Chaffin's office. If the ground floor is the studio of an artist or architect, then the upstairs is an art gallery. "Upstairs," says Jamie, "there are boards, charts, and photos everywhere down to the point where there's a *SF Chronicle* 1969 board with photos of typewriters and the little phones attached to the reporters' desks. Laray's office is on the second floor alongside her associate Mindy Bazar's office. Down a narrow hall are set decorator Victor Zolfo, a fabulous, generous guy, and Max Daly, an art department researcher. Max is organizing the material for the DVD document section, but Ron Frankel, a computer whiz who does motion, special effects pre-vis, and 3D models, is building it. Its budget is $1 million.

There is a screening room, Sally Sue Lander the second AD's office, and that of Hope Parrish, the tall blond prop master. Hope is using what will be David's future editing room. "We're just in here with

Fincher's future furniture," Hope says. She is an expert who has spent considerable months in Iraq and Canada working on such films as *The Aviator*. Like Max, she has a remarkably short time to do her work. "I had not seen a current script," she says, "and they told me three working days before I came on that I was hired. That was a Thursday and I was brought to work on Monday and given nine weeks to prepare everything in front of the camera and prepare the shooting schedule. Then they will probably give us a week to wrap it up at the end." Hope, Paul, Dana, Michelle, and Teri alternately are on eBay under an alias trying to buy a Zodiac watch. They keep being outbid by a staffer who doesn't know who he's bidding against. Hope's main prop, the one people will study to be certain they are accurate, are the Zodiac letters. It took a lot of time to make the first one — the paper had to be thin enough so that writing showed through on the other side. Hope's assistant, Jules Kmetzko, replicates the Zodiac skeleton card sent to Avery but the purplish ink is not black enough, and after she comes back in a flash with a perfect card notices something. At the *Chronicle* we thought the greeting card was folded in half, but Jules says, "No. Look. It actually had four folds so they can print everything on one side, *then* fold it."

Location Manager Rick Schuler considered four different possibilities for doubling Blue Rock Springs and finally decided on Bouquet Canyon Road in Angeles National Forest in Saugus for the Darlene Ferrin (Clara Hughes) and Mike Mageau (Lee Norris) shooting. Props include air mortars to simulate bullet hits, broken tempered glass for dressing and haze/smoke pots, a brilliant spotlight from inside Zodiac's car, a flashlight, headlights, a flashing turn signal, a balloon light with operator and the flash of a silencer. Trainers have a flock of geese ready to scream on cue.

On October 4, Mr. Ed Teen's hangout (George's 50s Diner in Long Beach) is filmed, and six days later, Shoot Day 22, filming on the *Chronicle* third floor editorial set commences. In August, Fincher had shown me computer-generated wide-frame photos of the *Chronicle*. Architect's floor plans reproduced three-dimensionally allow the director to plot camera tracking and angles through photogramity (a process where they establish certain points within three-dimensional space), and even pass through walls. Fincher envisions an opening sequence of a mail transport cart pushed into the *Chronicle* as seen as if the camera were in front of the cart and moving backward. Since the present *Chronicle* newsroom looks like an insurance company (with carpeting) Rick scouted not only San Francisco, but also different sites in LA that could stand in for the 1968 and 1978 *Chronicle*. His team had already created a fake watering hole (modeled after Hanno's in the Alley) behind the paper. The old newsroom is reborn perfectly on a block-long set inside the Terminal Annex Building on Alameda Street (its lobby is identical to the *Chronicle*'s). Everything is authentic: light fixtures, old typewriters, molding, U-shaped copy desk. Everything works—old phones, drinking fountains, elevators, and pneumatic mail tube stations. Hope even stocks the desk drawers with *Chronicle* notepads and Eagle pencils. Yet who would know the difference? David Fincher would.

Shorty, "an ill-tempered, white-haired little person," stands by his coffee setup and a sign that reads "Delicious as Hell Coffee." Scene 14A shows Jake Gyllenhaal rushing from the elevator into the chaos of the third floor editorial offices, talking to Shorty (James Caraway), and getting coffee. In Jake's cartoonist scenes he uses my actual drawing board, brushes, T-square, rough sketches, original sketchbooks (where I first drew Zodiac in costume), and glass ink bottle. The intricate pattern of sorting drawings at the right angle for the camera, delivering lines, inserting and shutting the portfolio clasp, then dashing across the office for the editorial meeting taxes the exhausted actor. Sometimes he forgets to lock the case. Once he dashes off without it. Running, missing, choosing and inserting, forgetting, he gives me a hapless shrug as he does it again. Yes, Jake Gyllenhaal has game.

Scene 17B, the *Chronicle* editorial conference room, stretches to Day 35, October 28. The scene includes Jake, Templeton Peck (John Getz), Al Hyman (Ed Setrakian), and publisher Charles Theriot (John Terry). Terry has researched his role to such depth he even knows about Theiriot's White House conference with President Lyndon Johnson to work out a newspaper joint operating agreement. Legend has it that at this meeting LBJ impolitely combed his hair in front of the impeccably mannered Theriot. Affronted, the elegant publisher returned to San Francisco and came out against LBJ's war in Vietnam. At Jamie's, I watch the rushes of Terry's moving performance when he hands Zodiac's letter off to Temp Peck because he cannot bear to continue to read it aloud. Terry catches the nobility and integrity of the doomed publisher. The massive *Chronicle* set is such a success it will be kept as a period newspaper set. For Shoot Day 36

Fincher is back at Blue Rock Springs, then on to the Culver City Court Building (the Riverside Police Station).

"So when Robert comes to you," Fincher asks my best friend, Dave Toschi, "and says, 'I'm interested in Zodiac,' he hasn't said to you, 'I'm gonna go to Vallejo and I'm gonna talk to those guys.' Obviously, you didn't know the kind of stick-to-it-tiveness Robert would later demonstrate but he comes to your office, and sits with you. By the time 1977 rolls around and you hear that he wants to write a book, is it somewhere in your mind that you kind of go, 'This has lost so much steam' and it's kind of come to an end for you in a way? Are you sitting there and thinking it needs somebody to come in and shake things up?"

"I was kind of spinning my wheels at that point," says Toschi, with a sad smile. "Nothing was forthcoming. Nothing good. I felt that when Robert left the *Chronicle* and didn't really cool off on Zodiac, he was going to do something. I believed in him."

"So you're not able to disclose information to him initially," says Fincher.

"I showed him the *closed* file cabinets full of the original letters and swatches of the shirt," Toschi replies.

"So, when you see Robert wants to be part of this thing," Fincher continues, "pick up where people left off and find something that might have been overlooked, is there some part of you that says, 'I always wanted to be able to have the manpower to go get in this guy's face, look over his shoulder, or put a flashlight up his ass, and this is the guy who might do it?' In a weird way the official route has all of these extraneous rules of engagement and suddenly somebody comes and offers to help. He is not governed by the same set of rules."

"He can pretty much do whatever he wants," says Toschi, "and he did as a concerned citizen."

"So you give him this thing. Now you don't know the half of the Vallejo stuff. You know something is not right in Vallejo. 'Here's something,' you say. 'There's this guy you might want to check out.' "

Toschi nods. "That's how it started," he says. "Our prime suspect was just about to get out of prison."

"What's great about David Fincher is he gets you to throw out all your preconceptions," a Hollywood source tells me. "And I love it when Fincher starts getting into his rants. He does not hold back. He comes across as a brilliant and talented man who on occasion can be exceedingly difficult, but only because he has no patience for any bullshit. Somehow he mixes with the film industry like oil and water, yet is one of the most talented filmmakers in the world. The great and terrible thing about David and what scares studios so much and the reason I love him so much is he does have commercial sensibilities, but in the end all he cares about is making a great movie. All he cares about is that in a hundred years someone will see his movie and say, 'This is a great movie.' In the end, a great film is more important than an opening weekend gross, but that's what studio executives live and die on in terms of their jobs, and makes David Fincher such an enigma to them."

Laray calls me. "The girl we got for Cecilia Shepherd, Pell James, is just so good, you'll freak out." *Zodiac* (under the code name *Chronicles*) began shooting on September 11, 2005, the darkest of dark days, the fourth anniversary of 9/11. The scene is Lake Berryessa, the sun creeping down. Penny and I make the long serpentine drive four days later, assured we will see not the violent stabbing scene, but a picnic idyll. Security is high. Napa County deputies drag an interloper in scuba gear from the lake. By helicopter Don Burt has flown in oaks weighing hundreds of pounds each and ensconced them on the peninsula. He has even gotten down on his hands and knees to plant grass blade-by-blade until the shore and hillside have been landscaped, resodded, regraded, and rebuilt until they look exactly as they did on September 27, 1969.

Penny and I walk along the bank toward the peninsula where the picnic blanket is laid out and David Fincher is waiting under a sun umbrella to shoot Scene 35. A heavily laden barge sits just off shore, packed with heavy equipment. Supervisor Engineer Wayne Tidwell and Data Capture assistant Derek Schweickart work over the Viper System S-2. Everyone is told to watch out for rattlesnakes. "I have a therapist who says, 'The trick is to learn you can't corral all the rattlesnakes,'" says Fincher. "'You just got to know where they are.'"

Captain Ken Narlow is there, healthy though favoring his hip. He quickly reminds me he was the one who actually took the aerial photos of Zodiac's footprints. Hope's props this time are a blanket, Bryan's car keys, a wallet, body plates (armor), ground pads, a quick-release hog-tie piece, a retractable blade knife with sheath, sun umbrellas for the cast, Zodiac's gun (doesn't fire), bullets, a holster, a knife and sheath, tears, and blood. A camera is buried at ground level.

A hooded man has Bryan Hartnell (Patrick Scott Lewis) and Cecilia hog-tied. Who is under the hood? Fincher will play with voice and build and different actors. He will play with our perception. "It gets cold at night," Bryan is saying, "we could freeze—" The man directs the gun at him at point-blank range: "Get down! Right now!" Later when Hope recalls the scene, tears appear in her eyes from Pell's heartrending cries echoing out over the lake waters.

Rain is falling outside the little restaurant. It's still the wettest year in memory and getting wetter. For Brad and Jamie this meeting is about discussing structure and the ancillary characters who will not make it to the screen but will provide some of David Fincher's truth. "I think we need to come up with some kind of way to subdivide [the material]," says Fincher. "We're going by department hierarchy. . . . Obviously once there's Blue Rock Springs, there's an ongoing Blue Rock Springs investigation. Did I tell you about the computer chronology that I wanted to make? We would create a movie basically that would allow us to 'zoom' into northern California and it would go—here's Vallejo, here's the street, here's what happens on this date/day/night. And literally take everything we have a police report for in the chronology between this hour and this hour, somewhere in this neighborhood and be able to build an entire chronology, including when letters are mailed." They could look at northern California hour by hour, day by day and see this happened here and that happened there and all in terms of geography. Calling up "Vallejo, July Fourth," Fincher would be able to see what Sergeant Ed Rust was doing at that time, the progress of the parade at that moment.

Later, Zodiac detectives Captain Roy Conway and Detective George Bawart join us. "The whole idea behind the Zodiac killings was to do something heinous and write letters about it," Conway says. He speaks positively, even bluntly at times.

"I agree," says Fincher. "But that is consistent also with somebody who is writing the *Chronicle* and *Vallejo Times* and Vallejo P.D. and saying, 'I'm responsible for this,' and they're saying, 'If you are, give us some more information.' That would be consistent with the self-righteous, 'I did do that, goddammit, and I'm taking my place in history. You cannot deny me my ink.'"

"That brings up another thing," says Conway, "this jurisdictional issue. If there would have been a task force formed like we did in later years, it would have been a slam-dunk."

"That's what Graysmith was doing," says Fincher.

"To this day every law enforcement agency in the world immediately forms a task force," says Bawart, "because the chief of police calls up the chief of police of someplace else and gets people assigned. We had marvelous results when we actually did that."

"The interesting thing about Leigh is that he's a guy who seems to be at turns and at moments aware of the fact that he's not as smart as he thought he was," says Fincher of a newly discovered one-and-a-half-hour-long interrogation tape. "And he gets upset. What he does, which is interesting because most people speed up, is he starts going slower, 'cause he realizes you have to give yourself time to get three more moves ahead."

By August 8, Laray had not yet cast ten to twenty of the seventy-six speaking parts. "I can't make offers until we've gotten the schedule, but we're letting people know who they are. Bijou Phillips is going to be Linda, Darlene Ferrin's sister. I love little Bijou." Candy Clark, who was in one of Fincher's favorite movies, *American Graffiti*, is up for the Carol Fisher part. So is Penny Wallace. "Jamie and I went over to David's office and Laray was showing us tapes of all the people she liked the best for the role," Brad tells me. "She made sure David sat there and watched Penny's tape [Scene 16: Carol Fisher going through letters and getting one from Zodiac]. She's good. She did a good job." Laray tells me, "David loves her." Penny responds, "I swear if I die tomorrow it would be okay because I could put a sign around my neck that says: David Fincher loves my work!" But Candy Clark gets the part. "It's not that I'm bitter," says Penny, "but it should really be me up there twelve-feet high on the silver screen. Instead I'm queued up here in the supermarket express lane holding two pesticide-free, sustainably farmed chickens, *aging*." At Fincher's office Laray decides Elias Koteas (*The Thin Red Line*) has a nose exactly like Jack Mulanax's and casts him. And Fincher thinks he knows who can play his secretary.

My phone rings. "Robert, honey, it's Laray calling. It's 4:30 on Thursday. I wonder if you can give me Penny's number. I have a role for her, but it works in LA and I don't know what the likelihood of her being able to come here to work as a local is going to be. It's Mulanax's secretary and she will be working with one of my favorite actors in the whole-wide world—Elias Koteas." Penny is at a Blue Grass Festival, out of cell phone reception. She calls later: "Robert! Robert! Robert!" It might be a single line but it is a David Fincher film.

Shoot Day 38, November 2—low clouds and fog. Call time to the closed set is 7:30 a.m. Stage One (the Lot in West Hollywood) at Warner Brothers is vast and dark. A batting of blue cloth is draped over the top of the open-roofed trailer like a cloth sky. The wood construction is rigged to come apart, walls opening up or sliding back to accommodate cameras just as Fincher's elaborate *Panic Room* set did. The furnished interior will be matched to exteriors of a real trailer on site. I walk into the trailer and look around, then go back out and see it on the monitor some feet away where Fincher and the great cinematographer Harris Savides sit side-by-side. They might as well be inside. The console shows every angle of the interior and every movement of the skittering squirrels and chipmunks (one caged on a stack of books, the other two roaming free, even a stand-in squirrel) silhouetted in the foreground. The set dressing is a bed, clothes, and clutter in every corner. Closed blinds allow a noirish light to creep into the dank trailer. Hope's prop list includes guns that do not fire, blue windbreakers, dildoes, vaseline, food in fridge, frozen squirrels (she has given them authentic freezer burn), gloves, old newspapers, shoes, porn, and even "squirrel shit."

For the part of Dave Toschi, Mark Ruffalo had been a favorite from the beginning. In Scene 171 Ruffalo's Toschi and Anthony Edwards's Inspector Bill Armstrong search the prime suspect's trailer. Ruffalo will put in a twelve-hour day and Tony Edwards even longer. Mary Ellen says, "First marks. Ready. Be attentive." They rehearse. "Stand by. Thank you," Fincher says, "Pictures up. Ready and Roll. And action!" He watches the first take in the monitor. "Cut it. Playback. Mary Ellen calls "Quiet!" Lighting: "Crank it back up."

Fincher's Viper, has been giving them trouble and so have the lights, flickering—an electrical problem. It is rental stuff and so there is a flurry of finger-pointing. Chris Strong and Brian "Fuzz" Fosnaugh have a battery instantly ready to change. "Reset," says Mary Ellen. "Very good," says Fincher. "A little tighter at the beginning. Boom down a little and action!"

The detectives enter and find a wooden dildo and a big jar of petroleum jelly under the bed. Next Toschi is in the kitchenette, opening the refrigerator door, then the freezer. "Jesus!" says Toschi. "What?" says Armstrong. "Squirrel," says Toschi. Armstrong comes to look. There is a frozen squirrel in the freezer. Each time Ruffalo opens the freezer and reacts: "Squirrel!" it is funny. He does it deadpan, with wonderment, with disgust, with resignation, and with a different inflection. It is always funny. Finally, after a break for lighting, Ruffalo opens the freezer and instead of a frozen squirrel sees a photo of Harris with a sunburned forehead. His double-take gets a big laugh. "Damn fine acting—I really believed you saw a squirrel," says Fincher.

On-set the director has a laser pointer. "Think you could blind a squirrel from here?" he jokes impishly as he points above the trailer. "Can we do one more—please." Fincher is always polite—he is a man who thanks waiters. Take 14 of the refrigerator search is terrific, especially the quality of light on Ruffalo's face. But Fincher is troubled. Did the vintage refrigerator actually have a light in the freezer? Yes, he is told. They would not add one if there wasn't. It's that authentic. Ruffalo goes to the freezer some eighteen times, but fourteen is a keeper. "The great thing about David," Jamie says, "and there are obviously a lot of great things about David, is that he is also known as being a perfectionist. He's one of those guys who'll do thirty-seven takes of a guy walking by just to get it right."

The trailer search continues as the inspectors find two windbreakers. "Hey, hey," says Toschi, "black gloves. Size seven, same as we found in the cab. He's got the same shoe size and glove size as Zodiac—I'm sure it's just a coincidence." "Cut it. Playback," says Fincher. Ruffalo spent two days with Toschi at his Daly City security office. "This guy is great," says Ruffalo. "No one could invent a Dave Toschi." When we met in Hollywood, Ruffalo did Toschi until I told him he was dead-on—the voice, the mannerisms—everything, perfect. "The trenchcoat is starting to remind me of Columbo," he tells Casey Storm, the costume designer. "I asked for a little bit shorter coat, and though it is already a short coat it is still very Columboesque." But Toschi has one just like it. He's also the world's biggest Columbo fan. "What's Toschi's hair like?" Ruffalo asks earnestly. "Is it curly?" "It is," says Jamie, who suddenly realizes, "Oh, yeah, Ruffalo's got naturally curly hair. Mark's got Dave Toschi's hair in real life!" I tell Ruffalo how, at the height of the Zodiac case, a news camera left Toschi's face and instead focused on his hand grinding a disposable cup. "Like this?" Ruffalo says, demonstrating and filing away the information.

Anthony Edwards is personable, tall, slender, pale, and well briefed—perfect to play Bill Armstrong, the intelligent, straight-arrow investigator. "I see Armstrong as a man of integrity who would never let the department down or let the case down," he says. "And I see the killer as someone who has disassociated himself from the actual killing. He is not there." Edwards, a local boy, once played Richard Eugene Hickock in Truman Capote's *In Cold Blood*. When Tony rifles through a stack of adult magazines in the trailer Fincher bullhorns: "Put down the porn! Step away from the trailer!" The magazine covers do not appear on screen, not because of their content, but because of copyright considerations. As they pick their way through the trailer, Toschi tries to step over caged squirrels. "Very good," Fincher says. Some of his direction extends to Edwards, shot from the waist up. "Give the feeling you are walking through clutter."

Finally, Armstrong in his search goes to the end of the hall and in the slanting light from outside turns and looks back over his shoulder—at what? Even without sound, the scene is ghostly and chilling. Fincher's compositions have the feel of old master paintings and his tonal palette is that of his *Se7en*, his groundbreaking, blockbuster film that took in $300 million worldwide at the box office. The men unleashing the atmospheric smoke inside the trailer add too much and Fincher goes into the trailer and comes right back out. "It's two hundred degrees in there and smells like ass!" he cries.

But when Fincher has shot a dozen-plus versions of the same scene, he is anxious to use that energy and gets the actors back on their marks. "Mark, can we do one more, please. Reset right away! Get it back. Shut up, please. Cut it—quickly!" Finally, "Good. I'll take that one." Then cut. Over again. "You're just like the Wizard of Oz behind the curtain, David," says one of the crew, "only more irritable." Fincher doesn't want the actors to be comfortable. "Very nice. Right away, again!" The acting (and directing) takes remarkable endurance and energy. And so the speed builds on the retakes so Fincher can keep the energy in his full frame, discarding as he goes, making room for the keepers. Finally he has an unbroken full-frame scene that is flawless and uneditable. In one scene Ruffalo has trouble cocking a .30-caliber carbine (no one knows guns like Fincher—

"Fincher knows a little too much," says Brad ruefully). Finally they shoot a scene where you see Ruffalo from his chest up, looking down and moving his arms, as the sound of a rifle being expertly cocked is dubbed in. In character, Ruffalo smiles at the sound of a car pulling up outside in the daylight. A lovely explosion of exterior noon light from the windshield bisects his face.

On November 7 they shoot the dinner party scene at Mel Belli's townhouse (the Enright Residence) and then over the next two days shoot backstage and onstage at the TV studio while Belli talks to "Zodiac" on the *Jim Dunbar Show*. After Armstrong and Toschi discuss Sherwood Morrill's handwriting results at Callahan's Restaurant in Santa Monica, the set is updated to 1978 as Graysmith shows Toschi the stolen cipher books. Shoot Day 50 is the Ace Hardware store (Southgate), then the Avenue Theatre (the Warner Grand Theatre in San Pedro). Shoot Day 52 means Fincher has met the halfway mark, but now the number of days is raised to 103. Weeks nine, ten and part of eleven pass—the TV studio, the hardware store, and finally VPD.

On a monitor, Harris Savides watches impassively in the beautiful morning light. "Up an eighth," says Harris. He scrutinizes the dapple play of shadow across what has become the Vallejo Police Department. His eye is calculating, more precise than any mechanical optics. "A sixth." He barely stirs in his chair as he shoots the exterior of the Old Jail on 126th Street in Hawthorne. Vintage black-and-whites pass. One parks in front behind a conspicuous orange 1975 VW Rabbit like the one I owned while writing *Zodiac*. As we waited, dawn broke at 6:32 a.m., cold, dank, the anniversary of JFK's assassination. There is a slight risk of a shower (a later scene involves rain) but it does not materialize and so, at 3:00 p.m., the Tech water truck will be brought in to ensure Graysmith is soaked. Inside the jail, Fincher, in a white T-shirt, begins rehearsal for Sergeant Jack Mulanax (Elias Koteas) and his secretary (Penny Wallace). Penny has a trailer, stand-in, makeup, and costumer—Casey, Stacy, Sally, Trish, and Amy. "In my 1969 dress and heels and Trish's teased hairstyle," Penny says, "I was 1969 adorable." Elias's wig is uncomfortable and soon discarded with an apology to Fincher. Makeup pats Elias's forehead down as he takes up the phone and begins an imaginary conversation. On the monitor Elias fills the left hand foreground; to the right Penny is seen busy in her office. Penny and Elias rehearse. "Very good," says Fincher. He is in good spirits this morning. They go again. "First marks. Ready. Be attentive. Action!" He watches on the wide monitor. Good, I'll take that one [Take 4]. He stars or diamond marks the best ones and deletes other takes to make room in the digital memory for what will be thirty-three takes. "OK," he says, "could you move Penny's mark over a bit to the left." The cable and the door frame begin to impede her as do her ill-fitting high heels. "Let's move her mark about one foot to the doorway." They act out Scene 14. "Boom down a little and action!" After Fincher moves the mark again, he changes her line. "The fact that the call is from the *Chronicle* is a big deal. Don't put too much emphasis on anything. Just throw it away. Let's change the word 'guy.' It's too modern sounding. Don't gesture with both hands. One's enough. Turn back in on the end of the line. Walk straight. You're veering into the doorway a little too wiggly." In the monitor Fincher watches her every movement. Then another line change. He changes the line from #2 to #4 because the live phone system has gone out and must be replaced on the spot by Hope and her crew. "Cut it. Once again—very nice. Right away, again." The cadence and movement of the scene improve immediately as Fincher adds the word "sorry" to her interruption of Elias's phone call. For Takes 32 and 33 her shoes are changed, and in flats she completes two perfect takes using the smoother line. In a scene set later, Penny is in the background filing. She is in a David Fincher film.

After a break for Thanksgiving, shooting resumes through November 30 at the Standard Oil Refinery (the Nabisco Plant on Artesia Boulevard in Buena Park) as police question the prime suspect. It is hazardous work for the actors. "Beware of steam," the cast is warned. "Do not get close, and watch for slippery floors. When at this location do not touch any breakers, electrical outlets, or switches. Do not wander around the building at all!" They film on a bus, in a prison, at a chicken shack, at a carwash, at the Bechtel Lobby, and at Questioned Documents and then are off for the holidays. On January 3, 2006, Shoot Day 75, they return to Questioned Documents and three days later complete a difficult scene along the docks—Avery's houseboat. The interior will be set up on Stage 2 at the Lot. Weeks 18 and 19 are at the Graysmith apartment.

In the morning on January 16, on Stage 7, Toschi, Ken Narlow (Donal Logue), and Mel Nicolai (Zach Grenier) are flying to the secret Riverside conference when they look up in disbelief. "Paul Avery," says Downey, "good to meet you. Can I catch a ride with you gents when we land?" In the afternoon Fincher moves to Stage 3, the Graysmith apartment. My ex-wife, Melanie, is played by Chloe Sevigny, and our daughter, Margot, is played at six months by Kiley and Keely Hanson and at age two by Jessica Baltutis. One scene shows my boys, David (Jack Sampson) and Aaron (Zachary Sauers), working on Zodiac charts; Jake leaves the dinner table to watch TV news, but the two kids keep breaking up because it is so hard to keep a straight face when Chloe is pretending to be stern.

The *Dirty Harry* premiere at the Westwood Theatre is moved a day ahead to January 24. Days 93 through 102 are spent at the Hall of Justice and, finally, with a retake of a Bawart scene, Fincher is done with 111 days of shooting. But his team is still sleuthing. Max studies a catalogue recovered by the VPD from the prime suspect's basement home in 1991. He discovers a photo of a black costume with a square black hood like Zodiac's. The catalogue says it can be ordered by mail. He turns quickly to the front. The publication date predates the Zodiac murders.

To celebrate the tenth anniversary of Phoenix Pictures, Mike Medavoy, Brad's boss, throws a glittering party. "It is really the twelfth anniversary," Brad says, "but in Hollywood everyone lies about their age." Medavoy embraces cofounder Arnie Messer, Brad, and executive producer Lou Phillips. "In my long career," the legendary Medavoy says, "this is the best team I have ever had." Bryan Hartnell and his son, Benjamin, are at the gala too. Bryan, 280 pounds and six foot eight, is healthy and successful. He is more than a survivor. Bryan draws me aside and tells me this story: One day he and Mike Mageau found themselves in the same Southland courtroom, Bryan a well-dressed defense attorney, Mike in an orange jumpsuit, still a troubled victim and a former street person. "Look at you and look at me," says Mageau. "Touched by the same killer and look what you have become. Look what I have become."